city-pick

NEW YORK

Oxygen Books

Published by Oxygen Books Ltd. 2011
Reprinted 2012

A CIP catalogue record for this book is available from the British Library.

ISBN 978–0–956787–61–3

Typeset in Sabon by Bookcraft Limited, Stroud, Gloucestershire

Printed and bound in Great Britain by
Henry Ling Ltd, The Dorset Press, Dorchester

Praise for the series

'Brilliant ... the best way to get under the skin of a city. The perfect read for travellers and book lovers of all ages'

Kate Mosse, author of *Labyrinth*

'This impressive little series'

Sunday Telegraph

'It's like having your own iPad loaded with different tomes'

The Times

'An attractive-looking list of destination-based literature anthologies ... a great range of writers'

The Independent

'There are some books that you spot and immediately curse under your breath – "Why didn't I think of that? What a great idea!" ... The editors have scoured the literature and compiled a miscellany of observations by writers, famous and insignificant, which describes the beauty, the unique character and the essence of the chosen city'

Sydney Morning Herald

'The excellent *city-pick* series which uses descriptions of a city penned by writers, both living and dead, to illuminate the metropolis in question.'

Condé Nast Traveller

'All of a sudden the traditional travel guide seems a little dull. ... *city-pick* offers a more soulful guide to the metropolises of the world in the company of journalists, musicians, playwrights, bloggers and novelists past and present.'

The Good Web Guide

'An inviting new series of travel guides which collects some of the best writing on European cities to give a real flavour of the place ... Such an *idée formidable*, it seems amazing it hasn't been done before'

Editor's Pick, *The Bookseller*

'The beauty of this clever series is the breadth and reach of its contributors.'

Real Travel Magazine

'Wonderful.'

The Guardian

'Esseential – slip it into your bag alongside a *Rough Guide*.'

Waterstone's Books Quarterly

Contents

Contents

On the waterfront

Contents

I am a stranger here myself

Good times, bad times

And all that jazz

Contents

Big weather

Happy holidays

Big yellow taxis etc

Contents

Village life

Celebrity city

Editor's Introduction

How to create a portrait of a subject that will scarcely keep still long enough for even a digital snap? As New York hurtles past us out of its improbable history (was it really bought for a handful of beads?) and on into an unforseeable future, all we can do is gather a modest selection of the millions of words that have been written about this city of superlatives and contradictions – a city that half the world feels it knows, even if it hasn't been there.

'This beautiful bedlam and chaos of New York,' writer Alfred Kazin called it, while in *City of God* E. L. Doctorow recalls Walt Whitman's description of the 'bustle and din, the sublimity, the exuberant arrogance, of the living moment' which defines the city. But Emerson referred to it as 'a sucked orange', and Saul Bellow called it 'stirring, insupportable, agitated, ungovernable, demonic' (but then *he* preferred Chicago). It has been called a place where you need to wear your heart on your sleeve and your tongue in your cheek – a place where, according to Quentin Crisp, 'everyone who isn't shooting you is your friend'. If New York were a person, it would be an implausible one, so full of contradictory impulses and origins as to necessitate a great deal of time with its analyst, no doubt ...

Quite early on in the editing process I gave up trying to cover every aspect of this astonishing city or to include every possible text. There is enough good writing on New York to make a dozen anthologies and, as usual, a number of worthy and/or well-known books didn't make it through to the final selection. In some cases this was the difficulty of extracting relevant material from texts set in New York but which tend

1

to take the city as a 'given' and so do not include much in the way of useful description but concentrate on human relationships and actions (as a writer native to the desert would omit descriptions of sand). Thus, for example, there is nothing from Edith Wharton or Henry James, and only a snippet from Sylvia Plath's *The Bell Jar* and Truman Capote's *Breakfast at Tiffany's*. Other omissions are the result of 'permissions' problems, and I would direct the reader particularly to Toni Morrison's wonderful novel, *Jazz*, Betty Smith's *A Tree Grows in Brooklyn*, J. D. Salinger's *The Catcher in the Rye*, Nora Ephron's *I feel bad about my neck*, Patti Smith's *Just Kids*, and Tony Judt's *The Memory Chalet* for more good reading on New York.

The added complication is that the *city-pick* anthologies attempt not just to collect 'good writing' but to act as an alternative kind of guidebook to the city. Partly for this reason, some writers appear a number of times: in certain cases, several short extracts add up to no more than a single substantial one from another writer. And sometimes – as with Edward Rutherfurd's long saga, *New York* – a number of long extracts are used because they explain or illuminate so well some key aspects of the city or its history.

Like every major city, New York has its darker side – its poverty and its terrible tragedies: it would not give an accurate picture of the place to ignore them. While working on the book I became aware that this year marks the tenth anniversary of 9/11 and have been remembering my late brother-in-law, Frederick J. Kuo Jr. Hard-working, kind, gentle, a second-generation immigrant, he loved his city and especially the magnificent view from his office, high up in the South Tower of the World Trade Center.

To offset the weightier pieces, I have tried to ensure a suitable New York 'fizz' by including plenty of very short extracts – which need to be read like mini poems – along with some surprises ... such as Maxim Gorky on Coney Island. As an illustrated reading list, this collection can serve as a starting point for the exploration of New York and the vast wealth of writing about it.

Whether you're travelling to the Big Apple by plane or boat, or simply in your imagination and your favourite armchair, we hope *city-pick NEW YORK* will enrich the journey.

Heather Reyes, 2011

I ♥ NY

For many of us, New York is the opening shot of Woody Allen's film Manhattan, *that incredible view of the sparkling, night-time city accompanied by George Gershwin's jazz-inspired* Rhapsody in Blue *... And fireworks, too! It's an image that speaks of a great love for all the excitement offered by this incomparable city – a city that plenty of people have fallen in love with, whether New Yorkers by birth or adoption, or simply visitors. We start with a cluster of little gems on some of the many reasons people adore the Big Apple.*

But God I was happy to be back in New York! I liked being able to find people on the street at two and three in the morning. I liked calling up all my friends and talking for hours on the phone. I liked the feeling that everything in New York was being *observed*. If I saw something strange on the street, it would end up in a cartoon in the *New Yorker* the following week. If the subway stalled, an article about it would be in the *New York Times* the next morning – and after all it was a national newspaper. If I got up in a restaurant and passed four tables on the way to the loo, there would be at least three conversations I'd be dying to join in.

Edmund White, *City Boy* (2009)

✱ ✱ ✱

As the Mercedes ascended the bridge's great arc, he could see the island of Manhattan off to the left. The towers were jammed together so tightly, he could feel the mass and stupendous weight. Just think of the millions, from all over the globe, who yearned to be on that island, in those towers, in those narrow streets! There it was, the Rome, the Paris, the London of the twentieth century, the city of ambition, the dense magnetic rock, the irresistible destination of all those who insist on being *where things are happening*.

Tom Wolfe, *The Bonfire of the Vanities* (1987)

✱ ✱ ✱

He'd liked the job, but he missed New York every single day he was out there. Portland was a good place, it had a lot to offer, but it wasn't New York, and that was the thing about New York – if you loved it, if it worked for you, it ruined you for any place else in the world.

Lawrence Block, *Small Town* (2003)

✱ ✱ ✱

A poem compresses much in a small space and adds music, thus heightening its meaning. The city is like poetry: it compresses all life, all races and breeds, into a small island and adds music and the accompaniment of internal engines. The island of Manhattan is without doubt the greatest human concentrate on earth, the poem whose magic is comprehensible to millions of permanent residents but whose full meaning will always remain elusive.

E. B. White, *Here is New York* (1949/1976)

❊ ❊ ❊

It's no accident that Parisians adore New York. Its orthogonal street grid notwithstanding, they feel right at home here, since one of the things that makes Europe Europe is that its urban centres are still attractors, rather than repellers, of public life. Conversely, for an American Midwesterner like me, hungry for a feeling of cultural placement, New York is the next best thing to Europe.

Jonathan Franzen, *How To Be Alone* (2002)

❊ ❊ ❊

Through Fifteenth Street ran a warm spring current. Lilacs and sewage. There were as yet no lilacs, but an element of the savage gas was velvety and sweet, reminiscent of blooming lilac. All about was a softness of perhaps dissolved soot, or of air passed through many human breasts, or metabolised in multitudinous brains, or released from as many intestines, and it got to one – oh, deeply, too! Now and then there came an appreciative or fanciful pleasure, apparently inconsequent, suggested by the ruddy dun of sandstone, by cool corners of the warmth. Bliss from his surroundings!

Saul Bellow, *Mr. Sammler's Planet* (1970)

I ♥ NY

*   *   *

For some people, the city just seems to give them more of life, more of 'themselves'.

There are mornings I awake and, somehow, I have more of myself. I swing my legs over the side of the bed, draw up the blind, and, from my sixteenth-floor window, feel the city spilling itself across my eyes, crowding up into the world, filling in the landscape. Behind it, there in the distance, where it belongs, is the Hudson River and, if I want it, the sky. But I don't want it. What I want is to take this self I now have more of down into those noisy, dirty, dangerous streets and make my way from one end of Manhattan to the other in the midst of that crowd that also may have more of itself. There is no friend, lover, or relative I want to be with as much as I want to swing through the streets being jostled and bumped, catching the eye of the stranger, feeling the stranger's touch. In the street I am grinning like an idiot to myself, walking fast as everyone coming my way. Children stare, men smile, women laugh right into my eyes. The tenderness I encounter in that mood! The impersonal affection of a palm laid against my arm or my back as someone murmurs, 'Excuse me,' and sidles skilfully past my body: it soothes beyond reasonable explanation. I feel such love then, for the idea of the city as well as the reality. And everyone looks good: handsome, stylish, interesting. Life spills over without stint and without condition. I feel often that I am walking with my head tipped back, my mouth thrown open, a stream of sunlight on water pouring into my throat.

Vivian Gornick, *Approaching Eye Level* (1996)

*   *   *

Frances Trollope (1779–1863) was a prolific English novelist and travel writer and mother of the more famous novelist Anthony Trollope. Possessing a strong social conscience as well as an acerbic wit, her own anti-slavery novel is said to have influenced Harriet Beecher Stowe's Uncle Tom's Cabin. *Despite misgivings about America and Americans in general (rather typical of an English person of her class at the time), she nevertheless falls under the spell of New York.*

I have never seen the bay of Naples, I can therefore make no comparison, but my imagination is incapable of conceiving any thing of the kind more beautiful than the harbour of New York. Various and lovely are the objects which meet the eye on every side, but the naming them would only be to give a list of words, without conveying the faintest idea of the scene. I doubt if ever the pencil of Turner could do it justice, bright and glorious as it rose upon us. We seemed to enter the harbour of New York upon waves of liquid gold, and as we darted past the green isles which rise from its bosom, like guardian sentinels of the fair city, the setting sun stretched his horizontal beams farther and farther at each moment, as if to point out to us some new glory in the landscape.

New York, indeed, appeared to us, even when we saw it by a soberer light, a lovely and a noble city. To us who had been so long travelling through half-cleared forests, and sojourning among an "I'm-as-good-as-you" population, it seemed, perhaps, more beautiful, more splendid, and more refined than it might have done, had we arrived there directly from London; but making every allowance for this, I must still declare that I think New York one of the finest cities I ever saw, and as much superior to every other in the Union, (Philadelphia not excepted,) as London to Liverpool, or Paris to Rouen. Its advantages of position are, perhaps, unequalled anywhere. Situated on an island, which I think it will one day cover, it rises, like Venice, from the sea, and like that fairest of cities in the days of her glory, receives into its lap tribute of all the riches of the earth.

Frances Trollope, *Domestic Manners of the Americans* (1832)

* * *

For Nick Carraway, the narrator of Scott Fitzgerald's
The Great Gatsby, *it seems not to have been love at*
first sight. But the atmosphere of New York City grad-
ually works its spell.

I began to like New York, the racy, adventurous feel of it at
night, and the satisfaction that the constant flicker of men and
women and machines gives to the restless eye. I liked to walk
up Fifth Avenue and pick out romantic women from the crowd
and imagine that in a few minutes I was going to enter into
their lives, and no one would ever know or disapprove. Sometimes, in my mind, I followed them to their apartments on the
corners of hidden streets, and they turned and smiled back at
me before they faded through a door into warm darkness. At
the enchanted metropolitan twilight I felt a haunting loneli-
ness sometimes, and felt it in others – poor young clerks who
loitered in front of windows waiting until it was time for a
solitary restaurant dinner – young clerks in the dusk, wasting
the most poignant moments of night and life.

Again at eight o'clock, when the dark lanes of the Forties were
lined five deep with throbbing taxicabs, bound for the theatre
district, I felt a sinking in my heart. Forms leaned together in
the taxis as they waited, and voices sang, and there was laughter
from unheard jokes, and lighted cigarettes made unintelligible
circles inside. Imagining that I, too, was hurrying toward gaiety
and sharing their intimate excitement, I wished them well.

F. Scott Fitzgerald, *The Great Gatsby* (1926)

* * *

One of the most famous New York novels has to
be Truman Capote's Breakfast at Tiffany's. *Audrey*
Hepburn (as the naïve and eccentric Holly Golightly)
wielding an outsized cigarette-holder, in the film

based on the book, has become an iconic image of twentieth-century American cinema. In this snippet, Holly's fantasies reflect her love of the city.

We spent entire evenings together during which we exchanged less than a hundred words; once, we walked all the way to Chinatown, ate a chow-mein supper, bought some paper lanterns, and stole a box of joss sticks, then moseyed across the Brooklyn Bridge, and on the bridge, as we watched seaward-moving ships pass between the cliffs of burning skyline, she said: 'Years from now, years and years, one of those ships will bring me back, me and my nine Brazilian brats. Because yes, they *must* see this, these lights, the river – I love New York, even though it isn't mine.'

Truman Capote, *Breakfast at Tiffany's* (1958)

✳ ✳ ✳

While on the subject of children and returning to New York by ship, we meet an excited couple sailing back to the city they love – from another great New York novel, John Dos Passos's Manhattan Transfer.

The baby with tiny shut purplishpink face and fists lay asleep on the berth. Ellen was leaning over a black leather suitcase. Jimmy Herf in his shirtsleeves was looking out the porthole.

"Well, there's the Statue of Liberty … Ellie we ought to be out on deck."

"It'll take ages before we dock … Go ahead up. I'll come up with Martin in a minute."

"Oh come ahead; we'll put the baby's stuff in the bag while we're warping into the slip."

They came out on deck into a dazzling September afternoon. The water was greenindigo. A steady wind kept sweeping coils of brown smoke and blobs of white-cotton steam off the high enormous blueindigo arch of sky. Against a sootsmudged horizon tangled with barges, steamers, chimneys of powerplants, covered wharves, bridges, lower New York was a pink and white tapering pyramid cut slenderly out of cardboard.

"Ellie we ought to have Martin out so he can see."

"And start yelling like a tugboat ... He's better off where he is."

They ducked under some ropes, slipped past the rattling steamwinch and out to the bow.

"God Ellie it's the greatest sight in the world ... I never thought I'd ever come back, did you?"

"I had every intention of coming back."

"Not like this."

"No I don't suppose I did."

"S'il vous plaît madame ... "

A sailor was motioning them back. Ellen turned her face into the wind to get the coppery wisps of hair out of her eyes. "C'est beau, n'est-ce pas?" She smiled into the wind and into the sailor's red face.

John Dos Passos, *Manhattan Transfer* (1925)

✳ ✳ ✳

And a great view of the city to provoke affection in the viewer – from Tom Wolfe's great novel of the 1980s. The Bonfire of the Vanities.

'Come here,' said Weiss. He got up from his great chair and walked over to the window behind him and beckoned to Kramer. From up here on the sixth floor, at the top of the hill, the view was grand. They were up high enough so that all sordid details receded and the Bronx's lovely rolling topology took over. They looked out over Yankee Stadium and John Mullaly Park, which from here actually looked green and sylvan. In the distance, straight ahead, across the Harlem River, was the skyline of upper Manhattan, up where Columbia-Presbyterian Medical Centre was, and from here it looked pastoral, like one of those old landscape paintings in which they put some fuzzy trees in the background and some soft grey clouds.

Tom Wolfe, *The Bonfire of the Vanities* (1987)

* * *

But it isn't just the look of the city that stirs the heart. The smells and the sheer scale and variety are what move Ian Frazier, who is particularly fond of Brooklyn and its inhabitants.

The smells in Brooklyn: coffee, fingernail polish, eucalyptus, the breath from laundry rooms, pot roast, tater Tots. A woman I know who grew up here says she moved away because she could not stand the smell of cooking food in the hallway of her parents' building. I feel just the opposite. I used to live in a converted factory above an army-navy store, and I like being in a place that smells like people live there. In the mornings, I sometimes wake to the smell of toast, and I still don't know exactly whose toast it is. And I prefer living in a borough of two and a half million inhabitants, the most of any borough in the city. I think of all the rural places, the pine-timbered canyons and within-commuting-distance farmland that we are preserving by not living there. I like the immensities of the borough, the unrolling miles of Eastern Parkway and Ocean Parkway and Linden Boulevard, and the dishevelled outlying parks strewn with tree limbs and with shards of glass held together by liquor bottle labels, and the tough bridges – the Willamsburg and the Manhattan – and the gentle Brooklyn Bridge. And I like the way the people talk; some really do have Brooklyn accents, really do say 'dese' and 'dose'.

Ian Frazier, *Gone to New York* (2005)

* * *

A writer who certainly appreciates the cultural variety of the city and the smells (especially those of a particular shop) is food writer and memoirist Colette Rossant.

On warm, sunny days Jimmy and I would walk across the Brooklyn Bridge into Brooklyn Heights, where we had friends. With them we would parade down the promenade over-looking the East River, and sit in the sun admiring the vista of skyscrapers of Lower Manhattan. I liked Brooklyn Heights with its narrow streets and lovely town houses; it reminded me more of Europe than my Upper West Side neighbourhood. It was on one of our walks in Brooklyn that I discovered Atlantic Avenue and its Middle Eastern food stores. The discovery would change my life.

After leaving Egypt in 1947 for Paris, I had consciously shunned my Egyptian past, desperately wanting to be French. I had worked hard to lose my singsong Egyptian accent, learned to dress as I imagined a French young woman would, and never looked back at my Egyptian past. Now being French in the United States seemed to be my passport to a better life; in New York, everything French had cachet. As Jimmy and I walked past a store on Atlantic Avenue, I stopped short as I noticed a cascade of loofas hanging on a nail. Loofas! These were the vegetable sponges that Aishe, my maid, washed me with when I was a six-year-old girl until my skin was as red as a lobster!

As I stepped into the shop – the Oriental Pastry and Grocery – the smell of cumin and coriander hit me with such force that I staggered. I was back in Cairo in the kitchen with Ahmet, sitting on the counter, eating a pita filled with warm, lemony *ful medamas* (richly braised fava beans).

Colette Rossant, Madeleines in Manhattan (2007)

Michael Cunningham's The Hours *(a film as well as a book) is a contemporary update of Virginia Woolf's great novel of 1920s London,* Mrs Dalloway. *The glorious June day on which it is set is transferred to New York at the end of the century, but the love of life it inspires springs from the same appreciation of the city's vibrancy and variety.*

There are still the flowers to buy. Clarissa feigns exasperation (though she loves doing errands like this), leaves Sally cleaning the bathroom, and runs out, promising to be back in half an hour.

It is New York City. It is the end of the twentieth century.

The vestibule door opens onto a June morning so fine and scrubbed Clarissa pauses at the threshold as she would at the edge of a pool, watching the turquoise water lapping at the tiles, the liquid nets of sun wavering in the blue depth. As if standing at the edge of a pool she delays for a moment the plunge, the quick membrane of chill, the plain shock of immersion. New York in its racket and stern brown decrepitude, its bottomless decline, always produces a few summer mornings like this; mornings invaded everywhere by an assertion of new life so determined it is almost comic, like a cartoon character that endures endless, hideous punishments and always emerges unburnt, unscarred, ready for more. This June, again, the trees along West Tenth Street have produced perfect little leaves from the squares of dog dirt and discarded wrappers in which they stand. Again the window box of the old woman next door, filled as it always is with faded red plastic geraniums pushed into the dirt, has sprouted a rogue dandelion.

What a thrill, what a shock, to be alive on a morning in June, prosperous, almost scandalously privileged, with a simple errand to run. She, Clarissa Vaughan, an ordinary person (at this age, why bother trying to deny it?), has flowers to buy and a party to give. [...]

Clarissa crossed Eighth Street. She loves, helplessly, the dead television set abandoned on the curb alongside a single white patent-leather pump. She loves the vendor's cart piled with broccoli and peaches and mangoes, each labelled with an index card that offers a price amid abundances of punctuation: "$1.49!!" "3 for ONE Dollar!?!" "50 Cents EA!!!!!" Ahead, under the Arch, an old woman in a dark, neatly tailored dress appears to be singing, stationed precisely between the twin statues of George Washington, as warrior and politician, both faces destroyed by weather. It's the city's crush and heave that moves you; its intricacy; its endless life.

Michael Cunningham, The Hours (1998)

Building the Big Apple

I wondered, as I burped my way up Broadway, I wondered how this town ever got put together. Some guy was dreaming big all right.

Martin Amis, *Money* (1984)

✳ ✳ ✳

The first light of the morning outlines the towers of the World Trade Center at the tip of the island. You turn in the other direction and start uptown. There are cobbles on the street where the asphalt has worn through. You think of the wooden shoes of the first Dutch settlers on these same stones. Before that, Algonquin braves stalking game along silent trails.

Jay McInerney, *Bright Lights Big City* (1985)

✳ ✳ ✳

*First, a little bit of basic geography and history from
Edward Rutherfurd's mammoth saga of the city.*

Manna hata: it was an Indian name. So far as he knew, it just
meant "the Island". The place was a narrow peninsula, really;
except that at its northern tip, a small, steep gorge allowed a
channel of water from the North River to snake round into the
long island's sound, converting the peninsula of Manhattan,
technically, into an island.

Had it not been for the great breakwater of the long island
protecting its ocean side, Manhattan would have been exposed
to the full force of the Atlantic. But thanks to this happy circumstance, as the North River came down to the tip of Manhattan,
it entered a splendid, sheltered harbour about four miles wide
and seven long – a spacious anchorage known to mariners as
the Upper Bay. Better yet, as one passed through the narrows
at the harbour's southern end to encounter the Atlantic, two
huge sandbars, one on each side, served as outer breakwaters
against the ocean swell, creating the calm waters of the Lower
Bay, so vast that all the ships in the world could well have lain
at anchor there. [...]

White men had been coming there since the days of Christopher Columbus. At first they had been seeking gold, or trying
to find a route to the Orient. One, Verrazano, who arrived
in 1524, was known by name; others had been forgotten.
And not always white men either: the Portuguese sea captain
Gomez had been black. He'd come, grabbed nearly sixty of
the local Indians to sell as slaves, then disappeared over the
horizon. But it was the arrival of another man which had
changed everything for the people of the great North River
and its harbour.

Henry Hudson had been an Englishman, employed by the
rival Dutch, to find a shorter route to China by sailing east.
Having had a look for this fabled North-East passage above
Russia and decided it was useless, he'd ignored all his orders,

doubled back across the Atlantic, and looked for a passage round the North-West instead. It was Hudson who had ventured into the bay below Manhattan, and gone up the big river for several days before concluding: "It isn't the way to China."

"It may not lead to China," he'd told his Dutch employers upon his return, "but the land is magnificent. And full of beavers."

And the people of northern Europe had an insatiable greed for beavers.

"The beaver," van Dyck would tell his children, "is a most useful creature. Beaver oil cures rheumatism, toothache and stomach pains. A beaver's testicles, powdered and dissolved in water, can restore an idiot to sanity. Its fur is thick and warm." But it was the soft pelt under the outer fur that men really desired. And why? Because it could be made into felt.

Hats. Everyone wanted a felt hat, though only the richer souls could afford one. It was the height of fashion. The hatters who made them sometimes went mad, poisoned by the mercury that used to separate the felt from the fur. And perhaps, van Dyck admitted to himself, there was a certain madness in this – that a whole colony, an empire perhaps, could be founded, men risk their lives and kill in turn – all on account of a fashionable hat. But such was the way of the world. The coast of north-eastern America might have been colonised for the Atlantic fishing trade, but the great harbour of New Amsterdam and its big North River were settled because of the felt hat.

And it was in gratitude to the intrepid explorer that van Dyck and fur traders like him would often refer to the big river not as the North, but as Hudson's River.

"There it is. New Amsterdam." The Dutchman smiled to see his daughter's shiver of excitement. Ahead, the southern tip of Manhattan jutted out into the harbour's watery immensity.

Seabirds wheeled over the small waves. There was a bracing saltiness in the air.

Edward Rutherfurd, *New York* (2009)

* * *

New Yorker Washington Irving (1783–1859) was America's first internationally recognised author. Much admired by Dickens, Irving was the author of many short stories (including 'Rip Van Winkle') as well as essays, biographies and histories. The extract below is from his satirical A History of New York from the Beginning of the World to the end of the Dutch Dynasty, *supposedly written by one Diedrich Knickerbocker – a hoax that was part of a clever marketing campaign when the author was widely advertised as having disappeared mysteriously from his hotel room, leaving an unpaid bill. (The hotel proprietor was allegedly threatening to publish a manuscript found in the room to recoup the lost money.) 'Knickerbocker' was to become a nick-name for Manhattan residents in general.*

The island of Manna-hata, Manhattoes, or as it is vulgarly called Manhattan, having been discovered, as was related in the last chapter; and being unanimously pronounced by the discoverers, the fairest spot in the known world, whereon to build a city, that should surpass all the emporiums of Europe, they immediately returned to Communipaw with the pleasing intelligence. Upon this a considerable colony was forthwith fitted out, who after a prosperous voyage of half an hour, arrived at Manna hata, and having previously purchased the land of the Indians, (a measure almost unparalleled in the annals of discovery and colonization) they settled upon the south-west point of the island, and fortified themselves strongly, by throwing up a mud battery, which they named FORT AMSTERDAM. A number of huts soon sprung up in the neighbourhood, to protect which, they made an enclosure of strong pallisadoes. A creek running from the East river, through what at present is called Whitehall street, and a little inlet from Hudson river to the bowling green formed the original boundaries; as though nature had kindly designated the cradle, in which the embryo of this renowned city was to be nestled. The woods on both sides of the creek were carefully cleared away, as well as from the space of ground now occupied by the bowling green. – These precautions were taken to protect the fort from either the open attacks or insidious advances of its savage neighbours, who wandered in hordes about the forests and swamps that extended over those tracts of country, at present called broad way, Wall street, William street and Pearl street.

Washington Irving, A History of New York (1809)

But let's fast-forward to when New York first started
to become architecturally interesting.

As I understand it, the first large buildings on the Upper West Side rose up at the end of the nineteenth century on speculation of the city's growing uptown. The Dakota was named after a frontier state and plunked down between farms and shanties where goats wandered near the edges of Central Park. After the building of the IRT, dreamboat buildings sprouted on Broadway, for instance the Ansonia, that Beaux Art wedding cake later home to Babe Ruth. Soon construction spread to Riverside Drive, solid brick apartments next door to the mansions of cigar-rolling millionaires. These had views of the Hudson and the Jersey palisades, but were within earshot of the trains on the riverbank. Soot caked the high windows and in summer you could smell the sewage seeping out to sea. In hot months the fetid water bubbled.

Gabriel Brownstein, 'The Curious Case of Benjamin Button,
Apt. 3W' (2003)
(title story of the collection)

❋ ❋ ❋

At the beginning of the twentieth century, an architectural paroxysm shook New York City. Gigantic towers called skyscrapers soared up one after the other, higher than anything built by the hand of man before. At a ribbon-cutting on Liberty Street in 1908, the top hats applauded as Mayor McClellan declared the forty-seven-storey redbrick and bluestone Singer Building the world's tallest structure. Eighteen months later, the mayor had to repeat the same ceremony at the fifty-storey Metropolitan Life tower on Twenty-fourth Street. But even then they were already breaking ground for Mr Woolworth's staggering fifty-eight-storey ziggurat back downtown.

On every block, enormous steel-beam skeletons appeared where empty lots had been the day before. The smash and scream of steam shovels never ceased. The only comparison was with Haussmann's transformation of Paris a half century earlier, but in New York there was no single vision behind the scenes, no unifying plan, no disciplining authority. Capital and speculation drove everything, releasing fantastic energies distinctly American and individualistic.

The masculinity of it all was undeniable. On the ground, the implacable Manhattan grid, with its two hundred numbered east-west streets and twelve north-south avenues, gave the city a stamp of abstract rectilinear order. Above this, in the immensity of the towering structures, with their peacock-like embellishments, it was all ambition, speculation, competition, domination, even lust – for height, size, and always money.

The Balmoral, on the Boulevard – New Yorkers at the time referred to Broadway from Fifty-ninth to 155th Street as the Boulevard – was one of the grand new edifices. Its very existence was a gamble. In 1909, the very rich still lived in houses, not apartments. They 'kept' apartments for short or seasonal stays in the city, but they failed to comprehend how anybody could actually live in one. The Balmoral was a bet: that the rich could be induced to change their minds if the accommodations were sufficiently opulent.

The Balmoral rose seventeen storeys, higher and grander than any apartment building – any residential building – had ever climbed before. Its four wings occupied an entire city block. Its lobby, where seals cavorted in a Roman fountain, shone with white Carrera marble. Chandeliers in every apartment sparkled with Murano glass. The smallest dwelling had eight rooms; the largest boasted fourteen bedrooms, seven baths, a grand ball-room with a twenty-foot ceiling, and full maid's service. This rented for the appalling sum of $495 dollars a month.

Jed Rubenfeld, *The Interpretation of Murder* (2006)

❋ ❋ ❋

The most iconic of New York's many great constructions was, and still is, the Empire State Building. In one of Alistair Cooke's 'Letters from America' he recalls telling the famous literary critic Cyril Connolly that the most crucial thing to do while in New York is to go to the top of the Empire State Building at sunset – winter is the best time as the office lights will be on and the skyscrapers will appear as a succession of jewel curtains. Here are some facts and figures, along with a sense of the wonder and excitement of its building.

It was a hot morning in August and Salvatore Caruso was high in the sky. He was setting bricks rapidly and with precision. [...]

He'd been on several sites in the last eighteen months, but this one was easily the most exciting. The job was on Fifth Avenue, down at 34th Street. At the start of the year it had still been magnificently occupied by the Waldorf-Astoria Hotel. By March there had been nothing but a huge hole, forty feet deep, down to the solid bedrock below. Now, arising from that bedrock with astonishing speed, was the skyscraper to surpass all the skyscrapers that had gone before.

The Empire State.

Everything about the project was larger than life. The entrepreneur, Raskob, had risen from poverty to be the right-hand man of the mighty du Pont family, and chairman of the General Motors finance committee. The frontman, Al Smith, was still poor, but he'd been New York's Democratic governor, and might have been elected President of the USA if he hadn't been a Catholic. Both men were flamboyant. Both hated the hypocrisy of Prohibition. Both loved a challenge.

And if Walter Chrysler thought that his clever, stainless-steel spike was going to leave him king of the New York skyline, then he'd better watch out. The Empire State Building was going to top it, and soon. [...]

The site was organised to perfection. In order not to disturb the residents of Fifth Avenue, the roadway was always kept clear. Every morning, on a strict schedule, the trucks swung in to the site from one street and left by the other, while their loads were hastily raised to the floor where they were needed.

The materials came from so many places. The big T girders from Pittsburg, limestone from Indiana, timber from the Pacific coast, marble from Italy and France, and when those suppliers couldn't keep up, the contractors had bought a whole quarry in Germany.

Most dramatic of all was the speed of the work. As the vast steel framework climbed steadily into the sky, the bricklayers

23

and stonemasons followed right behind it. The Empire State Building was going up almost a floor per day.

Just then, a few floors up and to the left, a large iron girder swung silently into view. Sitting astride it were a couple of men.

"There go the Injuns," one of the gang remarked.

There were scores of Mohawk Indians on the site. Whole families of them had learned their ironworking skills on Canada's bridges half a century before. Now they had come down from their reservation to work on the skyscrapers of New York. Salvatore liked to watch the Mohawks sitting calmly on the girders as they were swung up to dizzying heights in the sky. There, they guided them into the building's mighty frame, where the riveters, working in teams of four, went about their deafening work. The Mohawks and the riveters were some of the most highly paid men on the site.

Salvatore's own pay as a bricklayer was excellent: more than fifteen dollars a day. Most important of all, he was employed. For there were plenty of good men who couldn't find work, these days.

It was a strange irony. Just as the Empire State Building had started to go up, America itself had begun to stagger. The country wasn't hit by another stock market crash – there was no sudden crisis – but like a boxer who has taken a series of heavy blows, and starts to lose his legs, the mighty American economy had finally begun to sag.

From its April high, the stock market had given up its new year rally. Each day, as the Empire State Building went up another floor, the market went a little lower. [...]

By Friday 19 September, the great steel cage of the Empire State Building was nearly complete. It was almost two weeks ahead of schedule. The bricklayers had been keeping pace, and they only had about ten floors to go. Eight-five floors in six months from the start of the construction. A staggering achievement. [...]

The construction of the Empire State Building had proceeded rapidly because its design was so simple. First came the network of huge steel girders which carried the building's entire weight. Some of the vertical steel columns would support a weight of ten million pounds, but they could have taken far more. The building was massively over-engineered. Between the girders were curtain walls, whose only structural function was to keep the weather out.

But here the architects had shown their genius. The outer edges of the vertical girders were given a chrome-nickel trim that rendered them a soft grey. Apart from that, the entire working façade of the mighty tower contained only these principal elements: first, pairs of rectangular, metal window frames; second, above and below each frame, a single aluminium panel, called a spandrel; third, between each pair of windows, large slabs of pale limestone. Thus the façade soared up in pure stone and metal vertical lines. Only at the very top of each high column of stonework or window was there an elegant art deco carving with a vertical direction to satisfy and uplift the eye. Essentially, therefore, the men working on the façade just moved up behind the girder riveters and, as it were, clipped the frames, spandrels and blocks of limestone into place.

And then there were the bricklayers.

"We work from inside, you see," Salvatore explained. "Two courses of brick, eight inches thick." The brick went in behind the limestone and the spandrels, supporting and insulating them. But the brick had another important function. "The brick protects the girders," Salvatore pointed out. Being fired when they were made, the bricks were flame-resistant. In high heat, even steel girders are vulnerable. The brick would clothe and protect them. "The building is strong as a fortress, but it would be almost impossible to burn it down as well."

Edward Rutherfurd, *New York* (2009)

* * *

And a passing, idiosyncratic glance at it from Todd McEwen.

Isidor headed in his natural direction, down Fifth, moving southward – pausing at the corners only as sensibly as anyone else – diminishing rapidly and becoming an ant along with the rest of them by the time he shouldered by Empire – which looked rather upright, stiff and presentable today, not *drooping* like it sometimes does. You couldn't have seen much of what Izzy was thinking now, but as he walked under the canopy when is this f***ing thing going to get fixed, *finally fixed?* – and wondered as usual why the EMPIRE STATE BUILDING has *discount drug stores* in its clay feet – he noticed a certain aluminium gleam to the Empire's sides which seemed like modern light-weight coffins.

Todd McEwen, *Who Sleeps With Katz* (2003)

❊ ❊ ❊

Edward Rutherfurd again, this time on the Chrysler building.

You had to hand it to Walter Chrysler. He had style. When the automobile man had taken over the building project that now bore his name, he had insisted on daring art deco designs that incorporated images of wheels, radiator caps and much else besides. The top of the building, which was under construction now, consisted of a beautiful series of arches rising to a capstone, all to be covered in stainless steel. Supremely elegant, there would be nothing like it in the world when it was done.

And then there was the question of height. The tallest building in the world, of course, was the Eiffel Tower in Paris. But the daring men of New York were getting close.[...]

Far above, at the top of the Chrysler Building, the pyramid of arches, still unclad, rose as a network of girders into the sky.

But now, as William Master watched, something extraordinary was happening. Suddenly, from the centre of the building's peak, a metal framework tower began to push its way out. Foot by foot it was rising, like the section of a slender telescope. Ten feet, twenty, thirty. It must have been concealed inside the main structure, and now, by some mechanism, it was being raised. Forty feet, fifty now, it was pushing its way up towards the clouds. There was a Stars and Stripes attached to the tip, streaming out in the high wind. [...]

Cunning Chrysler, by this brilliant ploy, must have added the best part of two hundred feet to the height of his building, taking his rivals completely by surprise and vanquishing them. Master wasn't certain, but he was pretty sure the Chrysler Building had just surpassed the Eiffel Tower itself.

How fitting that it should be so. New York was the centre of the world. The market was soaring. The skyscrapers were soaring. It was the spirit of the age.

Edward Rutherfurd, *New York* (2009)

❖ ❖ ❖

It was just before the crash of 1929 that the fabu-
lously wealthy John D. Rockefeller began the vast
Fifth Avenue project that was to become the Rock-
efeller Center. The great complex of office buildings
with roof gardens and an attractive central plaza
(taken over by an ice-rink each winter) was originally
to have included an opera house, but this plan was
abandoned after the crash. Here's Todd McEwen's
humorous take on one of the Centre's features ...

Last year, standing outside the Rockefeller Plaza entrance with Shelby, who was smoking one of his legion 'Pall Malls': MacK looked up at the sculpted beardy above them, '*Wisdom and Knowledge Shall Be The Stability Of Thy Times*', and said: – Wait a minute, is this Zeus or Prometheus? – Beats me, said Shelby, I always thought it was Santa. MacK ignored this. But you have to get the pantheon straight. – So *that's* Prometheus, he said, looking out at the gold rink hunk. Shelby hissed his last lungful between his teeth and threw the butt so that it landed just behind the heel of the real door man, a character in a top hat who had been trained to wait for celebrities with an umbrella. [...] He looked out at Prometheus with his slightly yellow eyes. – Yeah well *my* liver ain't so good either, and stalked off under Sert's great mural, *Time*.

Todd McEwen, *Who Sleeps With Katz* (2003)

❄ ❄ ❄

Other great architectural projects in New York include the Lincoln Center for the Performing Arts (more on that in the 'And all that jazz' section), Frank Lloyd Wright's magnificent, curvy Guggenheim Museum and the impressive New York Public Library. And here's Tom Wolfe on the Criminal Courts Buildinge.

On this balmy day in June, 100 Centre Street was an easy walk uptown from Wall Street. In all the years he had lived in New York and worked downtown, Sherman had never noticed the Criminal Courts Building, even though it was one of the biggest and grandest buildings in the City Hall area. An architect named Harvey Wiley Corbett had designed it in the Moderne style, which was now called Art Deco. Corbett, once so famous, had been forgotten except by a handful of architectural historians; likewise, the excitement over the Criminal Courts Building when it was completed in 1933. The patterns of stone and brass and glass at the entrance were still impressive, but when Sherman reached the great lobby within, something put him on red alert. He could not have told you what. In fact, it was the dark faces, the sneakers and the warm-up jackets and the Pimp Rolls. To him it was like the Port Authority bus terminal. It was an alien terrain. Throughout the vast space, which had the soaring ceilings of an old-fashioned railroad station, were huddles of dark people, and their voices created a great nervous rumble, and around the edges of the dark people walked white men in cheap suits or sport jackets, watching them like wolves monitoring the sheep.

Tom Wolfe, *The Bonfire of the Vanities* (1987)

✳ ✳ ✳

And so to Times Square. In 1903 it was still called Longacre Square, though the impressive façade of the Times Tower was already in place. Underground, work was going on to complete the New York Times' high-tech printing presses as well as on the IRT subway tunnel running close by. But both were finished by the winter of 1904–5 – which is when the square acquired its present name and came to resemble the place we know today. First, Adam Gopnik reflects on the changing nature of the place, then Marshall Berman tells us a lot more. Anyone who wants to make a thorough study of the place should see the excellent book by Berman, On the Town: one hundred years of spectacle in Times Square *from which our extracts are taken.*

No other part of New York has had such a melodramatic, mood-ring sensitivity to the changes in the city's history, with an image for every decade. There was the turn-of-the-century Times Square, with its roof gardens and showgirls; the raffish twenties Times Square of Ziegfeld and Youmans tunes; the thirties Times Square of *42nd Street*, all chorus lines and moxie; the forties, V-J *On the Town* Times Square, full of sailors kissing girls; the wizened black-and-white fifties Times Square of *Sweet Smell of Success*, steaming hot dogs, and grungy beats; and then the sixties and the seventies Times Square of *Midnight Cowboy* and *Taxi Driver*, where everything fell apart and hell wafted up through the manhole covers. No other place in town has been quite so high and quite so low. Within a single half decade, it had Harpo Marx in the Marx Brothers' valedictory movie, *Love Happy*, leaping ecstatically from sign to sign and riding away on the flying Mobilgas Pegasus, and, down below, the unforgettable image of James Dean, hunched in his black overcoat, bearing the weight of a generation on his shoulders.

Now we have the new Times Square, as fresh as a neon daisy, with a giant Gap and a Niketown and an Applebee's and an ESPN Zone and television announcers visible through tinted windows, all family retailing and national brands. In some ways, the square has never looked better, with the diagonal sloping lines of the Reuters Building, the curving Deco zipper, even the giant mock dinosaur in the Toys "R" Us. There are people who miss the old Times Square, its picturesque squalor and violence and misery and exploitation. Those who pointed at the old Times Square as an instance of everything that capitalism can do wrong now point to the new Times Square as an instance of everything that capitalism can do worse. Where once Times Square was hot, it is now cold, where once varied, now uniform, where once alive, now dead. [...]

One of the things that make for vitality in any city, and above all in New York, is the trinity of big buildings, bright lights, and weird stores. The big buildings and bright lights are there in the new Times Square, but the weird stores are not. By weird stores one means not simply small stores, mom-and-pop operations, but stores in which a peculiar and even obsessive entrepreneur caters to a peculiar and even an obsessive taste. (Art galleries and modestly ambitious restaurants are weird stores by definition. It's why they still feel very New York.) If the big buildings and the bright signs reflect the city's vitality and density, weird stores refract it; they imply that the city is so varied that someone can make a mundane living from one tiny obsessive thing. Poolrooms and boxing clubs were visible instances of weird stores in the old Times Square; another, slightly less visible, was the thriving world of the independent film business, negative cutters and camera-rental firms.

There is hardly a single weird store left on Broadway from Forty-second Street to Forty-sixth Street – hardly a single place in which a peculiar passion seems to have committed itself to a peculiar product. You have now, one more irony, to bend east, toward respectable Fifth Avenue, toward the diamond merchants and the Brazilian restaurants and the kosher cafeterias that still fill the side streets, to re-create something that feels a little like the old Times Square.

Adam Gopnik, *Through The Children's Gate* (2007)

✻ ✻ ✻

In America's "nation of nations," from Jolson's time to our own, Times Square has always been the capital. You can see it on the street or in the subway, any hour of the day or night. You can hear it everywhere, inside and outside. (In my youth you could hear it underground, at the great Times Square Records in the IRT subway arcade.) Today's ingredients are different from those of the Jazz Age – for one thing there are a lot more ingredients, come from a far greater range of places – but now as then it's a *mix*. A mix means more than just different people "side by side". It means integration, but also intercourse, blending and fusion that changes everybody. In the Square the mix is insistently *there*, it's on the street, it's in your face. When you are in the mix, under the Square's spectacular light, ego-boundaries liquefy, identities get slippery. You won't be able to avoid the question, "Who are these people?" And brushing against them will raise the collateral question, "Who are you?" You will be changing them just as they will be changing you; you know everybody will change, even if you don't know how. How Americans feel about Times Square, and about New York as a whole, often depends on how ready they are for a liquefication of their being. [...]

The two most famous people in the history of Times Square are anonymous. They are a man and a woman locked in each other's arms. They were part of the enormous crowd that gathered in the Square on August 15, 1945, V-J Day, the day and night of Japan's surrender and the end of World War Two. The *PBS History of New York*, produced by Ric Burns, shows marvellous newsreel footage of that moment. When I first saw this footage in 2001, drawn from the National Archives, I was amazed I'd never seen it before, yet in another sense I felt I'd been seeing it all my life. It was a moment well choreographed. Around twilight, Mayor LaGuardia announced the surrender, and then, at a prearranged signal, after four years of blackout, all the lights in the Square went on. An earthshaking roar went up. A big band on a bandstand nearby (I have read it was Artie Shaw's) began to swing, and thousands of men and women instantly started to dance, holding each other, jitterbugging, men throwing women into the air. The dancing is said to have gone on all through the night and past sunrise. Even when there was no music playing, couples moved to their own. As the camera pans the crowd, it is a thrill to see so many men and women who clearly are strangers embrace, hug and kiss, dance, squeeze the hell out of one another. Two of them, a sailor and a nurse, locked in a rapt embrace at the very centre of the Square, became the subjects of a great photograph. It was taken by the German Jewish refugee photographer Alfred Eisenstaedt, and it ran on the cover of *Life* magazine. They were also photographed at just about the same moment, from a slightly different (and less exciting) angle, by U.S. Navy photographer Victor Jorgensen; Jorgensen's photo was reprinted in the next day's *New York Times*. The sailor and the nurse and the crowd and the Square form one of the classic images of America and Americans in the twentieth century. [...]

One of the most stunning visions of Times Square comes at the climax of *The Jazz Singer* (1927), the first-ever sound movie, the first music video, and one of the great American *Bildungsromans*. The hero, played by Al Jolson, wants to sing to the whole world, and Times Square symbolizes that world. Here is where he breaks on through, becomes who he is, fulfils his crossover dreams, sings his heart out, and gets to have it all. His story began in the Lower East Side's grey day; it ends in Times Square's gaudy night, in brilliant contrasts of black and white. A long shot unrolls a three-part structure of space stretching to the horizon: at ground level, a parade of *people*; above them, pulsating neon and electric signs, a flood of *light*; over all, a great expanse of open *sky* that frames and embraces the people and the signs and fuses them into a whole. This is the great Times Square spectacle. These few frames – they last less than a minute – can help us see Times Square fresh, as if for the first time. This is America's gift to the modern world, the most dynamic and intense urban space of the twentieth century, the commercial sublime. [...]

There are some really good buildings in the new Times Square. The best buildings are the oldest, and they are live and lively theatres: the New Amsterdam, once home of the Ziegfeld Follies, now the Disney flagship; the neo-Baroque New Victory, now a terrific avant-garde and cosmopolitan children's theatre. They keep theatre crowds flowing and overflowing at the Square's core. The best new buildings are small, like the New 42nd Street Rehearsal Studios, whose delicate lighting blurs the boundary between building and sign. The big new buildings are more overbearing than the ones they replaced, but none of them is anywhere near as bad as the really dreadful skyscrapers that blasted into the Square's heart a generation ago (One Astor Plaza, killer of the lovely Astor Hotel; the Marriott Marquis Hotel that killed the Automat and the Helen Hayes; the blocks of giant slabs on Upper Sixth), or the four giant Egyptian tombs designed by Philip Johnson for developer George Klein in the 1980s, part of an immense, abortive plan to turn Times Square into "Rockefeller Centre South". (I called it "Albert Speer Plaza"; I still look back fondly on the hearings and demonstrations that kept it unbuilt.) The worst of the new buildings are mediocre, not monstrous, and they are oriented toward the street system, rather than being, like the Astor and Marriott buildings, blown against it. When I think of the appalling level of big buildings erected in my lifetime, the mediocrity of the new Times Square looks like progress. The Condé Nast Building and the Westin Hotel were designed to look dynamic and original from the angles at which they are most often seen, but utterly pedestrian from everywhere else. In the daytime, the sunlight reflects in striking ways off the skyscrapers' glass, and the total ensemble looks a lot more exciting than we had any reason to expect.

Marshall Berman, *On The Town* (2006)

❖ ❖ ❖

Joseph O'Neill explains why, unlike most people, he likes the recent changes to Times Square.

Unfashionably, I liked Times Square in its newest incarnation. I had no objection to the Disney security corps or the ESPN Zone or the loitering tourists or the kids crowded outside the MTV studios. And whereas others felt mocked and diminished by the square's storming of the senses and detected malevolence or Promethean impudence in the molten progress of the news tickers and in the fifty-foot visages that looked down from vinyl billboards and in the twinkling shouted advertisements for drinks and Broadway musicals, I always regarded these shimmers and vapours as one might the neck feathers of certain of the city's pigeons – as natural, humble sources of iridescence.

Joseph O'Neill, *Netherland* (2008)

❖ ❖ ❖

> *Even before their destruction in 2001, the Twin Towers of the World Trade Center had found their way into fiction (as in Don DeLillo's much praised 1997 novel* Underworld*). Post 9/11 they inevitably became a frequent subject in both non-fiction and fiction (as in the snippet from* Absurdistan *[2006] by Russian Gary Shteyngart).*

The World Trade Center was under construction, already towering, twin-towering, with cranes tilted at the summits and work elevators sliding up the flanks. She saw it almost everywhere she went. She ate a meal and drank a glass of wine and walked to the rail or ledge and there it usually was, bulked up at the funnelled end of the island, and a man stood next to her one evening, early, drinks on the roof of a gallery building – about sixty, she thought, portly and jowled but also sleek in a way, assured and contained and hard-polished, a substantial sort, European.

'I think of it as one, not two,' she said. 'Even though there are clearly two towers. It's a single entity, isn't it?'

'Very terrible thing but you have to look at it, I think.'

'Yes, you have to look.'

And they were out of ideas for a while, standing at the ledge and taking in the baleful view together.

Don DeLillo, *Underworld* (1997)

❊ ❊ ❊

As I soon found out that I couldn't rent an apartment in the actual World Trade Center, I decided to settle for an entire floor in a nearby turn-of-the-century skyscraper. My loft had a startling view of Miss Liberty greening the harbour on one side and the World Trade Center obliterating the rest of the skyline on another. I spent my evenings hopping from one end of my lily pad to the other: as the sun fell on top of the statue, the Twin Towers became a fascinating checkerboard of lit and unlit windows, looking, after several puffs of marijuana, like a Mondrian painting come to life.

Gary Shteyngart, *Absurdistan* (2006)

❊ ❊ ❊

On 7 August 19745, the Twin Towers became the site of probably the most heart-stopping high-wire acts in history as French-born Philippe Petit walked a wire strung between the two towers. He had previously walked between the towers of Notre Dame in Paris and between the two north pylons of the Sydney Harbour Bridge, but the walk between the Twin Towers was in another class of daring altogether. You can read his own story in To Reach the Clouds: my high-wire walk between the Twin Towers*, but here we give an extract from Colin McCann's account of the event, relating it to New York life in general.*

The theatre began shortly after lunch. His fellow judges and court officers and reporters and even the stenographers were already talking about it as if it were another of those things that just happened in the city. One of those out-of-the-ordinary days that made sense of the slew of ordinary days. New York had a way of doing that. Every now and then the city shook its soul out. It assailed you with an image, or a day, or a crime, or a terror, or a beauty so difficult to wrap your mind around that you had to shake your head in disbelief.

He had a theory about it. It happened, and re-happened, because it was a city uninterested in history. Strange things occurred precisely because there was no necessary regard for the past. The city lived in a sort of everyday present. […]

He had said to his wife many times that the past disappeared in the city. It was why there weren't many monuments around. It wasn't like London, where every corner had a historical figure carved out of stone, a war memorial here, a leader's bust there. He could only really pinpoint a dozen true statues around New York City – most of them in Central Park, along the Literary Walk, and who in the world went to Central Park these days anyway? A man would need a phalanx of tanks just to pass Sir Walter Scott. On other famous street corners, Broadway or Wall Street or around Gracie Square, nobody felt a need to lay claim to history. Why bother? You couldn't eat a statue. You couldn't screw a monument. You couldn't wring a million dollars out of a piece of brass.

Even down here, on Centre Street, they didn't have many public backslaps to themselves. No Lady Justice in a blindfold. No Supreme Thinkers with their robes wrapped around themselves. No Hear No Evil, See No Evil, Speak No Evil carved into the upper granite columns of the criminal courts.

Which was one of the things that made Judge Soderberg think that the tightrope walker was such a stroke of genius. A monument in himself. He had made himself into a statue, but a perfect New York one, a temporary one, up in the air, high above the city. A statue that had no regard for the past. He had gone to the World Trade Center and had strung his rope across the biggest towers in the world. The Twin Towers. Of all places. So brash. So glassy. So forward-looking.

Colum McCann, *Let The Great World Spin* (2009)

* * *

English-born Australian journalist Marian Edmunds recalls the incredible view from the top of the World Trade Center, and then reflects on her post–9/11 visit to Ground Zero.

We chose what would be the last warm day of the year although we didn't know it. *Go up on a clear day or you won't see a thing*. The guidebooks and everyone said so about the World Trade Center. I knew little about it except that the Twin Towers were among the world's tallest, and were commercially important. And I knew people were killed there in a terrorist attack in 1993. I was working that Friday night on the world news desk of the *Financial Times* in London and we were just about to put the second edition to bed when our reporter called.

Going to the top was one of those things visitors were supposed to do in NYC.

I remember the operator saying how fast the elevator travelled, and about the height of the tower and telling Alex, my son, to hold his nose until his ears popped. Forgotten is what it was like where we disembarked. Of the observation floor and its shops and food court I've no recall. It's all gone.

Perhaps it's because what I do recall was so stunning to me. It was the observation walkway on the very top. I remember the brilliance of the blue sky and the sound of light aircraft and helicopters, and how a city symphony of whirring traffic, jackhammers, with siren and car horn sections reached all the way up there.

We picked out the landmarks. Liberty was a crayon stroke in the Upper Bay, and on the Lower Bay, the horizon synchronised with the Earth's curvature. Or so I fancied. The breeze was light and the sun was bright. It was heavenly.

We looked across and downwards at the Uptown icons, the gleaming Chrysler Building, the Empire State Building, its seniority commanding respect, and the green lungs of Central Park.

Just across was the North Tower where men in hard hats worked on top – fixing or building – as if floating on a neighbouring pontoon. Their body language shouted they were foremen although we could not hear their words. I remember thinking they had a great view at their place of work and wishing afterwards that I had a photograph conveying the blue of the sky. All I have is a handful of black and white snaps.

Ten years after my first visit to NYC I return alone. I emerge from the PATH train that comes up from under the Hudson

River and see Ground Zero – such a big footprint. At the bottom of Greenwich Street I meet a dear friend from home. It's an easy rendezvous point from where we are each staying. I imagine I will feel something very deep that will move me profoundly. I don't. Nor do I on subsequent visits.

I hear banging of metal and welding, and jackhammers, and I see construction workers in hard hats, and heavy equipment and hoardings. People stop to peek through tiny square viewing flaps to the site. So I look up and try to recall how it was.

And then we head off to Century 21, the temple of bargain retail with many followers. It's my first time. I pick out a few things ... but dump them on a rack and leave, having bought nothing.

The construction extends to the subway and here it feels as if it all happened yesterday. There's a small rectangle of light and behind it a tableau of rebuilding, of starting over. I don't feel much of anything. I try to understand why I am unmoved to visit the exhibition beside the site. Perhaps I don't want the past to be constructed for me. Or was it that an exhibition would be so unequal to the job of memory?

Marian Edmunds, 'Blue, blue sky' (2011)

Taking a break from the city's massive built environment, we'll visit Central Park with two small gems, then a weightier piece from Alistair Cooke's much-loved 'Letter from America' radio series.

Central Park, just at sunset, the light, cold and liquid, leaking around and soaking the few leaves and bare branches of the trees.

Benjamin Markovits, *Either Side of Winter* (2005)

But Central Park, she must admit, is fantastically groomed and beautiful. All around are the trillings and cawings of wildlife, though rarely seeing any insects and birds gives the feeling of walking through some sort of nature-themed park, the noises emitted by carefully hidden radios. They walk into a place called Sheep Meadow. Bird sits and Anju lies on her stomach, watching the white people play their games of catch and kites, backed by a deep green border of trees and, beyond this, a bevy of handsome buildings against a fading sky. From Anju's vantage point, the meadow is broad, so subtle in its changes of velvety green that the land seems to curve with the earth. There is a beauty here of which she will never be a part, but this is the pleasant melancholy of witnessing anything beautiful, the wish to enter and become it.

Tania James, *Atlas of Unknowns* (2009)

✳ ✳ ✳

My workplace is a study that has the great luck to be perched on the fifteenth storey of an apartment house that looks out over the reservoir and the enclosing trees and meadows of Mr Frederick Law Olmsted's Central Park.

Olmsted was a remarkable Connecticut Yankee who wrote the classic, and still the fairest, account – on the verge of the Civil War – of life in the slave states of the South: *The Cotton Kingdom*. During the war, he ran the Union's sanitary commission. But before that, after a lively knockabout career, he had settled down a landscape architect. When the city fathers of New York were thinking, in the 1850s, of having a city park, and when – naturally – the real estate men and the cement contractors and the politicians were trying to guess at the likely location and buy up every acre in sight, Olmsted's plan won out over the plans of thirty competitors. Maybe, I suspect, because Olmsted brought great relief to the realtors by placing his park on empty, bosky ground way out of town. In fact,

Oliver Wendell Holmes, the father of the great Justice, wrote a satirical essay wondering why Olmsted should have christened the proposed park 'Central' Park, since it would be about two miles north of where everybody lived.

Olmsted had out-foxed them all. He privately, and correctly, figured that the next great lurch of residents would be north of the limit of populated Manhattan, which in the 1850s was the streets in the Forties. By the time the park commission had voted on the site and ordered the twenty-year job to begin, it was too late for the realtors to do more than buy up the surrounding fringes of what would become a precious breathing space in a jungle of cement and steel. Olmsted showed remarkable foresight in other ways. His original plan allowed for meadows and a lake for recreation, for a wriggle of footpaths, for carriage paths, and for so-called 'transverses' that would at three banked intervals allow the invisible passage of crosstown horse-buses. When the internal combustion engine arrived, nothing radical was required to adapt the original plan to the 1920s or the 1970s. The carriage paths and the transverses were paved over, and today the automobiles skim their winding way through the trees and meadows and the buses and trucks cut through and under the bridges without entering the park. Olmsted went on to lay out three more parks in New York, and the grounds around the Capitol in Washington, and those around Stanford University in California, and the now splendid lake front of Chicago. His masterpiece, to my mind, is the little-known but exquisite estate of trees, lakes, lawns, and rolling hills that now houses Emory University bang in the middle of Atlanta, Georgia.

Well, as I was saying, I have the luck to look out on Olmsted's first great work and, in moments of furious idleness, when I am trying to work up a little creative thought, I stare at the stark trees of the winter against the snowfields, or the heartening fuzz of the breaking spring, or the rioting forsythia and dogwood and cherry, and then the vast blobs of the summer's full foliage before the yellows and scarlets of the fall come on. I am just at the height of a plane coming in for a steady landing, but I am low enough to sit and envy the kids down there – in winter the little Brueghel dolls scudding downhill on their sledges, but now – in the steaming midsummer – tossing balls, lolling under trees with girls, gobbling ice-cream cones and, on the diamond off to the right, playing baseball.

Alistair Cooke, *Letter From America* (8 July 1977)

❊ ❊ ❊

And across the park to the area around the Museum of Natural History with Tom Wolfe.

He liked to walk across to Central Park West on Seventy-seventh Street and then walk up to Eighty-first, because that took him past the Museum of Natural History. It was a beautiful block, the most beautiful block on the West Side, to Kramer's way of thinking, like a street scene in Paris; not that he had ever been to Paris. Seventy-seventh Street was very wide at that point. On one side was the museum, a marvellous Romanesque Revival creation in an old reddish stone. It was set back in a little park of trees. Even on a cloudy day like this the young spring leaves seemed to glow. *Verdant* was the word that crossed his mind. On this side of the street, where he was walking, was a cliff of elegant apartment houses overlooking the museum. There were doormen. He got glimpses of marbled halls.

Tom Wolfe, *The Bonfire of the Vanities* (1987)

❊ ❊ ❊

While 'central', we'll visit one of the most famous train stations in the world – Grand Central Station – with Ian Frazier, followed by Beatrice Colin's period re-creation of it in her novel The Songwriter, *set in 1916.*

The vaulted ceiling of the main concourse rises a hundred feet or more above the station's marble floor – it's the heart-stopping altitude of the tightrope walker, the altitude of prophetic ascension and rocket liftoff. When visitors come into the station for the first time, their eyes go up to the ceiling, and, in the vast interior space the ceiling encloses, their prospects seem to expand. Looking up in Grand Central evokes feelings of vertigo and excitement and fear of heights and dizziness and exaltation that may recall the reasons you moved to New York City in the first place. The ceiling is the dark greenish-blue of a clear summer-night sky, studded with small lights representing stars in the constellations of the zodiac, with the figures of the zodiac outlined in off-white around them.

Ian Frazier, *Gone to New York* (2005)

＊ ＊ ＊

The four-faced clock on top of the information booth in the middle of Grand Central Station read five minutes to ten. Dusty sunlight fell in long slants from the windows, half moons of glass positioned high above the concourse. The air smelled of scorched coffee and brass polish, of engine grease and pomade. Two huge American flags had been hung on ropes from the vaulted ceiling and they billowed gently in the breeze from the street outside. […]

The train to Chicago was ready to depart. Inside, most of the passengers had already settled into their seats and were unpacking picnics or unrolling newspapers. A porter struggled up the metal stairs into a first-class compartment with a huge wooden chest while the owner, an elderly woman in a black coat, fussed and scolded. A guard with a silver whistle in his mouth began to slam every door shut, starting at the front of the train and working his way to the end. Those who had climbed on board to say their goodbyes took the slamming doors as a cue and hurried quickly off. The hands on the platform clock clicked into place and then, with his arms outstretched and his cap pulled down over his eyes, the guard finally blew his whistle, long and loud. With a scream of metal and a sigh of smoke, the train slowly shifted forward and began to pull away from the platform, away from the station, away from the scattering of people left behind who blew kisses and waved until their shoulders ached. [...]

The train from New Haven was due and with the ringing of bells and the dull rolling rumble of porters' trolley wheels, the platform slowly began to come to life again. The chewing gum machine swallowed coins and belched out packets with a dull metallic clank. The waiting room door swung open, an old woman hobbled in with a cat in a basket and sat down in the corner. Two porters hovered on the platform outside, the dark blue of their jackets mottled by the dirty glass of the window.

'I tell you, he didn't even offer a nickel,' one of the porters was saying. 'I said, "Sir, this is America. It is customary to reward those who assist you and make your stay in this fine country a pleasant one."'

'And what did he do? Pay up?'

'Did he? Hell no. He replied, "Eh downt believe in teeping. In Russia we think it demeaning." "Well, demean me," I replied. "I expect it."'

Their laughter overlapped with the long low whistle of the train as it made its slow approach into Grand Central.

'Here she comes,' yelled one of the porters. 'Right on time.'

Beatrice Colin, *The Songwriter* (2010)

✳ ✳ ✳

Having recently gone the way of many wonderful bookshops, Scribner's Bookstore, the retail outlet of the prestigious publisher, was once home to writers like Hemingway and Fitzgerald, and their editor, the great Maxwell Perkins. It was where people like the Rothschilds bought their books, maybe pausing to look at the paintings by Maxfield Parrish which hung

*in the stairwell. (A brief recollection of it appears in
the singer Patti Smith's memoir* Just Kids.*) But here's
Alan Bennett singing the praises of another famous
New York bookstore, happily still in existence.*

1 December, New York. ... We stop for some tea at Barnes and
Noble on Union Square. All the Barnes and Noble bookshops
have lately been transformed, turned into what are virtually
free libraries. There are easy chairs in which people are encouraged to read the books on display; tables at which students are
sitting, making notes from the books and, upstairs in the café, a
huge rack of every conceivable magazine and newspaper which
you are encouraged to take to your table to read with your tea,
reading all that is required. Nor is it simply patronised by what
one might think of as the reading public. A workman in overalls
is sitting looking at a book on Chardin, the little black boy in
Philip Roth's *Goodbye, Columbus* who came into the library to
look at a book on Gauguin now grown up. But it doesn't have to
be as worthy as that: the boy at the next table is leafing through
a muscle mag. The feeling is overwhelmingly democratic and lifts
the spirits. It's said that the experiment has improved business. I
hope so, as it's inspiring to see and, as so often in America, one
is shamed by a civic sense which, if we ever had it in England,
we don't have now. Dutifully readers clear their tables, put the
trash in the bin and the magazines back on the racks and behave
in a way that is both more civilised and considerate and (this is
where we would really fall down) unselfconscious than we could
ever manage. God bless America.

Alan Bennett, *Untold Stories* (2005)

✱ ✱ ✱

*Even a brief survey of New York's architecture would
not be complete without an account of the more
humble domestic dwellings known as 'brownstones'.*

It lay between the grandest stretches of Madison Avenue and Fifth Avenue, only a couple of minutes on foot from Central Park. It looked across the street to the north and was consequently rather dark, but that was its only major defect. It occupied the *piano nobile* of a brownstone house of 1876, which happened to be the year in which our house in Hammersmith, west London, was built as well – a reminder that New York, despite its many skyscrapers, remained, like London, essentially Victorian in character.

From the mid-nineteenth century onwards, property developers covered New York with rows of brick terraced houses faced with thin slabs of 'Jersey freestone', a reddish-brown sandstone from New Jersey which became dark-chocolate-coloured with time. Lots of these brownstones were quite small and depressing-looking, but I was glad to see it confirmed in the *AA Guide to New York City* of the American Institute of Architects that in this particular house and its two neighbours on 63rd Street 'the brownstone is elevated to mansion status, unlike the endless rows east of Park Avenue'.

It did have a certain faded grandeur, and the two rooms I was to occupy on the second floor (we would say first floor in England, but American houses don't have ground floors) were large and high and square, both with handsome working fireplaces. The whole house, I was told, had once been owned by Jolie Gabor, the mother of Zsa Zsa, which gave it a certain raffish glamour in my eyes. The former Miss Hungary had reputedly lived on my floor and her mother on the floor below, and I imagined that there must have been a lot of emotional comings and goings and shouting in Hungarian on the stairs.

Alexander Chancellor, *Some Times in America* (1999)

✳ ✳ ✳

In the somnolent July afternoon the unbroken line of brownstone houses down the long Brooklyn street resembled an army massed at attention. They were all one uniform red-brown stone. All with high massive stone stoops and black iron-grille fences staving off the sun. All draped in ivy as though mourning. Their sombre façades, indifferent to the summer's heat and passion, faced a park while their backs reared dark against the sky. They were only three or four storeys tall – squat – yet they gave the impression of formidable height.

Glancing down the interminable Brooklyn street you thought of those joined brownstones as one house reflected through a train of mirrors, with no walls between the houses but only vast rooms yawning endlessly one into the other. Yet, looking close, you saw that under the thick ivy each house had something distinctively its own. Some touch that was Gothic, Romanesque, baroque or Greek triumphed amid the Victorian clutter. Here, Ionic columns framed the windows while next door gargoyles scowled up at the sun. There, the cornices were hung with carved foliage while Gorgon heads decorated others. Many houses had bay windows or Gothic stonework; a few boasted turrets raised high above the other roofs. Yet they all shared the same brown monotony. All seemed doomed by the confusion in their design.

Paule Marshall, *Brown Girl, Brownstones* (1960)

❋ ❋ ❋

And here's a view across the city from the roof of a brownstone.

Abraham's out so Dylan's free to climb the ladder out of the painting studio, unhook the hatch to their roof and push it aside, crawl out across the mushy tar paper into the new summer's morning.

Dylan wouldn't have said he feared heights, but the brownstone's roof has always made him dizzy, not so much the view to the ground as the view across rooftops, out to Coney Island and beyond. Easier if you gaze on Manhattan's towers. Those place you, fix you in a firm relation of puniness and awe. Easier still to kneel at the roof's edge, hands gripping the ankle-high rim of masonry, and stare down at the contents of your own yard: ailanthus, brick pile, shoots of weed, a dirty spaldeen you can just make out like a speck of flesh. The grainy reality is reassuring.

What's unsettling is to put Manhattan at your back and face the borough. Up from the canyon floor, out of the deep well of streets, gazing out into the Brooklyn Beyond is like standing in a Kansas prairie contemplating distance. Every rooftop for miles in every direction is level with that where you stand. The rooftops form a flotilla of rafts, a potential chessboard for your knight-hops, interrupted only by the promontory of the Wyckoff housing projects, the skeletal Eagle Clothing sign, the rise of the F-train platform where it elevates past the Gowanus Canal. Manhattan's topped, but Brooklyn's an open-face sandwich in the light, bare parts picked over by pigeon and gulls.

Jonathan Lethem, *The Fortress of Solitude* (2003)

✵ ✵ ✵

But for the city's plentiful poor there were the infamous tenements …

The tenement is the bassic façade in New York. The face of the slums, a slab of tombstone proportions, four to six storeys, pocked by windows. Above is the towering tin cornice, a confection of scallops and curlicues, with foliaceous brackets, often topped by a semicircular peak, a disk enclosing a rayèd sun. Below this, on the cornice, there may be a name, that of the builder, the owner, a female relative, or an allegorical quality: Hope, Columbia, Gertrude. The cornice exists in disdain of practical qualities; it possesses one, vaguely, in adjusting the roof's pitch so that rainwater will run off to the rear of the building, but this function yielded to an aesthetic and then to a nearly heraldic role. It is the most conspicuous item in the tenement's equipment of fictitious grandeur. Below the cornice is the façade proper, a mosaic composed mostly of red brick, but with lacings of white trim; with entablatures greater and lesser; false columns and caryatids; faces, urns, and emblems in bas-relief. The window frames may vary per floor, often the result of the architect's giving full rein to his eclecticism, so that the upper storey might be severely classical and the others increase in ornamentation and exoticism as they near the street level. The oldest buildings are the plainest; as the years advance in the history of tenement-building, through the eighties, nineties, oughts, and teens up to the end of the boom just before World War I, each decade seems to bring a new twist to the frenzied denial of interior realities manifested by the exterior. There are tenements displaying parodies of portes-cochères, false lanterns, pseudo-portcullises, others that compose themselves vertically like wedding cakes, going beyond merely styling the window frames to pretending that each storey is a separate edifice. The façade is all: it is the aspect of the tenement visible to idlers and passersby, to the gentry. If these must, of necessity, glimpse the unavoidable fire escapes, those grim reminders of fatality must be wrought and bowed and garlanded with iron vines so that their respectable beholders can believe them to be Spanish balconies or trellises or creeper roses. The façade is a mask, not the domino or half mask or the upper classes *en travesti* but a giant sunburst or devil's head from animist ritual: behind it is the frail and wretched thing of kitchens and urinals. But then this was a period of façades, in American architecture as in other aspects of society – and here we are talking about the extremes of the reform tenement, the very idea itself being a sort of mask. This was the time when frontier towns presented Main Streets of imposing two- and three-storey fronts which were merely billboards; the actual edifices were single-storey shacks. From such pretence to the false fronts of the Western movie set was no great leap.

The fiction of the tenement's face to the street might continue briefly within the door, or mouth, of the building – usually up to the second door. Between the doors lay a pocket vestibule which might at a later date hold mailboxes. It would have a floor of mosaic tiles, sawtooth mouldings and possibly marble inlays on the walls. The doors might be carved, might have glass in them, might be curtained. Or not, depending on the expediency of the project; a single door might suffice, after all. Within, the ornamentation might not cease abruptly: the stairs might be balustraded, the hall floors tiled and their walls half covered with pressed-tin wainscoting; the walls of the rooms may boast complex mouldings at waist level and just below the ceiling. But then the rooms themselves were stingily proportioned, contained the bare minimum of natural light, with walls and ceilings of hastily slopped plaster sensitive to dampness and cold, and floors of rough-hewn boards that separated, splintered, jutted out. Plumbing was a joke, heating only slightly less so. And in most of these cases such elements were the result of reforms, from a time when comforts were yet more minimal, when interior lighting, plumbing, heating, ventilation, for example, scarcely existed at all.

In its prime, the tenement was to Manhattan as the tree to the forest, the basic and irreducible unit of measure. Between the Civil War and World War I, the tenement plantations spread up the whole of the East Side from just north of City Hall to the Harlem River and through the south and middle of the West Side, excepting only the patches of industrialisation here and there and some old streets of Greenwich Village.

Luc Sante, *Low Life* (1991)

* * *

In a city with its gaze so much on the future, the architectural heritage of New York has not always been adequately preserved. In 2003, Alistair Cooke

*recalled the destruction, forty years previously, of
what must have been one of the greatest architectural
wonders of the city – the old Pennsylvania Station.*

Forty years ago last Monday morning, a gentle southwest wind
carried up through Manhattan what many New Yorkers at first
thought was a series of explosions of some kind. Pretty soon
there came on television what to most New Yorkers was an
incomprehensible sight and sound. The picture showed jackhammers clawing away at the walls of a famous building, and
then at slow rhythmic intervals, a huge airborne shining ball
swung and crashed against – were they mad? – the long stately
Doric colonnade of – were they mad – the Baths of Caracalla?
Well, yes, not of course the original but a superb re-creation of
a Roman architectural masterpiece.

Why were they doing this, and who were *they*? What we
saw was America's most famous railway station, the Pennsylvania Station. It had been designed at the turn of the twentieth century during the finest hour of the new millionaires,
especially the robber barons who had made their fortunes
in coke, iron ore and railroads, and when little old Andrew
Carnegie was proclaiming the new age of steel. Once such a
man became a millionaire, he became eager to advertise the
grandeur of his social position by ordering up a new house,
a mansion, as like as possible not to the mansions of the new
rich of Europe, but to the ancient houses of the old aristocracy,
especially the nobles of France and Italy. Just after Goethe had
given an encouraging line to the poor or oppressed of Europe
who emigrated to America, 'Du hast es besser im Amerika'
(You have things better in America), an American journalist,
watching the robber barons fight each other to procure the Old
Master paintings and the models of the old aristocrats' houses,
wrote: 'Their motto was they do things better in Europe.'

Such was the temper of the time when the most fashionable
architectural firm of the day had an idea beyond the dreams

of the culture-vulture robber barons. McKim, Mead & White proposed to the owners of the Pennsylvania railroad that they would like to build, not a mansion for the chairman of the board, but a railroad station for the city. To do so, they proposed to re-create a jewel of a building of ancient Rome. [...]

But fashions in architecture, as in everything else, change. The European intelligentsia came to chuckle and to sneer. By the mid-twentieth century, America and American businessmen had been ordered to admire the revolutionary works of a German, Walter Gropius, a rebel against all classical, all romantic, all Victorian styles of architecture. He invented what he called an international style. [...]

When the Second World War was over, and the building of everything from cottages to skyscrapers could begin again, Gropius, Mies van der Rohe, the so-called Bauhaus school, became almost compulsory for any city contemplating a new airport, a city hall, a big business about to bloom. (The god himself ruled from his pulpit at Harvard.) The tycoons didn't have to like the style. It simply became essential to their social standing. [...]

In such an atmosphere, there was only one thing more ridiculous than designing a Victorian or Georgian house, and that was retaining the huge absurdity of a re-created Roman classical building. Such is the hypocrisy of fashion that since the end of the Second World War, I don't recall a visiting friend or tourist ever saying, 'I must go down to 34th Street and look at Pennsylvania Station' as their successors would always obediently pad off to the Museum of Modern Art, the Guggenheim, the Whitney. By that time nobody had heard of the Baths of Caracalla, and nobody cared.

Except the board of directors of the Pennsylvania railroad, who decided in 1960 or thereabouts that their Roman station was an expensive burden and also something of an embarrassment. They decided to destroy it. And so at 9 a.m. on 28 October 1963 the jackhammers clawed and the wrecking ball crashed down on the Doric pillars and would soon demolish what was the last reminder in New York of the grandeur that was Rome. [...]

But out of this calamity, out of that ill October wind, there came one great and good thing. In the last year of the demolition, when the long block at 34th Street began to look like a pre-vision of Ground Zero, the small clique of outraged artists, authors, art lovers and citizens, petitioned the Mayor and then the city council and formed a body called the Landmarks Preservation Commission. Since 1965, their agents have snooped around the city with the zeal of the FBI, ticketing period relics of every style to be preserved. There was a big move in the 1970s on the part of the owners of the brilliant and majestic Grand Central Station to have it demolished and replaced by a 54-storey glass-and-steel Gropism. The squabble was fierce and prolonged. Thanks, however, to the tenacity of two members of the Landmarks Commission (one, Brendan Gill, a witty, Irish-American staff writer on the *New Yorker* magazine in its heyday, the other, the Presidential widow Jacqueline Kennedy), the fight was taken all the way to the Supreme Court, which upheld the protest, and in 1978 decreed that Grand Central Station was to be immortal and never to be subjected to the jackhammer and the wrecking ball.

Alistair Cooke, *Letter From America* (31 October 2003)

✳ ✳ ✳

The following extract suggests there is something superficial (even 'fake') and too uniform about the new buildings of contemporary New York.

I come in from Brooklyn now occasionally to visit the Upper West Side. From Lincoln Centre past 72nd Street where Broadway swells and intersects with Amsterdam Avenue all the way up to 89th Street, new buildings reconfigure the landscape of my childhood. These are huge and glossy – glass, steel, and stucco – but they feel portable and weightless, like architectural models grown large. The terraces all stacked and identical, there's no brickwork variation. You know the marble in the lobby and bathrooms is laid on in strips like veneer, that the Sheetrock walls bruise easily. And in the glass bottoms, you find the same coffee shops, bookstores, houseware retailers, and clothiers that you would in Peoria or Dubuque, the same countertops and signs, identical merchandise.

> Gabriel Brownstein, 'The Curious Case of Benjamin Button,
> Apt. 3W' (2003)
> (Title story of collection)

❋ ❋ ❋

Adam Gopnik, newly returned from Europe, suddenly sees New York architecture as derivative, a sad imitation of European styles. But, happily, the moment doesn't last …

The first few weeks back from France are precious, because naïve vision is a capital sum, quickly depleted, and for a few months, New York – the Great Home, Our Place – can be seen again. On our first morning back, woken early by the jet lag, I took Luke for a long dawn walk down Fifth Avenue, past the University Club and St. Patrick's Cathedral and Saks. *This is all from another place*, I thought, shocked by the derivativeness of Fifth Avenue architecture. I felt, I *saw*, for the first time ever, the adolescent absurdity of so many Manhattan monuments – the sad, wilderness, opera-house-in-the-Arctic and Amazon pathos of copying old European styles in a New World city. *This isn't a true Gothic cathedral*, I thought, staring at St. Patrick's. *There are such things, I've seen them, and this is just a … copy, a raw inflated thing thrown up in emulation of a far-off and distant thing! That Renaissance palazzo on Fifty-fourth Street is no Renaissance palazzo – it's a cheap stage-set imitation!*

This perception – of New York as a blown-up Inflato city, aspirational rather than achieved, gawkily imitating its models, the proper cities of Europe – which was once so obviously and embarrassing (to Henry James, much less to Tocqueville), has faded away now, and I no longer see it that way. For that single early morning, though, it seemed that the architecture of New York was not quite real, not organic, coming from else-where and imposed, a delirium of old styles and other people's European visions: the Gothic vision of sublime verticality, or, for that matter, the Bauhaus vision of the glass tower. For a moment New York seemed unnatural, the anti-matter city. "You're not real!" I wanted to cry out, to the city. *"Yes, we are,"* the buildings cried back blankly. *"It is the old thing that is the lie, the true thing is our re-creation of it."* But the moment passed quickly, and now New York just looks like New York: old as time, worn as Rome, mysterious as life.

Adam Gopnik, *Through the Children's Gate* (2007)

On the water front

For many generations, the first sight of New York, for travellers or immigrants, was the magnificent harbour and, as with Venice, this would still be the preferred manner of arrival ... were it not for the speed and convenience of air travel. So we start this section with three spirit-lifting arrivals by sea, including that of a famous European whose theories were to have a huge impact upon America.

The harbour is the most beautiful of New York's possessions, and nowadays it is one of the last refuges in an unhappy metropolis of that fizz and crackle, that sense of lovers' release, which once used to be synonymous with Manhattan. Here some of the American pageantry survives, and when the QE2 sailed in that day much of the old American generosity showed too, and the sentimental loyalty. The sea was choppy and the wind rough, but the sun came out just as the ship passed through the Narrows, and so in a bright flurry of flags and foam our procession passed through the Bay. The liner towered above high, bright and very new, almost fragile. The sky was thick with helicopters and seaplanes, idling happily about there like kites, or paper aeroplanes, and all around us scores of little ships noisily and exuberantly escorted the liner towards her berth.

On the forecastle of the QE2 the ship's cooks, in their chefs' hats, gazed impassively towards Manhattan, and in an open door in the flank of the liner a solitary white-clad sailor stood silhouetted nonchalant, even bored, against the black inside, as though such spectacles were observable on every voyage. For the rest, everybody seemed to be waving. We waved, all barriers down, at total strangers. We blew kisses all over the place. A girl in a blue dress jumped up and down with excitement on the boat deck, and through the slightly steamy windows of what I took to be some ferociously air-conditioned or centrally heated lounge, I could see pale elderly faces cautiously peering into the open air outside, looking wistfully nostalgic still, I fancied, for mahogany and Palm Court.

What fun it all was! The sirens constantly blew. The flags fluttered from every mast. The Staten Island ferry chugged by with a huge welcome sign hanging from its superstructure.

Jan Morris, *A Writer's World* (2003)

✻ ✻ ✻

It was three years before we saw New York again. As the ship glided up the river, the city burst thunderously upon us in the early dusk – the white glacier of lower New York swooping down like a strand of a bridge to rise into uptown New York, a miracle of foamy light suspended by the stars. A band started to play on deck, but the majesty of the city made the march trivial and tinkling. From that moment I knew that New York, however often I might leave it, was home.

F. Scott Fitzgerald, *The Crack-Up* (1945)

* * *

Which, I suppose, is how I came to be waiting in the swelter and mob of Hoboken harbour on Sunday evening, August 29, 1909, for the arrival of the Norddeutsche Lloyd steamship *George Washington*, bound from Bremen, carrying to our shores the one man in the world I most wanted to meet.

At 7 P.M. there was still no sign of the ship. Abraham Brill, my friend and fellow physician, was waiting at the harbour for the same reason as I. He could hardly contain himself, fidgeting and smoking incessantly. The heat was murderous, the air thick with the reek of fish. An unnatural fog rose from the water, as if the sea were steaming. Horns sounded heavily out in the deeper water, their sources invisible. Even the keening gulls could be only heard, not seen. A ridiculous premonition came to me that the *George Washington* had run aground in the fog, her twenty-five hundred European passengers drowning at the foot of the Statue of Liberty. Twilight came, but the temperature did not abate. We waited.

All at once the vast white ship appeared – not as a dot on the horizon, but mammoth, emerging from the mist full-blown before our eyes. The entire pier, with a collective gasp, drew back at the apparition. But the spell was broken by the outbreak of harbourmen's cries, the flinging and catching of rope, and bustle and jostle that followed. Within minutes, a hundred stevedores were unloading freight.

Brill, yelling at me to follow, shouldered through to the gangway. His entreaties to board were rebuffed; no one was being let on or off the ship. It was another hour before Brill yanked at my sleeve and pointed to three passengers descending the bridge. The first of the trio was a distinguished, immaculately groomed, grey-haired, and grey-bearded gentleman whom I knew to be the Viennese psychiatrist Dr. Sigmund Freud.

Jed Rubenfeld, *The Interpretation of Murder* (2006)

❋ ❋ ❋

But the harbour was not always the scene of joyful or apprehensive arrivals: it was also the place from which 'undesirables' were deported. The 'land of the free' wasn't free for everyone.

Bright flakes of cloud were scaling off a sky of crushing indigo over the Battery where groups of dinky dark-dressed people stood round the Ellis Island landing station and the small boat dock waiting silently for something. Frayed smoke of tugs and steamers hung low and trailed along the opaque glassgreen water. A threemasted schooner was being towed down the North River. A new-hoisted jib flopped awkwardly in the wind. Down the harbour loomed taller, taller a steamer head on, four red stacks packed into one, creamy superstructure gleaming. "*Mauretania* just acomin in twentyfour hours lyte," yelled the man with the telescope and fieldglasses ...

"Tyke a look at the *Mauretania*, farstest ocean greyhound, twentyfour hours lyte." The *Mauretania* stalked like a skyscraper through the harbour shipping. A rift of sunlight sharpened the shadow under the broad bridge, along the white stripes of upper decks, glinted in the rows of portholes. The smokestacks stood apart, the hull lengthened. The black relentless hull of the *Mauretania* pushing puffing tugs ahead of it cut like a long knife into the North River.

A ferry was leaving the immigration station, a murmur rustled through the crowd that packed the edges of the wharf. "Deportees ... It's the communists the Department of Justice is having deported ... deportees ... Reds ... It's the Reds they are deporting." The ferry was out of the slip. In the stern a group of men stood still tiny like tin soldiers. "They are sending the Reds back to Russia." A handkerchief waved on the ferry, a red handkerchief. People tiptoed gently to the edge of the wall, tiptoeing, quiet like in a sickroom.

Behind the backs of the men and women crowding to the edge of the water, gorillafaced chipontheshoulder policemen walked back and forth nervously swinging their billies.

"They are sending the Reds back to Russia ... Deportees ... Agitators ... Undesirables." ... Gulls wheeled crying. A catsupbottle bobbed gravely in the little ground-glass waves. A sound of singing came from the ferryboat getting small, slipping away across the water.

> C'est la lutte finale, groupons-nous et demain
> L'Internationale sera le genre humain.

"Take a look at the deportees ... Take a look at the undesirable aliens," shouted the man with the telescopes and fieldglasses. A girl's voice burst out suddenly, *"Arise prisoners of starvation,"* "Sh ... they could pull you for that."

The singing trailed away across the water. At the end of the marbled wake the ferryboat was shrinking into haze. *International ... shall be the human race.* The singing died. From up the river came the longdrawn rattling throb of a steamer leaving dock. Gulls wheeled above the dark dingydressed crowd that stood silently looking down the bay.

John Dos Passos, *Manhattan Transfer* (1925)

✳ ✳ ✳

Helen Keller was surely one of the most amazing women in history: being blind and deaf from the age of nineteen months did not stop her from achieving great things. A prolific writer, she here recalls the pleasure of sailing around the city.

One of my never-to-be-forgotten experiences was circumnavigating New York in a boat. The trip took all day. I had with me four people who could use the hand alphabet – my teacher, my sister, my niece and Mr. Holmes. One who has not seen New York in this way would be amazed at the number of people who live on the water. Someone has called them "harbour gypsies". Their homes are on boats – whole fleets of them, decorated with flower boxes and bright-coloured awnings. It is amusing to note how many of these stumbling, awkward harbour gypsies have pretty feminine names – *Bella*, *Floradora*, *Rosalind*, *Pearl of the Deep*, *Minnehaha*, *Sister Nell*. The occupants can be seen going about their household tasks – cooking, washing, sewing, gossiping from one barge to another, and there is a flood of smells which gives eyes to the mind. The children and dogs play on the tiny deck, and chase each other into the water, where they are perfectly at home.

Helen Keller, *Midstream: My Later Life* (1929)

✳ ✳ ✳

As lovely as the view of the city from the water might be to some, Edgar Alan Poe regrets what humans have done to spoil Nature's gift to the city.

In point of *natural* beauty, as well as of convenience, the harbour of New York has scarcely its equal in the northern hemisphere; but, as in the case of Brooklyn, the Gothamites have most grievously disfigured it by displays of landscape and architectural *taste*. More atrocious *pagodas*, or what not – for it is indeed difficult to find a name for them – were certainly never imagined than the greater portion of those which affront the eye, in every nook and corner of the bay, and, more particularly, in the vicinity of New Brighton. If these monstrosities appertain to taste, then it is to taste in its dying agonies.

Edgar Allan Poe, *Doings of Gotham* (1844)

✳ ✳ ✳

Where there are rivers there are bridges. A number of New York's bridges are among the most famous in the world. The Brooklyn, Queensboro and Manhattan bridges in particular have inspired some good writing.

The New York tower of the Brooklyn Bridge was completed the year that I was born, and I often heard my mother say – she having knowledge of what was going on, because we lived directly under that tower – that if the people of New York City had had any idea of the number of human lives sacrificed in the sinking of the caissons for the towers of the Brooklyn Bridge in all probability they would have halted its progress.

The Brooklyn Bridge was built by hand. Pneumatic tools and compressed air were unknown. All the riveting of the steel in the structure of that great bridge was done by hand, and it was the pride of New York and Brooklyn when, on Queen Victoria's birthday, on the twenty-fourth of May, 1883, it was opened to the public. Newspapers of the time contained a great many stories about the character of its construction, its strength, the load it could carry, and the other details of its construction. Militia crossing it in step or too many elephants crossing it at one time, because they are known to keep in step, were mentioned as dangerous because of the rhythmic vibration they would cause.

It must have been these newspaper stories stirring in the minds of some of the pedestrians on Decoration Day, 1883, six days after the opening of the bridge, which caused the cry that the bridge was falling. Regiments of the national guard, in celebration of the opening of the bridge as well as in celebration of Decoration Day, were crossing it. The cry of alarm started a stampede for the New York end and twelve people were killed and thirty-five injured in the mad scramble to get to the masonry work and away from the suspended steel.

I was a boy of ten, and with other boys was standing under the bridge in South Street. We were unable to discover what was the matter when we saw hats, coats, parasols, umbrellas and pocketbooks dropping from the bridge into the street, until we later found that there was an emergency call to all the hospitals of the city to send ambulances to the New York end of the bridge. We learned then that it was due to what was called the 'crush', in the effort of the people to get to what they considered to be a place of safety.

In its early days the bridge served as more than a utility for transportation between the two cities. It soon became a place of recreation and of pleasure. So much so that it was referred to in songs and popularised on the variety stage.

Al Smith, *Up To Now* (1929)

* * *

Queensboro Bridge, seen from the foot of East Fifty-third Street late at night, is a marvellous spectacle. There is light in the sky above and wandering light on the river below. There is all the grandeur which circumambient shade can give. 'What have I come to?' you ask, astonished after the sordidness of the Avenue, with its many garbage cans. Suddenly you see a mirage. It is called Queensboro Bridge. It takes the mind to the finest parts of the Seine and the Thames. You feel you must be at the centre of a great city, near its Parliament, its palaces, its pontifical grandeurs. But this is Rome without a Pope – a mere bridge, beautiful and awe-inspiring by accident, a convenience whose formal magnificence goes unheeded in the daytime, when business absorbs all the interest and takes the first and only place in men's eyes.

Stephen Graham, *New York Nights* (1927)

* * *

Cut off as I am, it is inevitable that I should sometimes feel like a shadow walking in a shadowy world. When this happens I ask to be taken to New York City. Always I return home weary but I have the comforting certainty that mankind is real flesh and I myself am not a dream.

In order to get to New York from my home it is necessary to cross one of the great bridges that separate Manhattan from Long Island. The oldest and most interesting of them is the Brooklyn Bridge, built by my friend, Colonel Roebling, but the one I cross oftenest is the Queensborough Bridge at 59th Street. How often I have had Manhattan described to me from these bridges! They tell me the view is loveliest in the morning and at sunset when one sees the skyscrapers rising like fairy palaces, their million windows gleaming in the rosy-tinted atmosphere.

I like to feel that all poetry is not between the covers of poetry books, that much of it is written in great enterprises of engineering and flying, that into mighty utility man has poured and is pouring his dreams, his emotions, his philosophy. This materialising of his genius is sometimes inchoate and monstrous, but even then sublime in its extravagance and courage. Who can deny that the Queensborough Bridge is the work of a creative artist?

Helen Keller, *Midstream: My Later Life* (1929)

❋ ❋ ❋

Just beyond the intersection of Canal and the Bowery, across an asphalt expanse of traffic lanes and concrete dividers and yellow stripes painted on the pavement, is the arch at the entrance to the Manhattan Bridge. Traffic going to and coming from the bridge drives on ramps around long, columned wings extending from either side of the arch. Depending on the time of day, traffic going one direction or the other drives under the arch itself. The arch is maybe forty feet high, embellished with goddesses of victory, shields, fasces, tridents, spears, flags, helmets, winged lion heads. Across the top of the arch, in bas-relief, is a frieze of Indians on horseback hunting buffalo. The Indians draw their bows all the way back among a galloping herd of adults and calves. One horse prances on its hind legs. At the keystone of the arch, a buffalo head looks down on the tops of passing trucks. An afterthought of twin steel cables stretched from one leg of the arch to the other holds yellow traffic-signal boxes. Along the wings of the arch, in between the columns, people with no place to live store folded-up cardboard cartons, plastic bags of clothes, a laundry cart, sneakers, a broom. Sometimes sanitation men come along and clean this out, and then all that is left, on a ledge at the base of a column, is a single plastic vial of those scented oils people sell in the subway. Windrows of trash pile up on one side of the traffic dividers that route the cars coming off the bridge. As you approach, pigeons leap from the trash like flames.

Actually, Canal Street does not stop at the bridge but angles off to the east for eight blocks. Here it is not an artery but just a Lower East Side street. Guys lie in it to work on their cars. The gutter holds blue safety glass from a shattered car window, birdseed, a squashed gherkin, puddles of fluorescent-green radiator coolant. Nobody yells at trucks that double-park. A Chinese man standing at the back of a truck loads garments that come to him down a long cord strung directly from the truck to a window on the top floor of a nearby building. Pastel sports shirts on hangers descend one after another in five-storey swoops. On this part of Canal Street, Chinese businesses mix with kosher delis, locksmiths, upholstery stores, and Hasidic hardware stores, which are closed on Saturday. Just below Canal is a network of narrow streets centuries older than the bridge roaring above them. It is Chinatown, but not the part where conventioneers come to eat Chinese food. Some of the side streets are so narrow they barely have curbs, much less sidewalks. Flatiron buildings almost small enough to put your arms around occupy tiny wedge-shaped lots. Gentrification has left this place untouched; rents here are probably about the same as they were in Carthage, or Nineveh, or Peking under the Tangs. Shoes have worn shallow depressions in the stone of apartment-house steps; hands have polished the paint off railings. Ancient paint on door lintels is cracked and ridged like alligator hide. This is the basic city that people have always lived in, of which the rest of New York is only the twentieth century's approximation. Market Street, which runs parallel to the bridge just south of it, angles down to the blue of the East River like a lane in a seacoast town.

Ian Frazier, *Gone to New York* (2005)

✲ ✲ ✲

Water has always provided the opportunity for fun ...
though the perils of pollution now make it unadvis-
able to cool off in the way described here by Al Smith.
A vivid miniature of past pleasures.

The East River was the place for swimming, and as early as April and as late as October the refreshing waters of the East River, free entirely at that time from pollution, offered the small boy all the joys that now come to the winter or summer bather on the shores of the Atlantic Ocean. [...]

The popular swimming place was the dock at the foot of Pike Street, built well out into the river, and there was a rather good-natured caretaker who paid no attention to small boys seeking the pleasure and recreation of swimming in the East River.

In the warm summer days it was great fun sliding under the dock while the men were unloading the boat-loads of bananas from Central America. An occasional overripe banana would drop from the green bunch being handed from one dock labourer to another, and the short space between the bock and the boat contained room enough for at least a dozen of us to dive after the banana.

Al Smith, *Up To Now* (1929)

✲ ✲ ✲

Nigerian-born writer and photographer Teju Cole
describes an unplanned boat trip to the Statue of
Liberty, and provides some fascinating details about the

*problems encountered by New York's birds in relation
to the 'beacon of freedom'. One cannot help reading
it metaphorically as the fate of a certain percentage of
the immigrants who flock to what they hope is liberty,
security, and full acceptance into American society.*

When I came off the subway, instead of going directly home, I
crossed the West Side Highway. I intended to see the water, and
approached the Chelsea Piers building. Coming around it on the
right, to where the yachts and tourists boats were docked, I saw a
man in uniform. He raised his arm in greeting. We are just about
to leave, he said. I presumed he was in charge of the boat, and I
explained I wasn't part of the party. It's okay, he said. The boat
isn't at capacity yet. And you don't have to pay anything; they've
covered the costs. He smiled, and added, I can tell you'd love to
hop on. Come on! We'll be back in under an hour. I followed
him to Pier 66, and stepped onto the long white boat, which was
already noisy with college-age revellers. It was almost eleven, and
there was no rain. In the brightly lit interior cabin, someone in a
waiter's uniform was checking ID cards before letting the students
take filled plastic champagne flutes from his tray. He offered me
one, and I declined. Most people were watching the view from
inside the cabin, as the wind was by now brisk. I made my way to
the back deck. There were a handful of couples and some solitary
individuals, and I found a place to sit near one of the railings.

The engine emitted a low grumble, and the boat pitched back
a little and trembled, as though it were inhaling air in readiness
for a dive. Then it pushed off the pier, and soon, the water
between us and the docking piers widened, and the chatter of
the revellers floated up from the glassed-in cabin. We traced a
fast arc south, and the taller buildings in the Wall Street area
soon loomed into view on our left. Closest to the water was
the World Financial Center, with its two towers linked by the
translucent atrium and lit blue by night lights. The boat rode
the river swells. Sitting on deck, watching the frothy, white

wake on the black water, I felt myself pulled aloft and down again, as if by the travel of an invisible bell rope.

Within a few minutes of our entering the Upper Bay, we saw the Statue of Liberty, a faint green in the mist, then very quickly massive and towering over us, a monument worthy of the name, with the thick folds of her dress as stately as columns. The boat came close to the island, and more of the students had by now moved up onto the deck, and they pointed, and their voices, which filled the air around us, fell echolessly into the water. The cruise organiser came up to me. Glad you came, aren't you? I acknowledged his greeting with a faint smile, and he, sensing my solitude, went away again. The crown of the statue has remained closed since late 2001, and even those visitors who come close to it are confined to looking upward at the statue: no one is permitted to climb up the 354 narrow steps and look out into the bay from the windows in the crown. Bartholdi's monumental statue has not, in any case, done particularly long service as a destination for tourists. Although it has had its symbolic value right from the beginning, until 1902, it was a working lighthouse, the biggest in the country. In those days, the flame that shone from the torch guided ships into Manhattan's harbour: that same light, especially in bad weather, fatally disorientated birds. The birds, many of which were clever enough to dodge the cluster of skyscrapers in the city, somehow lost their bearings when faced with a single monumental flame.

A large number of birds met their death in this manner. In 1888, for instance, on the morning after one particularly stormy night, more than fourteen hundred dead birds were recovered from the crown, the balcony of the torch, and the pedestal of the statue. The officials of the island saw an opportunity there and, as was their custom, sold the birds off, at low cost, to New York City milliners and fancy stores. But it was to be the last time they would do so, because one Colonel Tassin, who had military command of the island, intervened and was determined that any birds that happened to die in the future would not be disposed of commercially, but would be retained in the service of science. The carcasses, each time two hundred or more of them had been gathered, were sent to the Washington National Museum, the Smithsonian Institution, and other scientific institutions. With this strong instinct for public-spiritedness, Colonel Tassin undertook a government system of records which he ensured were kept with military regularity and, shortly afterward, he was able to deliver detailed reports on each death, including the species of the bird, date, hour of striking, number striking, number killed, direction and force of the wind, character of the weather, and general remarks. On October 1 of that year, for example, the colonel's report indicated that fifty rails had died, as had eleven wrens, two catbirds, and one whip-poor-will. The following day, the record showed two dead wrens; the day after that, eight wrens. The average, Colonel Tassim estimated, was about twenty birds per night, although the weather and the direction of the wind had a great deal to do with the resulting harvest. Nevertheless, the sense persisted that something more troubling was at work. On the morning of October 13, for example, 175 wrens had been gathered in, all dead of the impact, although the night just past hadn't been particularly windy or dark.

Teju Cole, *Open City* (2011)

* * *

So we return to the image of New York's harbour, in 1945, and the arrival of ships still occasionally bringing immigrants from a war-torn Europe. The second paragraph of this extract by Jan Morris is actually a footnote in the book from which it is taken, bringing the reader up-to-date.

Such was Manhattan the haven. It was the greatest of all seaports in 1945, but like the city itself it was also an allegory. Even then an immigrant ship occasionally docked on the West Side, and passers-by might glimpse its passengers wide-eyed, shabby-clothed and emaciated from Europe, stumbling through the customs formalities in the echoing arrivals shed: out of the sea like so many before them, bewildered and tongue-tied, but ready to accept, as they stepped with their bags and blankets into the street outside, the island's limitless chance and bounty.

Today the maritime business of New York has been dispersed far more widely around the Bay, and many of the Manhattan piers have been obliterated by landfill, depriving the island of its corrugated outline. The peak year for the passenger liners was 1957, and the peak day, September 3, 1957, when twelve liners disembarked 9,000 passengers: but in that same year, for the first time, as many people left New York for Europe by air as by sea, and in 1984 the *New York Times* discontinued its daily listing of shipping arrivals and departures. As to the immigrants, for another twenty years they continued to come in ships, but nowadays, like the rest of us, they nearly always reach their haven out of the skies.

Jan Morris, *Manhattan '45* (1987 / 2011)

✳ ✳ ✳

And even more up-to-date is this May 2011 article from The Guardian *reporting on the latest projects for renewing New York's amazing though neglected waterfront. If the projects are achieved, the transformation will be amazing and the city once more able fully to enjoy the pleasures and beauties of its watery location.*

The view from pier six on the Brooklyn side of the East River is breathtaking: the majestic skyline of downtown Manhattan boasts its latest addition, a new residential tower designed by Frank Gehry. In the distance to the right, the spires of the Empire State and the Chrysler buildings reflect the sunlight as if dipped in molten gold.

But the pier itself is not such a happy sight. A wasteland of concrete, rusty steel frames, rotting blocks of wood and mounds of gravel, it is testament to the decline of this stretch of Brooklyn, as well as the neglect that for many years has defined New York's relationship with its waterfront.

There are few cities in the world that can compete with New York for the extent and diversity of its water. It has 520 miles of shoreline – more than Chicago, Portland, San Francisco and Seattle combined. The city is embraced by two powerful tidal rivers, the Hudson and the East river, and two major bays, Long Island Sound and the Atlantic, affording New Yorkers the pleasures of 16 miles of beaches.

Yet until recently, you would hardly have noticed it. New York City looked inward to its famous buildings and Central Park, away from the gift of its waterways. As the mayor, Michael Bloomberg, has said: "At some point in our history, we literally and figuratively turned our back on the waterfront."

Now Bloomberg and his team have declared that they are determined the waste will be brought to an end, that New York will be reconnected with its water. Bloomberg has announced a $360m (£215m) three-year action plan that aims to bring the shoreline back into the heart of the community.

"The water is the connective tissue of this place – we see it as our sixth borough," said Amanda Burden, the city's chief planner. "The ambition is to make New York City once again one of the world's great harbour cities and to reclaim that water as part of New Yorkers' everyday lives." [...]

Under the new plan, 130 projects have been funded including 14 new greenways and esplanades and 20 hectares (50 acres) of new waterfront parks. New Yorkers will be encouraged not just to go to the water, but to go on to it. Within three years, there will be 60 launching pads around the city for those who want to go canoeing or sailing.

From this summer, a high-speed ferry service will run every 20 minutes between Manhattan, Brooklyn and Queens, which Burden says will blur the boundaries of the five boroughs. Economic incentives will be used to revitalise the port, which remains the largest on the US east coast, providing $6.8bn in business revenues.

The paradox is that New York became the powerhouse that it is today largely because of the water, both in terms of its population, which swelled with the arrival of European immigrants landing at Ellis Island, and economically, with the triangle trade in cotton and slaves between Africa and the American Deep South.

"It's incredible given its origins that the waterfront has become such a dead loss to New York," said Lisa Keller, a historian at the State University of New York and executive editor of the Encyclopaedia of New York City.

The trouble began, Keller explained, in the 1840s when railway lines were laid along the shoreline, cutting off New Yorkers from their rivers. That was accentuated in the early 20th century when the main roads through Manhattan, the East River Drive and the West Side Highway, were carved in concrete swathes all the way along the respective perimeters of the island. "You have just two arteries in Manhattan – only two – and they put them both on the water. That was crazy!" said Keller.

When low-cost housing was built after the second world war, that too was put on the water. Industrial decline in turn took its toll, leaving large stretches in the Bronx, Queens and Brooklyn derelict and dangerous to the public. [...]

But the change is palpable, and spreading steadily across the city. In June, on the Manhattan side of the East river, a new Waterfront Park will open within walking distance of Wall Street. And within a year or so pier six on the other side of the river will no longer be the concrete wasteland it is today. Work has begun that will transform it into a park where Brooklynites will be able to watch open-air films on balmy summer nights or stroll up to Brooklyn Bridge, where the waterfront has already been converted into glorious green space.

Ed Pilkington, *The Guardian* (2 May, 2011)

I am a stranger here myself

Watching the boats come in from the harbour-side was one thing, but what was it actually like for those arriving in New York hoping for a better life?

When the fourth day dawned even those who had spent the whole trip cooped up in their cabins showed up on deck. We saw the lights of New York even before the morning mist rose. As the boat entered the harbour the sky was clear and clean. The excitement grew the closer we got to the docks. We recognised the Statue of Liberty in the distance. Countless smaller boats were sailing about in the harbour. In front of us rose the imposing sight of skyscrapers – the same skyline we had admired so often on postcards. Many of the passengers had only heard talk of New York, and stood with their mouths open, spellbound.

Bernardo Vega, Memoirs (1955)

❊ ❊ ❊

"There it is, Toto." Anna was pointing. The bridge of the ship had obscured the great monument from view, but now the passengers were all pressing towards the port side to get a better look as it approached. "The Statue of Liberty."

There was hardly any need to move to the rail. The mighty statue towered over them. Its upraised arm, torch in hand, seemed to scrape the sky. Salvatore gazed up in silence. So this was America.

Salvatore didn't know much about America. He knew it was big, and that the people there spoke English, of which Uncle Luigi spoke a few words, and that when you worked, they gave you dollars to send home. He had never heard of the Anglo-Saxon Puritans or the Dutch settlers, or the God-fearing farmers of New England. His family had never spoken of the Boston Tea Party, or Ben Franklin, or even George Washington. Nor, gazing at the Statue of Liberty, could he have derived any clue as to the existence of such a Christian or democratic tradition.

Yet instinctively, as the Mediterranean boy looked up, he understood what he saw.

Power. The colossal, pale green, pagan god rose alone on its huge pedestal above the waters. Hundreds of feet up, under its mighty diadem, the blank, heroic face stared with Olympian indifference across the clear blue sky, while its upraised arm signalled: Victory. If the statue bade him any welcome at all, the little boy sensed, it was to an empire like that of his ancestors. Only one thing puzzled him.

"Is it a man," he whispered to Anna, "or a woman?"

She also gazed, uncertain. The huge face seemed to belong to a male god, yet the massive drapery that fell over the statue's body might have suggested a stately Roman matron. Anna tugged at Uncle Luigi's arm, to ask him.

"She is a woman," said Uncle Luigi. "The French gave her to the Americans."

Had Uncle Luigi known it, he could have added that the sculptor came from Alsace, on the Franco-German border, had studied in Egypt as well, and that therefore it was not so surprising if this monument to Liberty, timeless as the pyramids, should also echo that modern version of the classical spirit, the French Second Empire – with a hint, perhaps, of German power as well.

They sailed straight past Ellis Island. The first- and second-class passengers, the people with cabins, did not have to pass through that ordeal. They had already been given a brief and courteous inspection on board before the ship entered the harbour, and were free to disembark at their leisure.

On the starboard side, the ship passed Governor's Island, then the tip of Manhattan with its little fort and park. Beyond, in the East River, both the funnels of steamships and the huge masts of sailing ships graced the waters. On the port side, Salvatore saw the high cliffs of the Palisades up the Hudson. Then, moments later, the ship began to make its slow turn towards the Hoboken piers on the New Jersey side, where the German liners docked.

Across the river, New York stretched for miles. Street after street of brick and brownstone houses; here and there, clumps of office buildings, several storeys higher. Nearby, the dark spire of Trinity, Wall Street, and further off, the Gothic towers of the Brooklyn Bridge rose into the sky. Even more dramatically, nearly a dozen tall skyscrapers, each over three hundred feet high, soared into the heavens above them all.

Edward Rutherfurd, *New York* (2009)

✳ ✳ ✳

Alistair Cooke describes the harsh realities facing immigrants once they came ashore.

There can hardly be an American born here who cannot recite the five thundering lines inscribed on the Statue of Liberty: the hectoring command – 'Give me your tired, your poor, /Your huddled masses yearning to breathe free, /The wretched refuse of your teeming shore. – /Send these, the homeless tempest-tossed, to me: /I lift my lamp beside the golden door.' Generous words, almost arrogant in their bravery. Whether they constitute fine poetry or doggerel, they touched the hearts and minds of millions of Europeans – always the poor, often the persecuted, very often the fugitives from military service. They were spurred to pack a few belongings, often no more than a blanket, a cooking pot, a prayer book, a corset, to climb aboard box cars deep inside Russia or Hungary or Lithuania or Germany and be carried to the great ports: Constantinople, Piraeus, Antwerp, Bremen, and then put aboard. There, in enclosures outside the embarkation city, they were bathed, de-loused, fed, their baggage and clothes fumigated. They were prepared for the land of the free.

We are talking about the routine procedures employed with the fourteen and a half million immigrants who arrived here, mainly New York or Boston, in the first two decades of the twentieth century. Looking up in awe to the bosom of the colossal lady peering out towards Europe, they would very soon find out that the physical routine of getting into the United States was not quite what a poor foundling might expect of a new, compassionate mother.

Coming across the Atlantic, they were not so much allotted space as stowed aboard, as many as nine hundred in steerage. Sailing slowly up the lower bay of New York City, they would spot their first Americans climbing aboard from a Coast Guard cutter, two men and a woman: immigration inspectors, whose first job was to look over the ship's manifest and see if the captain had recorded cases of contagious disease. Considering the frequency and unpredictability at the time of ravaging epidemics across the continent of Europe, they looked out first for signs of cholera, typhoid, tuberculosis. If you showed any sign of these fearsome diseases, you were at once taken off to quarantine on an island in the bay and got ready for early deportation.

Once the newcomers had been herded into a large reception hall, they would be tagged with numbers and grouped according to their native tongue, which for the vast majority of them was the only one they spoke. They moved, shadowed by interpreters, in lines past a doctor in a blue uniform, a man with a chalk in his hand – an instant diagnostician. He was certainly a fast one and had the confidence that comes from not knowing anything about CT scans, or MRIs, or PSAs. He saw an ageing man with purple lips and chalked on his back: H – possible heart disease. Separate this man! Children in arms stood down to see if they betrayed the limp of rickets. T on the back was the expulsion sign of tuberculosis. Two other doctors dipped into a bowl of disinfectant and folded a suspect eyelid back with a buttonhook. Trachoma – very prevalent in Southern and Eastern Europe and a sure harbinger of blindness. You, too, were on your way back home.

We won't follow the release of most of the healthy rest to railroad agents, con men, honest bosses and sweatshop owners looking for, and getting in luscious numbers, an army of cheap labourers, for most of whom the prospect was better than life in the homeland.

The expectation, among the mass of the settled population, was that these strangers would settle in too. But with every wave of new immigrants there was always a booming counter-wave of protest, from the people who'd been here a long time, two, three or more generations of what we now call the Anglos and their collateral Nordics – Swedes, Norwegians, Germans. They had run the country, its government, its institutions for a hundred years or more. So every breaking wave of new immigrants made a rude sound to the residents, and they protested, then they discriminated. Often Washington legislated, as it did in the 1920s and again in the 1950s against what were called 'undesirable types', meaning Orientals, Southern and Eastern Europeans. Even as late as the time I first came here, in the early 1930s, there were still pasted on shop windows and employment agencies stickers left over from early in the century: 'No Irish Need Apply'. But now, equally new to me, just outside the entrance to an apartment building was a sign: a wooden post surmounted by a rectangle, a sort of mahogany plaque, very handsome, a meticulously printed sign of gold lettering on a black background. It said 'Apartments To Let, Three To Six Rooms. Restricted'. That last word was not put in as an afterthought. It was printed in the same fine style as the rest of the announcement. 'Restricted', I discovered, was shorthand for 'No Jews Need Apply'. This was standard practice here in New York, in Manhattan especially; the other four boroughs, getting most of their business and work from the legions of incoming Jews, could not afford to be so particular. That rather callous sign vanished. It came to be made illegal in the late 1940s, when a Republican Governor of New York, Thomas E. Dewey (who had two failing shots at the Presidency against Franklin Roosevelt), pushed through the state legislature the first (in this country) fair employment and fair housing Act. (The practice of exclusion was not totally abandoned. It continued in parts of the Upper East Side, unofficially, without the dreaded word, discreetly, on tiptoe, in the English manner.) Today there are no signs, except scurrilous ones painted by hooligans.

Alistair Cooke, *Letter From America* (25 June 1993)

❊   ❊   ❊

Despite wanting a new life and new chances, a firmly embedded culture and set of values cannot be changed overnight. And part of the rich variety of New York life depends upon the persistence of newcomers' different ways of doing things. Mario Puzo (best known for The Godfather*) describes something of the life of Italian immigrants.*

Each tenement was a village square; each had its group of women, all in black, sitting on stools and boxes and doing more than gossip. They recalled ancient history, argued morals and social law, always taking their precedents from the mountain village in southern Italy they had escaped, fled from many years ago. And with what relish their favourite imaginings! Now: what if their stern fathers were transported by some miracle to face the problems *they* faced every day? Or their mothers of the quick and heavy hands? What shrieks if *they* as daughters had dared as these American children dared? If *they* had presumed. […]

The truth: these country women from the mountain farms of Italy, whose fathers and grandfathers had died in the same rooms in which they were born, these women loved the clashing steel and stone of the great city, the thunder of trains in the railroad yards across the street, the lights above the Palisades far across the Hudson. As children they had lived in solitude, on land so poor that people scattered themselves singly along the mountain slopes to search out a living.

Audacity had liberated them. They were pioneers, though they never walked an American plain and never felt real soil beneath their feet. They moved in a sadder wilderness, where the language was strange, where their children became members of a different race. It was a price that must be paid.

Mario Puzo, *The Fortunate Pilgrim* (1965)

*   *   *

In the mid-nineteenth century, the great American philosopher, social campaigner, poet and early environmentalist, Henry David Thoreau, observes new arrivals from other parts of Europe.

I have crossed the bay 20 or 30 times and have seen a great many immigrants going up to the city for the first time – Norwegians who carry their old fashioned farming tools to the west with them, and will buy nothing here for fear of being cheated. – English operatives, known by their pale faces and stained hands, who will recover their birth-rights in a little cheap sun and wind, – English travellers on their way to the Astor House, to whom I have done the honours of the city. – While families of immigrants cooking their dinner upon the pavements, all sun-burnt – so that you are in doubt where the foreigner's face of flesh begins – their tidy clothes laid on, and then tied to their swathed bodies which move about like a bandaged finger – caps set on the head, as if woven of the hair, which is still growing at the roots – each and all busily cooking, stooping from time to time over the pot, and having something to drop into it, that so they may be entitled to take something out, forsooth. They look like respectable but straightened people, who may turn out to be counts when they get to Wisconsin – and will have their experience to relate to their children.

Henry David Thoreau, *Letters From Staten Island* (1843)

✽ ✽ ✽

Russian-born American Gary Shteyngart's first novel features the adventures of Vladimir Girshkin whose Jewish family had emigrated to New York from Russia when he was a boy. This brief, humorous extract reminds us that immigrants fleeing conflicts in their own countries sometimes come from opposing sides. All add to the amazing melting-pot that is New York.

His story begins in New York, on the corner of Broadway and Battery Place, the most dishevelled, godforsaken, not-for-profit corner of New York's financial district. On the tenth floor, the Emma Lazarus Immigrant Absorption Society greeted its clients with the familiar yellow water-stained walls and dying hydrangeas of a sad Thirds World government office. In the reception room, under the gentle but insistent prodding of trained Assimilation Facilitators, Turks and Kurds called a truce, Tutsis queued patiently behind Hutus, Serbs chatted up Croats by the demilitarised water fountain.

Meanwhile, in the cluttered back office, junior clerk Vladimir Girshkin – the immigrant's immigrant, the expatriate's expatriate, enduring victim of every practical joke the late twentieth century had to offer and an unlikely hero for our times – was going at it with the morning's first double-cured-spicy-soppressata-and-avocado sandwich. How Vladimir loved the unforgiving hardness of the soppressata and the fatty undertow of the tender avocado! The proliferation of this kind of Janus-faced sandwich, as far as he was concerned, was the best thing about Manhattan in the summer of 1993.

Gary Shteyngart, *The Russian Debutante's Handbook* (2002)

✳ ✳ ✳

Not all strangers, of course, come to stay for good. German writer Wolfgang Koeppen (1906–1996) describes his arrival in New York harbour on the ship 'Liberté'.

The New World greeted me with a cold wind and grey skies. Anticipation had driven our ship's passengers out of bed before daylight, but the closer we got to land, the less we yearned for the gradually approaching form. A herd of amateur photographers swarmed over the decks like frightened sheep. The Statue of Liberty reared up out of the sea in a ragged cloak of mist, a worthy sister to those beloved giantesses in Europe – Bavaria, Germania, and Berolina – whose hollow heads you can climb into, peering through their blind eyes at the mute, outspread horizon: a matron sullenly holding up a wet torch, but illuminating nothing.

Now the famous skyline stepped out from behind the homely symbol of freedom, the skyscrapers huddling together on the tip of that very solid and expensive rock. I thought of economic statistics, of success plotted with curves on a graph, I saw stock prices climbing, rockets taking off: the very heavens should be quaking! But you couldn't see paradise any better from here than anywhere else, and from the perspective of the visitor approaching the continent, the world's richest city seemed like a village with megalomania: the view looked familiar, and this painting was more true-to-life than outsized or overpowering.

The ship glided slowly, pulled by tugboats, toward the new Rome, the Rome of the fabled western hemisphere. Its towers weren't praising God, nor were they inquiring about an all-powerful Being, for they had arrived at their own omnipotence. I expected to feel a *frisson* as I confronted the enormity of human freedom and the acclaimed belief in human happiness through technical and material progress – but that shiver never materialized. New York City, stretching up in the morning mist, was a stage set of steel, concrete, glass, and brick which made me think of houses of cards and storms which might be brewing far away. Beneath its highest rooftops, other roofs cowered, looking as humble as they were: mere sheds, apparently, much like ground-level barracks, which drew down the giants and attempted to reduce them to their own level. Everything seemed temporary and arbitrary while appearing at the same time to follow the kind of easily-grasped order which a playful but not very imaginative child might have devised.

It pleased me, however, to see the chunky, old-fashioned ferryboats plying across the shallow harbour, and I was delighted to see their wheels turning, churning up foam, as they crossed the Hudson heavy with their human freight. This was the America I had anticipated: it made me think of Mark Twain and Walt Whitman, even if the Mississippi and the Camps of Green were far away and the era of those writers was past. The docks mentioned by Melville still encircled Manhattan like black honeycombs, and the *Liberté* was swallowed up in them as if by some huge maw.

Disembarkation proceeded according to an ancient, strict ritual. First the privileged people in first class were allowed into the country, then the cabin section with all its black-clad priests, and the emigrants had their turn at the very end, herded into the sacred precincts of the demigods, invited to the thick carpets and brocade armchairs of the great ballroom. Immigration officials were sitting here at tables cleared of those lavish suppers which were the pride of the shipping line. I wasn't asked whether I wanted to assassinate the President: that turned out to be a myth. The officials were friendly and informal, stamping documents left and right, and they left assassinations to the foreigners.

This mighty America trusted me – it trusted me right away. It expected me to recognize with my very own eyes that the U.S. was God's country. I was instinctively afraid of failing to live up to this expectation, and I was ashamed. Was I travelling with a false passport? I received my entry visa, walked down the gangplank, my last tangible connection to Europe, and stepped over a bridge into the huge customs hall.

The hall was America and yet it was like something out of Kafka, a space with such a vaulting roof, such far-flung boundlessness, that it seemed to disappear into thin air and become totally unreal. Pale sunlight fell through panes of frosted glass to form shimmering shafts of dust motes. The concrete floor was worn and scratched, and numerous crude wooden barriers and desks of the cheapest sort stood all around with small mountains of baggage lying scattered between them, like a harvest gathered on a field – the flotsam of Europe, raised out of the belly of the *Liberté* and somehow ordered alphabetically according to the owners' names. I looked for my own things, found them, and observed that they were shabby.

This is the moment when an immigrant has the urge to tear the clothes off his back and burn all the possessions he has brought along, so that he can step into his new life naked and unencumbered, anticipating different, more glittering trappings. But since such behaviour wouldn't be appropriate even in America, and might negate all my efforts to travel this far, I waited for the customs official, who approached unhurriedly. From the star on his chest I recognized him as the good-natured policeman of the film strips, but he took a stern, Prussian view of his duty. Every bag had to be opened and searched. What kind of contraband was he worried about in this land of abundance? I never found out. My baggage received the clearance stamp which was given out at the last barrier of the hall.

I went through the gate. I had arrived in America. I was standing in New York. I had often dreamed about this, and now it was like a dream. The dream of being here had fulfilled itself, and as in that dream there was no foreignness: I too was at home here, and America lay at my feet like my own personal property. I sensed freedom. I felt freedom. The wind was freedom. Nobody asked me where I was going, what I was going to do, or what I wanted to undertake from the Atlantic to the Pacific coast, from the Gulf of Mexico to the icebergs of Alaska.

Wolfgang Koeppen, *Amerikafahrt* (1959)
(In Gesammelte Werke in sechs Bänden Vol 4, 1986)
translated from the German by Susan Thorne

✳ ✳ ✳

Even New Yorkers can feel like strangers in their own city if they move from one borough to another – though the end result can be to raise one's appreciation of the city's incredible contrasts and variety.

So we moved to Brooklyn. It was August, the city was scorching and violent in that way it can get when the rich people have gone to the beach or the mountains and the people who are left are nearly naked. They played loud music in their cars and at night, along the West Side Highway, they set up barbecue grills in the parking lots and had parties. But that was Manhattan. Here we finally had some space, indoors – there was no way our new apartment would have cost less than a million and a half dollars in Manhattan, though it hadn't been a third of that price out here. It was a strange old building, with hundreds of apartments, and the tenants were mostly very old. It was a pre-Depression building, the original owner – and builder – had jumped from the roof just after the place was completed, in 1929, and though there was plenty of light there were all sorts of other peculiarities we discovered after we moved in. […]

I had never thought of myself – of us, my husband, Tim, and our little girl, Willow – as the kind of people who would live in Brooklyn. First I had fought against it, but now I no longer cared. Manhattan was boring. Everyone looked the same – they were all white, in their twenties, the women were the same shade of blonde and the men either the same gay man, apparently cloned (brown hair, small nose, tidy) or recent graduates from an American university where they had spent four years calling each other 'dude' and drinking beer before heading to Wall Street.

Every block had the same things: a Banana Republic clothing store, with window displays of black, white and khaki clothing; a Gap, with blue jeans and skinny, headless mannequins; a Starbuck's coffee shop and an upscale Italian restaurant. […]

In Brooklyn we were opposite the park, Prospect Park, but we weren't in one of the popular, fancier neighbourhoods. Around the corner was a Jamaican restaurant, operated by kids who were so stoned it could take an hour for them to prepare food-to-go. There was a Chinese take-away, with pictures of food displayed so you could point to whatever you wanted, and then slide your money through a window in a bullet-proof glass wall that kept the cooks safe, but visible, in the kitchen.

The liquor store had an armed guard by the door, and in the Everything 99¢ Or Less there was a box to donate money to the mosque.

I hadn't even noticed how rough it appeared until a friend who had grown up in the slums of Glasgow stopped by for a visit on his way to the airport and said he had walked around the block first but was able to defend himself, due to his upbringing. I guess I was so intrigued by living in a place that was like a foreign country I had forgotten to be nervous. But everyone was extremely friendly – much more so than in Manhattan. […]

After all that time in Manhattan, I had no idea I would enjoy Brooklyn so much. From this apartment I can see Manhattan, as well as Queens, Staten Island and New Jersey; I can view the entire panorama of Brooklyn, from Coney Island at the tip, with its run-down, antiquated amusement park and strip of grey beach, all the way over to Jamaica Bay. My free afternoons have been spent exploring Brooklyn: by subway and on foot. There is Ditmas Park with its huge mansions and grounds that resemble plantations in *Gone with the Wind* – only each parked on a tiny plot of land. Nearby are neighbourhoods of apartments, or other less grand houses, and each area contains a different ethnic group – I've found regions inhabited entirely by people from Haiti, from Guyana, from Russia, from the Ukraine, there are areas of Orthodox Jews wearing dress unchanged from the seventeenth century; there is a complete Chinatown (Sunset Park) and the Italian neighbourhoods known as Bensonhurst and Bay Ridge. There is the upscale area in which Norman Mailer lives – Brooklyn Heights – and a poor area, Bedford Stuyvesant, where until recently the film director Spike Lee lived, in a huge brownstone in a once-very-expensive neighbourhood.

To have lived in a city for so long and feel I knew the place completely – only to realise that my explorations have barely begun – has both humbled and inspired me.

Tama Janowitz, *Area Code 212* (2002)

❉ ❉ ❉

But let's return to the real 'strangers' in the city. What is life like for New York's new immigrants today? Where do they live? What are their lives like? What do they do? Two extracts that touch on the subject.

Queens is the largest New York City borough. It has the longest and widest avenues, the most freeways, and the most crowded subway stations. It has more ethnic groups and nationalities than any other borough; observers say it has more ethnic diversity than any other place its size on earth. Some of its schools are the city's most overcrowded. In one Queens school district, a dozen or more new pupils enroll every week during the school year, many speaking little English. Classes meet in bathrooms and on stairways; kids use stairs as desks when they practise their spelling, and teachers go home hoarse every night from trying to make themselves heard. Immigrants open stores along the avenues beneath the elevated-train tracks in Queens, the way they used to under the old Second Avenue El on the Lower East Side. Queens has more miles of elevated tracks than any borough, and the streets below them teem.

Ian Frazier, *Gone to New York* (2005)

❉ ❉ ❉

His first year in Nueva York he lived in Washington Heights, in a roachy flat above what's now the Tres Marías restaurant. As soon as he secured his apartment and two jobs, one cleaning offices and the other washing dishes, he started writing home. In the first letter he folded four twenty-dollar bills. The trickles of money he sent back were not premeditated like those sent by his other friends, calculated from what he needed to survive; these were arbitrary sums that often left him broke and borrowing until the next payday.

The first year he worked nineteen-, twenty-hour days, seven days a week. Out in the cold he coughed, feeling as if his lungs were tearing open from the force of his exhales and in the kitchens the heat from the ovens sent pain corkscrewing into his head. He wrote home sporadically. Mami forgave him for what he had done and told him who else had left the barrio, via coffin or plane ticket. Papi's replies were scribbled on whatever he could find, usually the thin cardboard of tissue boxes or pages from the bill books at work. He was so tired from working that he misspelled almost everything and had to bite his lip to stay awake. He promised her and the children tickets soon. The pictures he received from Mami were shared with his friends at work and then forgotten in his wallet, lost between old lottery slips.

The weather was no good. He was sick often but was able to work through it and succeeded in saving up enough money to start looking for a wife to marry. It was the old routine, the oldest of the post-war maromas. Find a citizen, get married, wait, and then divorce her. The routine was well-practiced and expensive and riddled with swindlers.

Junot Díaz, *Drown* (1996)

❊ ❊ ❊

Like many a new arrival in New York, Anne Matthews is overwhelmed by the noise and the general cut and thrust of the city. But she soon learns survival strategies from some unlikely teachers …

New York undid us. Three blocks from Penn Station, at Broadway and Herald Square, we clung together in a Macy's doorway, stunned, disoriented, drowning. Even when we shouted we could not hear each other; almost nothing is louder than midtown Manhattan, not even a jet engine at close range. The gray urban air smelled of sewers and diesel and burned pushcart chestnuts. The local signage was full of opinions: LITTERING IS FILTHY AND SELFISH. DON'T EVEN *THINK* ABOUT PARKING HERE. And no matter which way I looked to find a horizon, I saw only faces – near, nearer, gone:

Manhattan wedges 1.5 million residents plus three million commuters onto a granite island thirteen miles long by two miles wide. A band of city pigeons made a showy landing at the curb, barged over, and began to eat our shoelaces.

At least, they looked like pigeons; in truth, these were feral superdoves – immigrant New Yorkers descended from Old World rock doves and escaped racing birds, honed to urban perfection by urban pressures. New York City pigeons can breed year-round, eat meat, and see ultraviolet light. They perform alarmingly well on tests of symbolic logic. They produce droppings acid enough to snap the cables of the Brooklyn Bridge. I looked down at the iridescent necks of the flock surging about my ankles and up at the impossible Manhattan skyline and began to understand that in this magnificent and unforgiving place, this American Galapagos, adaptation – change – is the only law and only hope. My compatriot went home at midyear. He said the New York region was clearly uncivilized; you couldn't even get the noon farm prices on the radio. I stayed, became a commuter, and learned to barge and peck.

Anne Matthews, *Wild Nights* (2001)

✳ ✳ ✳

But most people arriving in the Big Apple are very temporary strangers in the city, there for no longer than a short holiday or business trip – like the Jewish writer from the former East Germany, Jurek Becker. Here's the diary of his week in New York.

Day One
New York gets off to a great start: due to a snowstorm, the airplane has to circle over Kennedy Airport for fifty minutes since there is no runway ready for us. I look out the window and try to be moved by the thought that right down there below me is New York.

It is evening and cloudy, and I know right away that I have

never before seen so many lights shining at the same time. One particularly bright strip makes me think the word "Broadway" to myself. But after twenty minutes of circling, those lights are just lights after all, and even the children don't bother looking out the window anymore.

My visa reveals that I am an individual not entitled to immigrate. The passport official studies it for a long time. Then he asks me whether I don't *really* intend to stay. There is an unmistakable note in his voice: *Come on, say it, just between ourselves.* I am glad that I understand the meaning of his words right away. I laugh and shake my head, saying that he needn't worry. But in the next instant I think: How do I already know that?

The customs official asks me what publications I am bringing with me. I suppress the reply that it is none of his business, as I have been accustomed to do at home for many years. I can tell that he will search my suitcase, whatever I say. I willingly show him my manuscripts and a paperback version of the Talmud which I had decided on as my reading material for America. He looks at me benevolently, as if he wouldn't have thought I had it in me. Maybe he is a Jew himself.

Day Two

I have been strongly advised by those in the know about America never to carry more than twenty dollars, and to immediately surrender them to robbers on demand. I am cleverly keeping forty-five dollars in my pocket as well as the key to the hotel safe. The rest of my money is there together with my East German passport – a prized possession, I suppose.

My first problem when I step out onto the street in the morning is that I don't know the formula for converting Fahrenheit to Celsius. It is definitely cold, but I don't know *how* cold. I don't know how cold I'm supposed to feel, and that is no joke. I've always assumed that you feel cold according to the thermometer, in the same way you get hungry according to the clock: a sort of opportunism of your sensations.

A second piece of advice was that I should go around New York on foot. So with that advice I walk along and come to the first corner. I don't ask myself which way to go because I just want to walk in any direction.

I am not unprepared for the run-down condition of the city, but I have the feeling that I am seeing an all-time high: the greatest achievable extreme of dilapidation. I wonder what it must be like in those districts that I have been warned about.

I put coins in a collection box that is blocking my way. A young woman smiles at me more compellingly than I have ever been smiled at right out on the street. I have no idea what she is collecting for, and I can't make up my mind to pull out my dictionary and translate the sentence that is written around the outside of her hat. I watch from a safe distance for ten minutes to see who else donates money: nobody.

In a quiet side street I turn around a few times, but no one is following me. The fire escapes on the fronts of houses are old acquaintances, for I've been familiar with them since I started going to the movies. All at once my stroll becomes difficult: I have a choice between clearing myself a path through a large number of trash cans and garbage bags or switching to the other side of the street. I also have to get past a meter-high barrier of dark grey snow, so I turn around. I come back to Broadway and buy myself a city map, then find the spot on it where I am standing with the city map.

I walk more in the afternoon, but with eyes which are only providing a kind of emergency service, as if there is no more room in the storage depot for first impressions. Late in the evening the age of Muhammad Ali comes to an end on the television, and the new man is called Spinks. I don't think a man can found a new era if he is missing all his front teeth.

Lying in bed, I am a long way from knowing what New York means. I tell myself that this is normal, that I am not in Jena here. I find it rather absurd to appear so lost to myself.

Day Three

During breakfast there is a show on television in which they pray three times: once for George Foreman, a defeated boxer; once for a crippled girl, who sits in front of the camera all spruced up in her wheelchair; and once for all America. I turn it off and then on again because I want to watch it to the end. Nasty thoughts circulate in my head. Imagine that in Middle Europe, I think ... [...]

I am struck by how often I suddenly think EUROPE, a word that has hardly come to mind before. Up to now I have given myself several detailed names: I was a Berliner, a resident of Kopenick, and a citizen of the *Deutsche Demokratische Republik*. Calling myself a German sounded exotic. And all at once I am a European, no less.

The main thing is to keep walking. People are patient with me if I want to buy something and take a long time with my English. It is no shame here not to speak good English. For example, in front of me at the travel agency were an ancient man and his wife who wanted to go to Las Vegas. Both of them had sloppy English, even I could hear that, it was even worse than mine. Still there was no doubt that they were Americans, you could spot it right away from their coats. I asked myself why the employee didn't take me for an American, too.

Up on top of the Empire State Building I stick a few dimes in the telescope and search in the mist for those world-famous sights. I find a heart on the railing, drawn with a thick blue felt pen. I immediately think of home, of tree trunks, of pines in the forest behind the bridge, of a certain girl – as if my memories were poised ready to spring out at the slightest nudge. Later I read the inscription inside the blue heart: *February 2, '78, Harry & Henry*.

Keep walking. In the afternoon a black woman speaks to me on the street, me in my leather coat with the fur collar. She invites me to her place, she lives close by. She names a price that is like a gift compared with the price for my hotel room. She is pretty. I have never held a black woman, I have only thought about it sometimes, most recently on the flight here. I turn around twice looking after her, but she has already forgotten me.

Day Seven: Departure

You come to a new city: you've heard a lot about it beforehand and your head is fsull of the prejudgments that you've brought along. You determine that every one of your preconceptions can be proven without much trouble; there is some truth in each of them, really. You collect observations like evidence. You want to show yourself how well you already knew the city before going there, and you manage to carry this off. The result is a lost week that could have turned out differently.

Leaving on the bus you ask yourself how you came to be going through the streets with a checklist, a pencil in your hand ready to tick things off: Poverty, check. Race problems, check. Criminality, check. An irreproachable, barren row of categories. You ask yourself: do you really need to keep wearing yourself out proving things that are already established? Who gave you this deadly-dull assignment? Your conscience? Absurd. You arrived here with the firm intention of looking only at superficialities, and as a result you saw absolutely nothing.

Now you are annoyed because you didn't immerse yourself in this exciting city for even a second. Because you never let yourself go when there were so many opportunities. You didn't even look them over, those opportunities. You walked faster every time, just wanting to get away. You automatically thought, Where is that going to lead? And now you are wondering where it all ought to lead. In the boring moments you kept your eyes wonderfully open. You only wanted to see what everybody knew already, not the things that no one knows.

Suddenly you are worried about your ability to be excited. Imagine somebody who diligently protects himself from surprises. Who figures everything out in advance and then tries to live so that this calculation will fit.

Maybe I will come back to New York someday; that would be nice. But for the time being I am going to ride the bus to La Guardia Airport. I will sit in my window seat and I will close my eyes the minute I see black people, run-down streets, policemen, whites, billboards, or traffic chaos.

Jurek Becker, *New Yorker Woche (A New York Week)* 1980,
in *Nach der ersten Zukunft (After the first Future)*
translated by Susan Thorne

Good times, bad times

Some would say that the best times in New York were the 1920s, between the end of the First World War and the stock-market crash of 1929. Scott Fitzgerald gives us a taste of what it was like.

The tempo of the city had changed sharply. The uncertainties of 1920 were drowned in a steady golden roar and many of our friends had grown wealthy. But the restlessness of New York in

1927 approached hysteria. The parties were bigger – those of Condé Nast, for example, rivalled in their way the fabled balls of the nineties; the pace was faster – the catering to dissipation set an example to Paris; the shows were broader, the buildings were higher, the morals were looser and the liquor was cheaper; but all these benefits did not really minister to much delight. Young people wore out early – they were hard and languid at twenty-one and save for Peter Arno none of them contributed anything new; perhaps Peter Arno and his collaborators said everything there was to say about the boom days in New York that couldn't be said by a jazz band. Many people who were not alcoholics were lit up four days out of seven, and frayed nerves were strewn everywhere; groups were held together by a generic nervousness and the hangover became a part of the day as well allowed for as the Spanish siesta. Most of my friends drank too much – the more they were in tune to the times the more they drank. And as effort *per se* had no dignity against the mere bounty of those days in New York, a depreciatory word was found for it: a successful programme became a racket – I was in the literary racket.

F. Scott Fitzgerald, *The Crack-Up* (1945)

✳ ✳ ✳

There were plenty of clubs in 'good times' New York. We visit a couple of them.

The Cotton Club was quite a scene. From the street, with its big corner site on Lenox Avenue, and brightly lit entrance, one would have thought it was a movie theatre. Only the patrons in evening dress getting out of their expensive cars gave a clue as to what it was really like inside.

The club was big and elegant. The clientele sat at small round tables, each with a single candle in the centre of a spotless white linen tablecloth. There was room for dancing, but the key to the place was the show. The proscenium stage was large and lit with footlights on each side. This evening, the front of the stage had a mirrored floor, so that the reflection of the chorus girls exploded into the space above. [...]

One never knew who would be at the Cotton Club. The mayor, of course – it was his kind of place. Music people like Irving Berlin and George Gershwin, singers like Al Jonson and Jimmy Durante. Anyone from the fashionable New York crowd. Charlie had recently started to write a novel. He liked taking note of any scenes he might be able to use some day, and he always made a point of talking to people – both because they interested him, and because they might give him useful dialogue.

"I wondered if Madden was here," Charlie said.

Did it worry any of these good people that the place was owned by Owney Madden the bootlegger, who had bought the club while he was still in Sing Sing, doing time for murder? It never seemed to. Madden might kill people who crossed him, but why worry about a few murders when he ran the best jazz club in town? Madden had friends, too. The police hadn't raided the club in a long time now.

Charlie had talked to Madden once or twice. Despite his Irish name, Madden was born and raised in northern England, and proud of it. The bootlegger and jazz club owner's accent was broad Yorkshire.

Edward Rutherfurd, *New York* (2009)

✳ ✳ ✳

Though a little later than the Cotton Club, the Stork Club (1929–1965) was one of the most elite establishments in the city.

He had started his Stork Club as an up-market speakeasy – the first, he used to say, with a carpet on the floor and a canopy out front. By 1945, although the club menu still felt obliged to advise its clients not to drink red wine with fish, and some people took their children to breakfast there after Sunday morning church, it had become a very symbol of Manhattan sophistication. It was "the New Yorkiest place in town," wrote Winchell, who spent every evening at his own Stork Club table, where people lined up to be interviewed by him. "Sherm" himself called it "a place unique to itself – the elite of the world have graced my tables."

Sometimes un-graced them too, for Billingsley, like Nash before him, could be severe upon patrons, however eminent, who misbehaved themselves in his eyes. Sometimes he banned them – Elliot Roosevelt the President's son was a black sheep of the Stork Club, and Humphrey Bogart was another.

Jan Morris, Manhattan '45 (1987/2011)

❊ ❊ ❊

One person's good time is another person's bad time. Joyce Johnson tells how the tenements of the Lower East Side, once the place from which the poor longed to escape, became the living place of choice for young bohemians.

Scuffling was what you did in my new neighbourhood, soon to be called the East Village. The original poor of the Lower East Side had scuffled without hope, of course, selling their labour for low wages. Their children grew up and fled to Queens or Jersey, leaving room in the tenements for middle-class children loosely defined as "artists," who believed for a while, under the influence of all the new philosophy and rejecting the values of their own parents, that they had no use for money. […]

Rents were low, you could eat for next to nothing, toilets were in the hallway, bathtubs were in the kitchen, and you never let the meter man in if you could help it. Con Ed trucks appeared on the streets on Friday mornings to turn delinquent payers off for the weekend, plunging them into penal darkness even if they could have paid up that very afternoon. Yahrzeit candles, or the

Puerto Rican kind with rainbow-coloured wax, were hoarded for such emergencies. Poems were written about roaches who lived in the stove, the woodwork, the innards of portable radios and shoes, and copulated in the chocolate-smelling gas heat of winter. Wives swapped recipes for chicken-back stew or lentil soup with gizzards; tofu had not yet been discovered in the West. [...]

Another approach to tenement life involved denial of the tenement as a tenement and insistence upon it as "a charming place" once it had been stripped to its core, taken back virtually to its prehistory as a dwelling. Plaster was laboriously scraped off brick that had always been plastered; windowsills and lintels were sanded raw; decades of linoleum were ripped up to reveal floorboards underneath, even parquet, sometimes, perfectly preserved by generations of housewives who, like my mother and Jack's, always put a covering on anything "good".

My mother couldn't understand why I'd returned to the streets my grandparents had struggled so hard to stay out of: "At least we never lived on the Lower East Side. We lived near Bronx Park when it was a beautiful area. At least we never lived in the slums."

I loved the slums, my slums, the sweet slums of Bohemia and beatnikdom, where sunflowers and morning glories would bloom on fire escapes in the summer and old ladies weighed down by breasts leaned on goosedown pillows in windows, self-appointed guardians of the street, and Tompkins Square with its onion-topped church had the greyness of photos of Moscow. Who would not wish to be a scuffler on Second Avenue? I bought seven-cent bagels and ten-cent half-sour pickles and sat up till dawn in Rappaport's, where they gave you a whole basket of rolls free, drinking coffee with a jazz trombonist from St. Louis and a poet just arrived from Chicago.

Joyce Johnson, *Minor Characters* (1983)

* * *

But like every city, New York has had plenty of bad times. Fire has always been a major hazard in a closely packed environment and in factories and workshops. One of the most famous was at the Triangle Shirtwaist factory, in 1911, in which 150 young women perished. Here is an earlier catastrophe vividly recorded by a diarist of the time.

(1835) THURSDAY, DEC 17 How shall I record the events of last night, or how attempt to describe the most awful calamity which has ever visited these United States? The greatest loss by fire that has ever been known, with the exception perhaps of the conflagration of Moscow, and that was an incidental concomitant of war. I am fatigued in body, disturbed in mind, and my fancy filled with images of horror which my pen is inadequate to describe. Nearly one half of the first ward is in ashes; 500 to 700 stores, which with their contents are valued at $20,000,000 to $40,000,000, are now lying in an indistinguishable mass of ruins. There is not perhaps in the world the same space of ground covered by so great an amount of real and personal property as the scene of this dreadful conflagration. The fire broke out at nine o'clock last evening. I was waiting in the library when the alarm was given and went immediately down. The night was intensely cold, which was one cause of the unprecedented progress of the flames, for the water froze in the hydrants, and the engines and their hose could not be worked without great difficulty. The firemen, too, had been on duty all last night, and were almost incapable of performing their usual services.

The fire originated in the store of Cornstock & Adams in Merchant Street, a narrow crooked street, filled with high stores lately erected and occupied by dry goods and hardware merchants, which led from Hanover to Pearl Street. When I arrived at the spot the scene exceeded all description; the progress of the flames, like flashes of lightning, communicated in every direction, and a few minutes sufficed to level the lofty edifices on every side. [...]

A calculation is made in the *Commercial* this afternoon that the number of buildings burnt is 570, and that the whole loss is something over $15,000,000. The insurance offices are all, of course, bankrupt. Their collective capitals amount to $11,750,000; but those downtown have a large proportion of the risks, and will not be able to pay 50 per cent of the losses. The unfortunate stockholders lose all. In this way I suffer directly, and in others indirectly, to a large amount.

Philip Hone, *Diary* (1835)

❊ ❊ ❊

And another diarist records one of the most famous assassinations in history.

APRIL 15, SATURDAY Nine o'clock in the morning. *LINCOLN AND SEWARD ASSASSINATED LAST NIGHT!!!*

The South has nearly filled up the measure of her iniquities at last! Lincoln's death not yet certainly announced, but the one o'clock despatch states that he was then dying. Seward's side room was entered by the same or another assassin, and his throat cut. It is unlikely he will survive, for he was suffering from a broken arm and other injuries, the consequence of a fall, and is advanced in life. Ellie brought this news two hours ago, but I can hardly take it in even yet. *Eheu* A. Lincoln!

I have been expecting this. I predicted an attempt would be made on Lincoln's life when he went into Richmond, but just now, after his generous dealings with Lee, I should have said the danger was past. But the ferocious malignity of Southerners is infinite and inexhaustible. I am stunned, as by a fearful personal calamity, though I can see that this thing, occurring just at this time, may be overruled to our great good. Poor Ellie is heartbroken, though never an admirer of Lincoln's. We shall appreciate him at last.

102

Up with the Black Flag now!

  [...]

APRIL 17 All over the city, people have been at work all day, draping street fronts, so that hardly a building on Wall Street, Broadway, Chambers Street, Bowery, Fourth Avenue is without its symbol of the profound public sorrow. What a place this man, whom his friends have been patronizing for four years as a well-meaning, sagacious, kind-hearted, ignorant, old codger, had won for himself in the hearts of the people! What a place he will fill in history!

George Templeton Strong, The Diaries (1865)

✳ ✳ ✳

> *When Charles Dickens undertook a lecture tour of America, he was rapturously received, but his response to his hosts' country – especially New York – was less than enthusiastic. Perhaps it was inevitable, being the kind of writer he was, that his social antennae would pick up mainly the negative aspects of the city.*

The beautiful metropolis of America is by no means so clean a city as Boston, but many of its streets have the same characteristics; except that the houses are not quite so fresh-coloured, the sign-boards are not quite so gaudy, the gilded letters not quite so golden, the bricks not quite so red, the stone not quite so white, the blinds and area railings not quite so green, the knobs and plates upon the street doors not quite so bright and twinkling. There are many bye-streets, almost as neutral in clean colours, and positive in dirty ones, as bye-streets in London; and there is one quarter, commonly called the Five Points, which, in respect of filth and wretchedness, may be safely backed against Seven Dials, or any other part of famed St. Giles's. [...]

We have seen no beggars in the streets by night or day; but of other kinds of strollers, plenty. Poverty, wretchedness, and vice, are rife enough where we are going now.

This is the place: these narrow ways, diverging to the right and left, and reeking everywhere with dirt and filth. Such lives as are led here, bear the same fruits here as elsewhere. The coarse and bloated faces at the doors, have counterparts at home, and all the wide world over. Debauchery has made the very houses prematurely old. See how the rotten beams are tumbling down, and how the patched and broken windows seem to scowl dimly, like eyes that have been hurt in drunken frays. [...]

What place is this, to which the squalid street conducts us? A kind of square of leprous houses, some of which are attainable only by crazy wooden stairs without. What lies beyond this tottering flight of steps, that creak beneath our tread – a miserable room, lighted by one dim candle, and destitute of all comfort, save that which may be hidden in a wretched bed. Beside it, sits a man: his elbows on his knees: his forehead hidden in his hands. "What ails that man?" asks the foremost officer. "Fever," he sullenly replies, without looking up. Conceive the fancies of a feverish brain, in such a place as this!

Ascend these pitch-dark stairs, heedful of a false footing on the trembling boards, and grope your way with me into this wolfish den, where neither ray of light nor breath of air, appears to come. A negro lad, startled from his sleep by the officer's voice – he knows it well – but comforted by his assurance that he has not come on business, officiously bestirs himself to light a candle. The match flickers for a moment, and shows great mounds of dusty rags upon the ground; then dies away and leaves a denser darkness than before, if there can be degrees in such extremes. [...]

From every corner, as you glance about you in these dark retreats, some figure crawls half-awakened, as if the judgment-hour were near at hand, and every obscene grave were giving up its dead. Where dogs would howl to lie, women, and men, and boys slink off to sleep, forcing the dislodged rats to move away in quest of better lodgings.

Here too are lanes and alleys, paved with mud knee-deep: underground chambers, where they dance and game; the walls bedecked with rough designs of ships, and forts, and flags, and American Eagles out of number: ruined houses, open to the street, whence, through wide gaps in the walls, other ruins loom upon the eye, as though the world of vice and misery had nothing else to show: hideous tenements which take their name from robbery and murder: all that is loathsome, drooping, and decayed is here.

Charles Dickens, *American Notes For General Circulation* (1842)

✳ ✳ ✳

This extract, from Lawrence Block's Small Town, *brings together a number of the worst events in New York's history.*

He had been reading about the Draft Riots in New York during the Civil War, when the city was essentially lawless for days, and when mobs lynched black men and beat policemen to death. The Draft Riots were a puzzle, an anomaly, and all the arguments trotted out to explain them – the animosity, born of competition for work, of Irish immigrants for freed African slaves, the resentment of white workingmen at being drafted to fight a war for black freedom, and others, so many others – all were valid, and all seemed beside the point.

But he'd looked at them in the context of the Civil War, or in the context of the city's ethnic and political realities, and he could see that he'd been completely wrong. The Draft Riots happened because they had to happen.

They were a sacrifice.

They were the city, New York, sacrificing itself for its own greater glory. They were a ritual bloodletting by means of which the city's soul was redeemed and renewed, rising from its own psychic ashes to be reborn greater than it had been before.

And the Draft Riots were not an isolated example. No, not at all. The city had been shocked over the centuries by no end of tragedies, great pointless disasters that were no longer point-less when viewed through the lens of his new perspective.

The *General Slocum* tragedy, for example, when a ship loaded to capacity with German immigrants and their chil-dren, bound for a holiday excursion, caught fire and burned and sank in the East River. Hundreds of men and women and children perished, so many that the Lower East Side neighbour-hood known as Little Germany ceased overnight to exist. So many residents had been lost that the survivors couldn't bear to stay where they were. They moved en masse, most to the Yorkville section of the Upper East Side.

Or the Triangle Shirtwaist fire of 1911, when 150 seam-stresses, most of them young Jewish women, died when the sweatshop they worked in went up in flames. They couldn't get out, the fire doors were locked, so they either jumped to their death or died in the fire.

Sacrificed, all of them. And each time the city, reeling in shock, bleeding from its wounds, had rebounded to become greater than ever. Each time the souls of the sacrificed had become part of the greater soul of the city, enriching it, enlarging it.

When this great insight came, this revelation, he stopped his front-to-back reading of the encyclopaedia and began skipping around, looking for further examples to support his thesis. They were there in abundance, tragedies great and small, from the city's earliest days to the eleventh of September.

The history of the city was the history of violent death.

The gang wars, from the pitched battles between the Bowery Boys and the Dead Rabbits to the endless Mafia palace coups and clan wars. Albert Anastasia, shot dead in the barber chair at the Park Sheraton Hotel. Joey Gallo, gunned down in Umberto's Clam House. Throughout the five boroughs, blood seeped into the pave-ment. The rain couldn't wash it away. It only made it invisible.

And fires, so many fires. You thought of the city as non-flammable, a city of glass and steel and asphalt and concrete, but hadn't the world watched as buildings of glass and steel burned like torches until they melted and collapsed of their own weight? Oh yes, forests could burn, and wooden houses could burn, but so could cities of concrete and steel.

Lawrence Block, *Small Town* (2003)

✳ ✳ ✳

The good times of the 1920s came to an abrupt end. Here it is in Edward Rutherfurd's historical saga New York. *At this point, no-one seemed to really grasp the depth and scope of the crisis.*

The start of the great crash of 1929 is usually given as Black Thursday, 24 October. This is incorrect. It began on Wednesday, the very day that the Chrysler Building became the tallest structure in the world, when stocks abruptly tumbled 4.6 per cent. Strangely, few people had yet noticed the clever trick that Walter Chrysler had played. But everybody noticed Wednesday's stock market collapse.

On Thursday morning, William Master went into the Stock Exchange as it opened its doors. The atmosphere was tense. Glancing up at the visitors' gallery, he saw a face he thought looked familiar. "That's Winston Churchill, the British politician," one of the traders remarked. "He's chosen a hell of a day to call."

He certainly had. As trading began, Master was aghast. The market wasn't just falling, it was in headlong panic. By the end of the first hour, there were cries of pain, then howls. Men with margin calls were being wiped out. A couple of times, sellers were shouting out prices and finding not a single buyer in the market. As noon approached, he reckoned the market would soon have fallen nearly ten per cent. The anguished hubbub from the floor was so loud that, unable to bear it any longer, he walked outside.

In the street, the scene was extraordinary. A crowd of men had gathered on the steps of Federal Hall. They seemed to be in shock. He saw a fellow come out of the Exchange and burst into tears. An old broker he knew passed him and remarked, with a shake of the head: "Ain't seen anything like this since the crash of 1907."

But in 1907, old Pierpont Morgan had been there to save the day. Maybe his son Jack could so something? But Jack Morgan was on the other side of the Atlantic in England, for the shooting season. The courtly senior Morgan partner Thomas Lamont was in charge.

As if on cue, at that moment, a group of men went up the steps of 23 Wall Street, the House of Morgan. He recognised at once the heads of the greatest banks. Could they stop the rot?

It seemed they could. At one thirty that day, Richard Whitney, the president of the Stock Exchange and a broker for Morgan, walked calmly out of 23 Wall Street, went straight to the floor of the Exchange, and started buying. Big money, big stocks, at well above the asking price. The banks had given him $240 million to use if he needed, but he only had to use a fraction. With a great sigh of relief, the market began to calm down.

The godlike spirit of Pierpont Morgan had descended from Olympus to rule the street once more.

That night William attended a big meeting of brokers. Everyone agreed the panic was unnecessary. On Friday, and on Saturday morning, the market suffered no further crisis.

He spent the rest of the weekend quietly. On Sunday, Charlie came by for lunch. "Technically," William told them, "this sell-off has left the market in better condition than it's been in for months." After that, asking Charlie to keep his mother company, he went for a walk in Central Park.

The truth was, he needed some time alone, to think.

What had really happened? The underlying problem, he reckoned, was that for the last few years, there had been too much cash in the stock market. Funnily enough, it wasn't that everything was booming. Farming and commodity prices had been weak, so instead of investing in those traditional staples, people had been looking for gains in stocks. Cash flowed in; brokers, banks and other finance houses mushroomed. Even in the huge American economy, there weren't really enough productive stocks for all this cash, so prices rose. And then, of course, giddy greed set in.

Small investors, who should have been putting some savings in solid stocks, were buying wildly. Out of the total population of a hundred and twenty million, two, maybe three million were in the market now. That was a hell of a lot. And more than half a million of these little guys were even buying on a ten per cent margin – putting down only a hundred dollars for every thousand they invested, with finance houses lending them the rest. Respectable brokerage houses like his own were lending clients two-thirds of the funds to purchase stocks. Money pushed stock prices ever higher. You couldn't lose. And not only stocks. William knew damn well that some of the banks were parcelling up their worst Latin American debt and selling it to suckers as valuable bonds. So long as everything went up, nobody noticed.

And not just the man in the street – the brokers and traders were not much better. Seduced by their own success, most of them had never seen a bear market in their lives.

William walked right across the park, until he was opposite the Dakota. Then, deep in thought, he walked slowly back.

Maybe this market shock was a good thing. Maybe it was time for a shock to the system. Not only to the market, but to the whole city as well.

The fact was, the whole of New York seemed to have forgotten its morals. What had happened to responsible investing? To hard work and saving? What had happened to the old puritan ethic in the world of speakeasies, and bootleggers, and gangland killings, and loose women? Life was too easy; they'd all gone soft. He himself was just as guilty as any of them. Look at Charlie. Charming, and all that, but at bottom, a spoiled rich kid. And it's my fault as much as his, he thought. I let him get this way.

So what was to be done? He was damned if he knew. But if this little crisis reminded people about the fundamentals of life, then maybe it was worth whatever it had cost him.

Edward Rutherfurd, *New York* (2009)

* * *

The worst of the Great Depression – the aftermath of the crash – was over by the early 1940s, but times were still bad if you were poor in New York and found yourself living in the infamous tenements.

The tenements could be terrible. The most unspeakable of them, of which a few were left, dated from the time when there were no building regulations at all, and unscrupulous agents and landlords could pack the maximum number of tenants into the most minimal accommodation – "lung blocks," they called them, because of their fearful incidence of tuberculosis. Many more were Old Law tenements, from the days when the law required only that a tenement should have an air shaft in the middle, and these were quite frightful enough; lavatories were shared, one to each floor, and inside rooms generally had no proper windows, only ventilators opening into the dark, narrow and foetid central air shaft, its walls stained with droppings, its inaccessible floor deep with garbage. The most diligent housewife could hardly maintain a decent home in a place like this. Damp got into everything, you could keep nothing clean, roaches were inescapable and rats brown, black and Alexandrian defied extermination – the only cure for rats, it was said, was to "build them out."

The survival of these cruel old structures, with all the crime, disease and unhappiness they fostered, was the worst of all indictments of Manhattan, at this happiest moment of its history. […]

The slums of New York were disgraceful slums, but there was no denying that they were interesting. They were among the most interesting slums on earth, and among the liveliest. Whether they were black slums, Puerto Rican slums, Jewish slums, they burst with vivacity. They were bursting with noise – shouts, swearings, radio music (they might have no lavatories, but 94 percent of Manhattan homes possessed a radio). They were bursting with things, from radio aerials and rooftop pigeon coops to the inevitable laundry lines, sometimes on sticks out of windows, sometimes trailing across streets. They were bursting most of all with people, especially in the hot weather, when there were people hanging from every window, people flat on the roofs, people sitting in pairs all down the diagonal fire ladders, people lounging on front steps, leaning against railings, sitting on the kerb or hilariously hosing themselves, if young enough, from the corner fire hydrant – hardly a book of photographs of Manhattan in the 1940s is complete without its statutory hydrant children. [...]

Foreign visitors in fact were struck by the sense of comradeship which, especially in moments of particular amusement, relief or difficulty, bound New Yorkers together in those days. On winter mornings the hoisted red ball announcing that ponds were fit for skating brought people of all classes sociably into Central Park. Conversely a mute acceptance of shared suffering wryly united commuters in the morning rush hour. When blizzards howled through Manhattan, piling its streets with snow, or when a heat wave left the whole city gasping and sweating, a powerful fellowship blunted the edge of the common misery, bridging the most insuperable linguistic barriers, or the most unclimbable social barricades, if only with a wink or a grimace. [...]

And anyway citizenship of this city in itself made for a bond beyond class. To be a citizen of Manhattan was an achievement in itself – it had taken guts and enterprise, if not on your own part, at least on your forebears'. The pressures of the place, its competition, its pace, its hazards, even the fun of it, demanded special qualities in its people, and gave them a particular affinity one with another. They were all an elite!

Jan Morris, *Manhattan '45* (1987/2011)

❊ ❊ ❊

An unforgettable year for many reasons, 1968 neverthe-less saw the start of a period of decline for the Big Apple.

With all its tragedy, 1968 had been an extraordinary year. There had been the failure of the Tet Offensive, and the huge demonstrations in New York against the Vietnam War. April had seen the terrible assassination of Martin Luther King, and June of Robert Kennedy. There had been the memorable candidacies of Nixon, Hubert Humphrey and Wallace for the presidency. In Europe, the student revolution in Paris, and the Russian crushing of the Prague Spring in Czechoslovakia had changed the history of the Western world. Andy Warhol had been shot and wounded, Jackie Kennedy had married Aristotle Onassis. So many iconic events in modern history had taken place that year, and Charlie Master had not been there to witness and comment upon them. It seemed so unnatural, so wrong.

Yet in some ways, Gorham was almost glad that his father had not lived to see the last few years. For that depressing garbage strike at the start of '68 had not been the culmination, but only the beginning of New York's troubles. Year after year the great city his father loved had deteriorated. Huge efforts had been made to market New York to the world as an exciting place. Taking a little-known slang term for a large city that dated back to the twenties, the marketing men called it the Big Apple, and invented a logo to go with the name. Central Park was filled with concerts, plays, every kind of activity. But behind all the razzmatazz, the city was falling apart. The park was turning into a dust bowl, where it was unsafe to walk after dark. Street crime continued to rise. As for the poor neighbourhoods like Harlem and the South Bronx, they seemed to be falling into terminal neglect.

Finally, in 1975, the Big Apple confessed it was bankrupt. For years, it seemed, the accounts had been falsified. The city had borrowed money against revenues it did not have. Nobody wanted to buy New York debt, and President Ford refused to bail the city out unless it reformed itself. "FORD TO CITY: DROP DEAD" the *Daily News* headline had memorably put it. Emergency help from Union funds had saved actual collapse, but the Big Apple was still in a state of ongoing crisis.

Edward Rutherfurd, *New York* (2009)

* * *

Ask me about New York in the 1970s and I'll remember it as a golden age, the city bankrupt and filthy but full of aspiration. Snowstorms and blackouts and strikes – garbage, transportation, teachers – all of this was ordinary, exciting, and incomprehensible.

Gabriel Brownstein, 'The Curious Case of Benjamin Button, Apt. 3W' (2003)

* * *

I'd lived through both of the blackouts in New York. The first one, in 1965, went more or less peacefully by since it happened when it was getting cold, but the second one occurred on July 13 and 14, 1977, and led to two days of rioting and looting. Some 1,616 stores were looted, and at certain points the looters were looting the other looters. Altogether 3,776 people were arrested – the largest mass arrest in the city's history – and 1,037 fires were reported.

New York was a mess by the late 1970s. The city had lost hundreds of thousands of jobs. It was from time to time incapable of paying teachers their salaries. Graffiti covered every square inch of the interiors of subway cars, which were awash with garbage. Passengers were subjected to the intolerably loud music coming out of boom boxes. Crime had risen faster in the sixties (and was continuing to rise in the seventies) than in any other American city since the 1930s. In 1975 Mayor Beame had furloughed thousands of city workers, including cops and garbagemen. When Beame asked President Ford for federal assistance to meet the payroll, Ford told New York to drop dead. New York had been called Fun City. Now it had become Fear City and Stink City. Garbage left on the streets would go weeks without being collected.

Edmund White, *City Boy* (2009)

✳ ✳ ✳

In City of Glass (1985), *the first novel in Paul Auster's* New York Trilogy, *the protagonist records a particular occasion when he walks the city and observes closely the lives and conditions of many of its inhabitants, committing his observations to his notebook. Here are some of them.*

Today, as never before: the tramps, the down-and-outs, the shopping-bag ladies, the drifters and drunks. They range from the merely destitute to the wretchedly broken. Wherever you turn, they are there, in good neighbourhoods and bad.

Some beg with a semblance of pride. Give me this money, they seem to say, and soon I will be back there with the rest of you, rushing back and forth on my daily rounds. Others have given up hope of ever leaving their tramphood. They lie there sprawled out on the sidewalk with their hat, or cup, or box, not even bothering to look up at the passerby, too defeated even to thank the ones who drop a coin beside them. Still others try to work for the money they are given: the blind pencil sellers, the winos who wash the windscreen of your car. Some tell stories, usually tragic accounts of their own lives, as if to give their benefactors something for their kindness – even if only words.

Others have real talents. The old black man today, for example, who tap-danced while juggling cigarettes – still

114

dignified, clearly once a vaudevillian, dressed in a purple suit with a green shirt and a yellow tie, his mouth fixed in a half-remembered stage smile. There are also the pavement chalk artists and musicians: saxophonists, electric guitarists, fiddlers. Occasionally, you will even come across a genius, as I did today:

A clarinettist of no particular age, wearing a hat that obscured his face, and sitting cross-legged on the sidewalk, in the manner of a snake-charmer. Directly in front of him were two wind-up monkeys, one with a tambourine and the other with a drum. With the one shaking and the other banging, beating out a weird and precise syncopation, the man would improvise endless tiny variations on his instrument, his body swaying stiffly back and forth, energetically miming the monkeys' rhythm. He played jauntily and with flair, crisp and looping figures in the minor mode, as if glad to be there with his mechanical friends, enclosed in the universe he had created, never once looking up. It went on and on, always finally the same, and yet the longer I listened the harder I found it to leave.

To be inside that music, to be drawn into the circle of the repetitions: perhaps that is a place where one could finally disappear.

But beggars and performers make up only a small part of the vagabond population. They are the aristocracy, the elite of the fallen. Far more numerous are those with nothing to do, with nowhere to go. Many are drunks – but that term does not do justice to the devastation they embody. Hulks of despair, clothed in rags, their faces bruised and bleeding, they shuffle through the streets as though in chains. Asleep in doorways, staggering insanely through traffic, collapsing on sidewalks – they seem to be everywhere the moment you look for them. Some will starve to death, others will die of exposure, still others will be beaten or burned or tortured.

For every soul lost in this particular hell, there are several others locked inside madness – unable to exit to the world that stands at the threshold of their bodies. Even though they seem to be there,

115

they cannot be counted as present. The man, for example, who goes everywhere with a set of drumsticks, pounding the pavement with them in a reckless, nonsensical rhythm, stooped over awkwardly as he advances along the street, beating and beating away at the cement. Perhaps he thinks he is doing important work. Perhaps, if he did not do what he did, the city would fall apart. Perhaps the moon would spin out of its orbit and come crashing into the earth. There are the ones who talk to themselves, who mutter, who scream, who curse, who groan, who tell themselves stories as if to someone else. The man I saw today, sitting like a heap of garbage in front of Grand Central Station, the crowds rushing past him, saying in a loud, panic-stricken voice: 'Third Marines ... eating bees ... the bees crawling out of my mouth.' Or the woman shouting at an invisible companion: 'And what if I don't want to! What if I just fucking don't want to!'

There are the women with their shopping bags and the men with their cardboard boxes, hauling their possessions from one place to the next, forever on the move, as if it mattered where they were. There is the man wrapped in the American flag. There is the woman with a Hallowe'en mask on her face. There is the man in a ravaged overcoat, his shoes wrapped in rags, carrying a perfectly pressed white shirt on a hanger – still sheathed in the dry-cleaner's plastic.

Paul Auster, *City of Glass* (1985), part one of *The New York Trilogy*

❋ ❋ ❋

And so, inevitably, to the blackest day in New York City's history.

11 September. Working rather disconsolately when Tom M. rings to tell me to switch on the television as the Twin Towers have been attacked. Not long after I switch on one of the towers collapses, an unbearable sight, like a huge plumed beast plunging earthwards. I go to put the kettle on and in that moment the other tower collapses.

15 September. Lynn in New York says that people in the city so want to be together they stand outside so that though New York is quiet there are many people on the streets, the atmosphere kindly and unthreatening, everyone courteous and not at all like New York. She had gone down to the Odeon when the first tower was hit and found the restaurant turned into a dressing station. She was out on the street when the second tower fell and had to flee the dust cloud, not stopping or looking behind her until she got to Canal Street.

Alan Bennett, *Untold Stories* (2005)

✳ ✳ ✳

It was not a street anymore but a world, a time and space of falling ash and near night. He was walking north through rubble and mud and there were people running past holding towels to their faces or jackets over their heads. They had handkerchiefs pressed to their mouths. They had shoes in their hands, a woman with a shoe in each hand, running past him. They ran and fell, some of them, confused and ungainly, with debris coming down around them, and there were people taking shelter under cars.

The roar was still in the air, the buckling rumble of the fall. This was the world now. Smoke and ash came rolling down streets and turning corners, bursting around corners, seismic tides of smoke, with office paper flashing past, standard sheets with cutting edge, skimming, whipping past, otherworldly things in the morning pall.

He wore a suit and carried a briefcase. There was glass in his hair and face, marbled bolls of blood and light. He walked past a Breakfast Special sign and they went running by, city cops and security guards running, hands pressed down on gun butts to keep the weapons steady.

Things inside were distant and still, where he was supposed to be. It happened everywhere around him, a car half buried in debris, windows smashed and noises coming out, radio voices scratching at the wreckage. He saw people shedding water as they ran, clothes and bodies drenched from sprinkler systems. There were shoes discarded in the street, handbags and laptops, a man seated on the sidewalk coughing up blood. Paper cups went bouncing oddly by.

The world was this as well, figures in windows a thousand feet up, dropping into free space, and the stink of fuel fire, and the steady rip of sirens in the air. The noise lay everywhere they ran, stratified sound collecting around them, and he walked away from it and into it at the same time.

There was something else then, outside all this, not belonging to this, aloft. He watched it come down. A shirt came down out of the high smoke, a shirt lifted and drifting in the scant light and then falling again, down toward the river.

They ran and then they stopped, some of them, standing there swaying, trying to draw breath out of the burning air, and the fitful cries of disbelief, curses and lost shouts, and the paper massed in the air, contracts, resumés blowing by, intact snatches of business, quick in the wind.

He kept on walking. There were the runners who'd stopped and others veering into sidestreets. Some were walking backwards, looking into the core of it, all those writhing lives back there, and things kept falling, scorched objects trailing lines of fire.

Don DeLillo, *Falling Man* (2007)

❊ ❊ ❊

That morning the city was as beautiful as it had ever been. Central Park had never seemed so gleaming and luxuriant – the leaves just beginning to fall, and the light on the leaves left on the trees somehow making them at once golden and bright green. A bird-watcher in the Ramble made a list of the birds he saw there, from the northern flicker and the red-eyed vireo to the rose-breasted grosbeak and the Baltimore oriole. "Quite a few migrants around today," he noted happily.

In some schools, it was the first day, and children went off as they do on the first day, with the certainty that this year we will have fun again. That protective bubble that, for the past decade or so, had settled over the city, and that we had come home to with a bubble's transparency and bright highlights, still seemed to be in place above us. We always knew that that bubble would burst, but we imagined it bursting as bubbles do: No one will be hurt, we thought, or they will be hurt only as people are hurt when bubbles burst, a little soap in your mouth. It seemed safely in place for another day as the children walked to school. The stockbroker fathers delivered – no, inserted – their kids into school as they always do, racing downtown, their cell phones already at work, like cartoons waiting for their usual morning caption: EXASPERATED AT 8 A.M.

A little while later, a writer who happened to be downtown saw a flock of pigeon rise, high and fast, and thought, *Why are the pigeons rising?* It was only seconds before he realized that the pigeons had felt the wave of the concussion before he heard the sound. In the same way, the shock wave hit us before the sound, the image before our understanding. For the lucky ones, the day from then on was spent in a strange, calm, and soul-emptying back-and-forth between the impossible images on television and the usual things on the street.

Around noon, a lot of people crowded around a lamppost on Madison, right underneath a poster announcing the Wayne Thiebaud show at the Whitney: all those cakes, as if to signal the impotence of our abundance. The impotence of our abundance! In the uptown supermarkets, people began to shop. It was a hoarding instinct, of course, though oddly not brought on by any sense of panic; certainly no one on television or radio was suggesting that people needed to hoard. Yet people had the instinct to do it, and in any case, in New York the instinct to hoard quickly seemed to shade over into the instinct to consume, shop for anything, shop because it might be a comfort. One woman emerged from a Gristede's on Lexington with a bottle of olive oil and said, "I had to get *something*." Mostly, people bought water – bottled water, French and Italian – and many people, waiting in the long lines, had Armageddon baskets: the Manhattan version, carts filled with steaks, Häagen-Dazs, and butter. Many of the carts held the goods of the bubble decade, hothouse goods: flavoured balsamics and cappellini and argula. There was no logic to it, as one man pointed out in that testy, superior, patient tone: "If trucks can't get through, the army will take over and give everybody K rations or some crazy thing; if they do, this won't matter." Someone asked him what was he doing uptown? He had been down there, gotten out before the building collapsed, and walked up.

People seemed not to much to suspend the rituals of normalcy as to carry on with them in a kind of bemusement – as though to reject the image on the screen, as though to say, *That's there, we're here, they're not here yet*, it's *not here yet*. "Everything turns away quite leisurely from the disaster," Auden wrote about a painting of Icarus falling from the sky; now we know why they turned away – they saw the boy falling from the sky, sure enough, but they did not know what to do about it. If we do the things we know how to do, New Yorkers thought, then what has happened will matter less.

The streets and parks were thinned of people, but New York is so dense – an experiment in density, really, as Venice is an experiment in water – that the thinning just produced the normal density of Philadelphia or Baltimore. It added to the odd calm. "You wouldn't put it in a book," a young man with an accent said to a girl in the park, and then he added, "Do you like to ski?" Giorgio Armani was in the park – Georgio Armani? Yes, right behind the Metropolitan Museum, with his entourage, beautiful Italian boys and girls in tight white T-shirts. "*Cinema*," he kept saying, his hands moving back and forth like an accordion player's. "*Cinema*."

120

Even urban geography is destiny, and New York, a long thin island, cuts off downtown from uptown, west side from east. And a kind of moral miniaturization is always at work, as we try unconsciously to seal ourselves from the disaster: People in Europe say "America attacked" and people in America say "New York attacked" and people in New York think "Downtown attacked.") For the financial community, this was the Somme; it was impossible not to know someone inside that building, or thrown from it. Whole companies, tiny civilizations, an entire zip code vanished. Yet those of us outside the world, hovering in midtown, were connected to the people dying in the towers only by New York's uniquely straight lines of sight – you looked right down Fifth Avenue and saw that strange, still, neat package of white smoke.

The city has never been so clearly, so surreally, sectioned as it became on Wednesday and Thursday. From uptown all the way down to Fourteenth Street, life is almost entirely normal – fewer cars, perhaps, one note quieter on the street, but children and moms and hotdog vendors on nearly every corner. In the flower district, the wholesalers unpack autumn branches from the boxes they arrived in this morning. "That came over the bridge?" someone asks, surprised at the thought of a truck driver waiting patiently for hours just to bring in blossoming autumn branches. The vendor nods.

At Fourteenth Street, one suddenly enters the zone of the missing, of mourning not yet acknowledged. It is, in a way, almost helpful to walk in that strange new village, since the concussion wave of fear that has been sucking us in since Tuesday is replaced with an outward ripple of grief and need, something human to hold on to. The stanchions and walls are plastered with home-made colour-Xerox posters, smiling snapshots above, a text below, searching for the missing: "Roger Mark Rasweiler. Missing. One WTC, 100th floor." "We Need Your Help: Giovanna 'Gennie' Gambale." "We're Looking for

Kevin M. Williams, 104th Fl. WTC." "Have You Seen Him?
Robert 'Bob' Dewitt." "Ed Feldman – Call Ross." "Millan
Rustillo – Missing WTC." Every lost face is smiling, caught
at Disney World or Miami Beach, on vacation. Every poster
lovingly notes the missing person's height and weight to the last
ounce and inch. "Clown tattoo on right shoulder," one says. On
two different posters, there is an apologetic note along with the
holiday snap: "Was Not Wearing Sunglasses on Tuesday."

Adam Gopnik, *Through The Children's Gate* (2007)

❉ ❉ ❉

From the suburb where I live in New Jersey, you can see the
skyline of Manhattan. When it appears through the trees or
beyond the edge of a hill, I find myself checking it and checking
it again, to see if the World Trade towers still aren't there. What
happened to them and to the people in them is unacceptable
to the mind, and we must use a lot of effort to get it straight.
To accommodate ourselves to the facts is to feel a weight that
gets no lighter no matter how we adjust it. The weight has a
particular heaviness in the early morning. After a troubled but
forgetful sleep, I wake up at five forty-five, before first light.
For a moment I don't remember what happened; in the next
moment, fully awake, I do.

There's a kind of impact as memory revives: yes, what I'm
remembering isn't a dreadful misgiving that ran through my
sleep; it's real. Outside the bedroom, the morning is quiet.
Traffic hasn't yet begun on the busy street in front of my house.
As I lie there listening, I know that millions of my neighbours
in the suburbs and the city are having the same experience I
just had. People are waking; there's a heartbeat of not remembering, and then, heavily, memory returns. For me, pain of it
is broad but not sharp, because no one close to me died in
the attack. But for many thousands of survivors – the paper
said hundreds of children lost a parent – the dawning memory

is specific and hard and unrelieved, poking through the early morning like a piece of angle iron among the pillows.

I think of the weight of memory falling in all those houses and apartments in the quiet half hour or so before the day begins. It's a weight that's continental in size, and it has a motion, heading westward as people there start to wake up, too. The weight consists of details – orange and black explosions, news clips run over and over, the smoke from something that shouldn't burn, the headlong verticality of the buildings' gigantic collapse, a rush of history like the *Titanic* going down. Each detail produces its own inward wince. It's an unusual feeling, and not a bad one, to know that at a particular moment millions of your fellow citizens are all thinking about the same thing.

Ian Frazier, *Gone to New York* (2005)

* * *

The recent global 'economic downturn' has brought bad times even to some of the most long-established symbols of New York's wealth and prestige. Adam Gopnik considers the commercial scene .

The great department stores of New York now lie on the avenues like luxury liners becalmed in a lagoon, big ships in shallow water. All around them, the dhows and junks and speedboats of the new national retailing, Staples and Victoria's Secret and Banana Republic and the Gap, honk at them and insult their sisters and get in their way. (And the newcomers hunt in pairs, so that no Duane Reade appears without a Starbucks nearby, no Staples without a Victoria's Secret minding its rear, as though the urge to tickle your husband and the urge to buy discounted stationery goods, the urge to caffeine and the urge to Coricidin were twinned deep in the desire system of the brain.) Saks and Bergdorf's and Bloomingdale's, immense and slow, look down at them and try to continue on a stately course, but the water is ebbing from around their keels.

Our sense of this, our mental image of it, is real and grounded in what we read – just this summer, Lord & Taylor, whose New York store is the southernmost ship of the Fifth Avenue fleet, and which is owned by the May company, lost nearly four thousand employees and thirty-two sister stores and was sent back to dry dock to be remade, nothing left but its signature. "Lackluster upon lackluster" is how a Piper Jaffray analyst describes the department-store sector. The professional retail trade papers worry about the disappearance of the department store exactly as the theater people worry about Broadway. But the decline is also intuitive and grounded in what we feel about the city. As recently as the early nineties, when Bloomies almost fell and women wept, department stores still mattered; they mattered as talk shows mattered then, as cable news matters now. One day we feel that something is big, and the next day we know that it is not. Without even looking at a receipt, we know somehow that the romance of the department store is fading, and we wonder what life will be like when it is gone.

Some of the department stores in town are in good shape – chiefly those that have been narrowly redefined as upscale clothing stores with small secondary lines in furniture and cosmetics. The seventh floor of Bergdorf Goodman hums, the eight floor of Saks sings, and there are few places that seem more entirely of Manhattan than Fred's at Barneys on a Saturday at noon. But we miss the big stores, because they defined a world, little duchies of commerce, with their faith in literal display: not the cunning and Duchampian show windows of a Simon Doonan but the things themselves shown as the things themselves, these shirts, these ties – the wooden escalators and crowded elevators, and the ghosts of elevator operators wearing small hats and announcing, "Notions." (There is a beautiful, forgotten song in the old Johnny Mercer show *Top Banana*, sung in the elevator of a department store, listing the contents of the floors as though they were poem enough: "Third floor rat-traps and radios, cheesecloth, cupcakes and cameos/Fourth floor peanuts and piccolos/left-over ushers from Loews.")

Lord & Taylor still gives one a sense of the department store as it once was, a last lingering resonance of the old dispensation. It is not a very distant world. The first floor of the store, at Thirty-eighth and Fifth, is laid out sweetly and expectantly, all mirrors and cosmetics; the salespeople in the Clinique department look serious in their white coats, as though actually about to attempt something cliniqual. There are no divisions, no urgency, no one spraying perfume – it is a ground floor seemingly arranged by the hand of God for displaying goods. There are striped men's ties placed like salmon fillets and men's shirts hanging like partridges. There are hats. The store plays the national anthem at ten o'clock every morning. On the sixth floor, the restauranteur Larry Forgione has opened a new café, complete with wine by the glass and a sweeping panoramic view of sturdy ladies' coats. The chowder is tasty, the wine decent. But there is something about Forgione himself – someone who has become a brand without ever quite having been a name – that extends the sense of a time warp, another era of hope. The old Lord & Taylor implies a rhythm of time, of women's time, in particular, a pace not slowed but purposeful and expansive: It takes a morning and lunch, or tea and an afternoon, to make a survey of the place, shopping as a setting out rather than a dropping in.

At last, up on the tenth floor, in the men's department, one can find an awe-inspiring demonstration of the sheer numbing stasis that capitalism can achieve – for it is insensitivity to the immediate pressure of the market that separates big-ticket capitalism from the rug bazaar and the vegetable stall. Capital slows down the market and places it within the shell of The Firm, firm in every sense, so that things can linger after their appeal to the market has passed. The brand names are Jack

Victor and Grant Thomas, name brands that are neither really names nor really brands, and seem to set off the commercial logic of brand-naming in a twilight zone of pure performance. No one wants to wear Jack Victor slacks, but there they are, hanging in poignant rows, their creases abjectly offered. It is a kind of installation piece: the department store as an abstract exercise in naming and branding and display, without commercial urgency and, mostly, without customers.

Adam Gopnik, *Through The Children's Gate* (2007)

✳ ✳ ✳

In his idiosyncratic style, Todd McEwen sums up a city made of good things and bad things, and comes to the only possible conclusion …

In classic and agreeable fashion, Central Park is a god and also the *abode* of the god.

Hundreds and thousands of TREES connect our island with the heavens.

We got complicated gods: the Chrysler Building, the Metropolitan Opera, the Board of Estimate, the Port Authority (Gee Whizz!). We got simple: eggs scrambled with calf brains by Hungarians on a winter morning, drums, *toupees* (the garment district their HQ). We got subterranean rivers from the old Underworld. […]

We got the all-seeing sun and the moon which peeks at you when you're doing something you shouldn't maybe. We got all kinds of statues replete with divinity.

We have our Mayors: divine kingship is a form of polytheism.

And – sadly – our gods are countered by demonic forces. The IRT wrestles with quite a few – no names need be named but there is sometimes a powerful demon at work in the token-booth at 50th Street. Wears a dirty blue shirt. The weather, in February, is a demon – or at least a bitch. There is Asbestos.

There is the guy who lived upstairs from Isidor with the dogs. The dogs themselves. F*** – *all dogs*. AND, as a kind of Miltonian-size counter to all the striving, scheming, smoking, buying, selling, thinking, stinking, drinking and LOVING in this our town, there is, across the river, NEW JERSEY. So it's a struggle – what isn't?

Todd McEwen, *Who Sleeps With Katz* (2003)

And all that jazz

*Ask anyone to say what kind of music they most asso-
ciate with New York and they're almost certain to say
popular music and jazz. We begin this taster of the
cultural and entertainment life in the city with a look
at its distinctive music industry, then move on to the
visual arts, theatre, classical music ... and sport. First,
'Tin Pan Alley' as explained in Beatrice Colin's novel*
The Songwriter.

Every time Monroe turned the corner on to Forty-Fifth Street,
he always paused for an instant and just listened, really listened.
Above the splutter of motor cars left to idle on the corner,
above the chitter and blurt of chorus girls and the bragging of
promoters, above the roar, even, of the printing presses that
churned out fifty pages of sheet music a minute, was the unmis-

takable, unforgettable sound of the piano, not just one, but ten, twenty, thirty, all playing different tunes at the same time.

Monroe was too young to remember the early days but the old-timers, the doormen and the veteran printers, talked about the first music publishers in the 1890s with reverence. They'd opened offices in Lower Manhattan, on the Bowery, before moving to Union Square and then up to the West Forties. Firms liker Shapiro's and Remick's followed the path of the entertainment industry uptown until they were settled in a triangle of high rises and brownstones called Upper Longacre Square, a triangle that was now surrounded by agents, bookers, theatres, music halls and vaudeville houses.

Although the whole industry was known collectively as Tin Pan Alley, only a handful of publishers still had their offices on West Twenty-Eighth Street, the street that had originally been given the name. If you went down to the 'Alley' now there would be little more than tourists and hustlers, ten-cent stores and sheet music wholesalers. But if you tried to describe it, and many had, you would eventually come to the conclusion that Tin Pan Alley was much more than a location. It was a flutter in the belly, the float of a crescendo followed by the crash of a minor seventh chord. It was the buzz of adrenalin or the first draw of a cigarette. Something new mixed with something old, it was a cocktail of melancholy mixed with a generous shot of pandemonium.

Beatrice Colin, *The Songwriter* (2010)

An insight into the craze for 'ragtime' from the auto-biography of James Weldon Johnson.

We at length secured places at a table in a corner of the room, and as soon as we could attract the attention of one of the busy waiters ordered a round of drinks. When I had somewhat collected my senses I realized that in a large back room into which the main room opened, there was a young fellow singing a song, accompanied on the piano by a short, thick-set, dark man.

Between each verse he did some dance steps, which brought forth great applause and a shower of small coins at his feet. After the singer had responded to a rousing encore, the stout man at the piano began to run his fingers up and down the keyboard. This he did in a manner which indicated that he was master of a good deal of technic. Then he began to play; and such playing! I stopped talking to listen. It was music of a kind I had never heard before. It was music that demanded physical response, patting of the feet, drumming of the fingers, or nodding of the head in time with the beat. The barbaric harmonies, the audacious resolutions often consisting of an abrupt jump from one key to another, the intricate rhythms in which the accents fell in the most unexpected places, but in which the beat was never lost, produced a most curious effect. [...]

This was ragtime music, then a novelty in New York, and just growing to be a rage which has not yet subsided. It was originated in the questionable resorts about Memphis and St. Louis by Negro piano players, who knew no more of the theory of music than they did of the theory of the universe, but were guided by natural musical instinct and talent. It made its way to Chicago, where it was popular some time before it reached New York. These players often improvised crude and, at times, vulgar words to fit the melodies. This was the beginning of the ragtime song. Several of these improvisations were taken down by white men, the words slightly altered, and published under the names of the arrangers. They sprang into immediate popularity and earned small fortunes, of which the Negro originators got only a few dollars. But I have learned that since that time a number of coloured men, of not only musical talent, but training, are writing out their own melodies and words and reaping the reward of their work. I have learned also that they have a larger number of white imitators and adulterators.

James Weldon Johnson,
The Autobiography of An Ex-Coloured Man (1912)

Enlightenment and flavoured with cold tea and Frigid® brand embalming fluid). No, the museums that make you feel loved! The museums where the pictures love YOU!

Always this coat-room madness; Izzy almost always refused to give up his coat – he thought the attendants rude – he wandered the museums of New York like they were bus stations – Not that the Metropolitan resembles anything else – but it is a god and must be placated – you cannot walk by.

Todd McEwen, *Who Sleeps With Katz* (2003)

* * *

Vanessa Threapleton-Horrocks takes us to the Frick – with a warm appreciation of this extraordinary gallery.

Picture this: you're living the Merchant's high-life in New York's Gilded Age. You've made your fortune in industrial deals and ruthless steel-worker exploitation, and, in honour of your achievements (notwithstanding a bit of healthy rivalry with a certain Andrew Carnegie), and paying due homage to the might of the masterpiece, you acquire a taste for the finer things in life. You're the Renaissance American living the American dream – which, in actual fact, is just a newer interpretation of European Old Money, but without the pedigree.

Henry Clay Frick, the "Pittsburgh Pit-bull" to his employees became the "Pittsburgh Pirate" to the genteel world of art collectors, and amassed an enviable collection of sumptuous spoils (think a litany of Old Masters, Renaissance wonders, fine French porcelain, Rococo panels, Limoges enamel, Oriental tapestries, Italian bronzes and sculptures, and all manner of antiquities). Then, in 1913, he erected a suitably splendid Beaux Arts mansion in New York within which to house them all. More than a match for the Carnegies!

Fortunately for the public, this steel-magnate-turned-art-enthusiast styled himself as a surprise posthumous

* * *

The enthusiasm for black musicians and the music they created triggered, in the 1920s, what became known as the Harlem Renaissance. (It was depicted in Wallace Thurman's novel Infants of the Spring.*) It seems to have begun with the musical review* Shuffle Along *and the popularity of the Charleston. But in* The Big *Sea, Langston Hughes (1902–67) – novelist, playwright and columnist who instigated the literary form known as 'jazz poetry' – reveals that the sparkling life of this so-called Negro Renaissance wasn't always so positive just beneath the surface.*

I was there. I had a swell time while it lasted. But I thought it wouldn't last long. (I remember the vogue for things Russian, the season the Chauve-Souris first came to town.) For how could a large and enthusiastic number of people be crazy about Negroes forever? But some Harlemites thought the millennium had come. They thought the race problem had at last been solved through Art plus Gladys Bentley. They were sure the New Negro would lead a new life from then on in green pastures of tolerance created by Countee Cullen, Ethel Waters, Claude McKay, Duke Ellington, Bojangles, and Alain Locke.

I don't know what made any Negroes think that – except that they were mostly intellectuals doing the thinking. The ordinary Negroes hadn't heard of the Negro Renaissance.

Langston Hughes, *The Big Sea* (1940)

* * *

Some more on the original jazz club scene from Jan Morris.

"Swing Street" was what they called West 52nd Street, between Fifth and Sixth Avenues, for in its hundred yards or so there flourished a dozen or more jazz clubs featuring some of the greatest performers of the day. These had started in the 1930s chiefly as resorts for jazz musicians themselves, after their evening gigs were done. They had been adopted by the Cafe Society, and had done much to project improvisational jazz as a popular art form, at a time when the regimented big bands were all-conquering. All kinds of jazz were played there cheek-by-jowl. At the Downbeat you might hear Charlie Parker and Dizzy Gillespie playing bop, bang next door at the Three Deuces Art Tatum was playing virtuoso swing, across the road Billie Holiday sang at the Onyx Club, immediately next door to the Onyx Dixieland and New Orleans jazz blared out from Jimmy Ryan's. Every sort of raffish and eccentric character mixed with the swells in those smoky brownstone premises, and for many young New Yorkers they offered the best night out of all – you paid no entrance fee, you were charged no fancy Broadway prices, and over a single beer you could spend half the night listening to some of the best popular music in the world played live before your eyes.

Jan Morris, *Manhattan '45* (1987/2011)

* * *

Some of those who couldn't afford to go in hung around the open doors to enjoy snatches of the music that so authentically expressed the life of the city.

Evenings always found her striding, head up, tam askew, through Times Square, that bejewelled navel in the city's long sinuous form. To Selina it was a new constellation, the myriad lights hot stars bursting from chaos into their own vivid life, shooting, streaking, wheeling in the night void, then expiring, but only to burst again – and the concatenation of traffic and voices like the roar from the depth of a maelstrom – an irresistible call to destruction.

She loved it, for its chaos echoed her inner chaos; each bedizened window, each gaudy empty display evoked something in her that loved and understood the gaudy, the

emptiness defined her own emptiness and that in the faces flitting past her. She walked with a swagger here, gazing boldly into those faces, always hoping to happen upon some violence, or to be involved in some spectacular brawl. For hours she stood outside the Metropole, listening to the jazz that poured through the open doors in a thick guttural flow that churned the air into a pulsating mass; sometimes the music was thin and reedy, sometimes brassy and jarring, yet often soulful, and always expressing the chaos in the street.

Paule Marshall, *Brown Girl, Brownstones* (1960)

* * *

We move on to the art scene, first with a whiff of poetry from Edmund White.

What was distinctive about New York in the 1970s was its uncompromising high culture masquerading as slouching, grinning gee-whiz – Wallace Stevens in sneakers. John Ashbery had lived in Paris for years, where he'd been the art critic for the *Herald Tribune*, and now wrote art reviews for *Newsweek*. When he gave a reading in the austere and large auditorium at the bottom of the Guggenheim Museum, it was packed with young people in black and older, art-world people. There were German women in full-length black leather coats and hennaed hair and men in faded blue work shirts, insect-eye glasses, white stubb and oversize porkpie hats. Ashbery was always surrounded art-world people, which brought a whiff of money and inter tionalism to the usual seedy gatherings of poor poets.

Edmund White, *City Boy* (2

* * *

The day was museum-cold, with the reflected quiet light pulls you into the Whitney or the Metropolitan or the M and lets you feel cosy about being there. (Not the Frick is surrounded by its own weather left over from the

philanthropist, bequeathing his home and all its contents to the city, metamorphosing it into one of the world's most exquisite museums.

Discreetly tucked away in a quiet corner of Fifth Avenue and 70th Street on the Upper East Side's Museum Mile, overlooking the verdant heart of Manhattan, Central Park, its clean architectural lines and neat landscaped gardens create an imposing first impression. Consider the prospect of a pocket-sized Hermitage – perfect, piquant, opulent and ornamental yet with a warm homely touch, as only a former family home can have, and you'll get the picture. Unlike the epic European altars to art and antiquities, where one can get lost in galleries upon galleries of ordered and chronicled art, one feels comfortable and in control here. The rooms and their contents are pretty much arranged as Frick himself would remember them and to his taste.

The awe that was audible back when the new museum first opened its doors in December 1935 remains for today's visitor. Degas, Gainsborough, Goya, Reynolds, Turner, Van Dyck, Velazquez and Whistler – the Frick has paintings by them all … not to mention the three Vermeers. But the most opulent, jaw-dropping rooms are those of the Rococo aesthetic (the Boucher and Fragonard Rooms) which certainly fulfil the movement's lust for a sensual, frivolous setting. But remarkable too is the glass-roofed Garden Court at the heart of the home, with its central fountain and a marble bench where one can claim a welcome retreat for the senses.

We tend to think New York and its modern veneer as favouring art of the edgy, pioneering contemporary set. After all, the Whitney and Guggenheim are celebrated bastions of the American modern art scene. So how does the Frick fit?

New York loves tradition as well as modernity (in fact nowhere does classical with a modern touch as well as the Big Apple). True, Old Masters and Renaissance devotional art are not everyone's preferred canvass, but a collection like the Frick's, in such a unique setting, cannot help but touch the aesthete in us all.

Vanessa Threapleton-Horrocks,
'The Frick: from frivolous to fabulous' (2011)

❋ ❋ ❋

And so to the theatre. The vast numbers of theatrical memoirs available to the enthusiast are impossible to choose between: one could create a whole anthology just on this aspect of New York. So, opting for mini-malism, here are just a couple of brief, less obvious extracts on the subject – an informational piece by Luc Sante, and a humorous one from Quentin Crisp.

The duality of Broadway and anti-Broadway began in the mists of New York's theatrical history, around the end of the eighteenth century. It quickly came to stand for a class distinction, in regard both to money (cost of tickets, wages paid to actors, production budgets, structural and land values of theatres) and to a perceived idea of quality (art vs. entertainment, sometimes; at other times, merely the slick vs. the rough-cut). Broadway was the theatre of the bourgeoisie, the standard, the temple, while the Bowery was the circus of the masses. The scenery-chewing productions of Shakespeare typical of the nineteenth century might be viewed by the press and by memoirists as art if they were produced on Broadway, as stunts if they played to the Bowery mechanics. When the Bowery finally folded as an entertainment venue just before World War I, Broadway nominally had the game all to itself, but actually the opposition merely changed its name and setting. There has consistently been some kind of dichotomy ever since: stage plays countered by moving pictures, the legitimate theatre countered by vaudeville and burlesque, the native drama by ethnic drama, "big" theatre by little theatre, Broadway by Off-Broadway, Off-Broadway by Off-Off-Broadway. Although some of these contrasts may appear to be of an innocuously practical mature, each of them also exemplifies the assumption of the standard of official culture by one party and the challenge to that standard by another.

Luc Sante, *Low Life* (1991)

✳ ✳ ✳

In all big cities, I suppose, there is a fringe theatre. In London, it is called 'Fringe Theatre'; in New York, it is called 'Off-Off-Broadway'. This secondary entertainment is usually too risqué (filthy) or too cultural (boring) to be presented at great expense to the public, which will reject it, but it serves the purpose of employing actors, set designers etc., and prevents them from becoming desperate. Now nothing can possibly be too risqué for modern audiences, so 'kinky' has become the mainstay of fringe theatre.

Mr John Glines has established a cartel in kinkiness at the Courtyard Theatre on Grove Street. I went there to see four 'gay' plays gathered into something called *Adjoining Trances* by a Mr Buck. This is very different from its last theatrical offering, which was a hilarious play about a televangelist tempted by the devil, who appears in drag for this purpose. The present play is a sober affair, an imaginary conversation between Tennessee Williams and Carson McCullers. It is only gay in that we know both parties were homosexual. It is cultural in that nothing happens.

Quentin Crisp, *Resident Alien* (1996)

✳ ✳ ✳

Even though the razzamatazz of Broadway may define New York's entertainment scene in the popular imagination, it is in fact the supreme city of 'high art'.

New York was still obsessed with the hierarchy of the arts and the idea of the Pure. Many of the figures of the international scene, active elsewhere in the world, remained present in the

137

imaginations of cultured New Yorkers – Nabokov, Beckett, Sartre, to name a few. In the 1960s a New York newspaper had asked American writers to identify the most important living writer – they chose Beckett.

The music of Stravinsky, though he'd recently died, was being played every week during the New York City Ballet season. The three great geniuses of the twentieth century, Stravinsky, Nabokov, and Balanchine, had all started off in imperial Russia, passed through France, and known a second (or third) creative flowering in America. Whereas later New Yorkers, and Americans in general, would turn their backs on Europe, in the 1970s we were all still reading Lacan, Deleuze, Foucault, Barthes, Derrida, and Lévi-Strauss. And many distinguished foreigners would live in rough, grimy, stimulating New York for long periods. Many French and Italian artists had studios in Manhattan; the French sculptor Alain Kirili and his photographer wife Ariane Lopez-Huici began to spend longer and longer sojourns in New York in the seventies, Kirili becoming a major collaborator with American jazz musicians.

The American literary avant-garde was very much in business, including such New Yorkers as Donald Barthelme. They were often published in the *New American Review*, and all made frequent appearances at the 92nd Street Y in New York, events that were well attended. A magazine such as *Esquire* in 1963 was able to generate sales by mapping out the "red-hot centre" of American literary life – and locating it in New York and among mostly white men. Norman Mailer, Gore Vidal, and Truman Capote, like Hollywood stars, all appeared on national TV and Mailer's movements or Philip Roth's were carefully charted by their fellow New Yorkers. David's boss Richard Poirier had written a book in the Modern Masters series about Mailer and Vidal and their contrasting chat styles on television (Vidal's was better suited to the medium, Poirier argued, since it consisted of sound bites rather than complex, sustained arguments). This was the backdrop of Woody Allen films featuring Jewish psychiatrists, of blue blazers worn over faded jeans, of Saul Steinberg cartoons. I remember seeing Steinberg at a party in the Hamptons in the late sixties, when he would glide up from behind a tree and try to spook my date, a girl from work. We thought it was glamorous to be a writer; a highly visible whiskey ad of the time showed a writer pounding his chic little Olivetti and asking his girlfriend, "While you're up, would you get me a Grant's?" We didn't pay much attention to television personalities (there were only three channels in those days); our celebrities were all writers and painters.

Edmund White, *City Boy* (2009)

❊ ❊ ❊

Nigerian-born Teju Cole's Open City *contains a wonderful description of seeing Sir Simon Rattle conduct Mahler's ninth symphony at Carnegie Hall. But it is what happens when he tries to beat the crowds and leave by an alternative exit that leads to an unforgettable New York moment and provides a cautionary tale for anyone not content to follow the usual route out.*

Only when the door clicked behind me did I realise what I had done. I had used the emergency exit, which led directly from the fourth tier to the fire escape outside the building. The heavy metallic door that had just slammed shut had no external handle: I was locked out. There was to be no respite from the rain and the wind because I had also left my umbrella in the concert hall. And, added to all this was the fact that I was standing not on an exit staircase, as I had hoped, but on a flimsy fire escape, locked out on the unlit side of Carnegie Hall on a stormy evening. It was a situation of unimprovable comedy.

The slick wirework was all that separated me from the street level of the city, some seventy feet down. The lights directly below were visible between my feet, and my head and coat were already wet. My fellow concertgoers went about their lives oblivious to my plight. It was farther than the distance of a shout, even in clement weather; at night, with rain lisping through the streets, it was futile. And a few minutes before this, I had been in God's arms, and in the company of many hundreds of others, as the orchestra had sailed toward the coda, and brought us all to an impossible elation.

Now, I faced solitude of a rare purity. In the darkness, above the sheer drop, I could see the lights of Forty-second Street flashing in the visible distance. The railings of the fire escape, which were probably precarious at the best of times, were slicked with water and inimical to the grip. I moved carefully, taking step after premeditated step. The wind pushed around the building noisily, and I took some grim comfort in the idea that, if I were to fall from that height, there was no question of being maimed: death would be instant. The thought calmed me, and I stepped and slid down the metal steps, a few modest inches at a time. My high-wire act continued for long minutes in the darkness. And then I saw that the fire escape went only halfway down the building, ending abruptly at another closed door. The rest of the way down to the ground, some two flights, was air alone. But luck was with me: this second door had a handle. I tried it and it opened, into a hallway.

Before I entered the door, holding it open with relief and gratitude, it occurred to me to look straight up, and much to my surprise there were stars. Stars! I hadn't thought I would be able to see them, not with the light pollution perpetually wreathing the city, and not on a night on which it had been raining. But the rain had stopped while I was climbing down, and had washed the air clean. The miasma of Manhattan's electric lights did not go very far up into the sky, and in the moonless night, the sky was like a roof shot through with light and heaven itself shimmered. [...]

I gripped the rusted railing of the fire escape with one hand and tightened my hold on the open door with the other. The night air clipped my ears. I looked down, a steep drop, and the blurred yellow rectangle of a taxicab sped by, and then an ambulance, its wailing reaching me from seven floors below, and stretching out as it headed toward Times Square's neon inferno.

Teju Cole, *Open City* (2011)

* * *

One of the unmissable 'high art' experiences New York has to offer is the Metropolitan Opera House. (Listeners to BBC Radio Three on a Saturday evening will be familiar with the Met's ability to attract the world's top singers and the most stunning productions.). Vanessa Threapleton-Horrocks takes us along ...

As night falls, I leave behind the hum and haste of the city and join the crowds collecting outside the Metropolitan Opera House. Caught up in a riot of suits and furs, I enter the foyer and the communal frisson of adrenaline and expensive perfume fill the air. Though a child of the '60s, the Met has some surprisingly traditional touches – deep crimson, velvety carpets, a grand, sweeping staircase – uniting the old world with the new. Its signature contemporary cool was sealed at the beginning in 1966 when the House summoned the Russian painter, Marc Chagall, to provide the elegant foyer with two monumental murals, titled "The Triumph of Music" and "The Sources of Music", replete with ethereal, seraphic figures and exotic creatures astride a sea of striking gold and vermillion. My favourite vantage point from which to contemplate the Chagall close-up is the white spiral staircase, but the murals can also be marvelled at outside, from the Lincoln Center Plaza – at their kaleidoscopic best at night.

The Metropolitan Opera House may lack the historical romance of La Scala or The Bolshoi Theatre, but what it lacks in age it makes up for in size: one of the largest operatic stages in the world, and seating for 3995. I take my place in the Grand Tier, savouring the generous seating space and relaxing into velvet, gazing upwards at the exquisite chandeliers. As the performance is about to begin, the excitement is palpable.

With the magnificence of the music, the complexity of the plots, the huge sets, the sparkling, scene-stealing costumes, and the intricate lighting, opera at the Met can be a kind of "extreme sport" – not just for the singers but for the audience too: one needs the combined constitution, stamina and patience of a Scots Guard to survive three-to-five hours of intense passion without keeling over! Keeping stationary for an extended period must surely be a challenge for the average New Yorker always on the go, but with such a dazzling spectacle, they seem to think it's worth it. Certainly, cultured residents from every walk of life consider their opera house, and the wider Lincoln Center complex, a national treasure.

The Metropolitan Opera secured its celebrated home when it partnered eleven other premiere New York institutions in forming the Lincoln Center for the Performing Arts. Maybe New York hasn't got a Parthenon or an Alhambra, but the largest performing arts venue in the land has made its mark on the Manhattan map as its very own "Citadel of Culture". Some may argue that it is epic folly to lump such celebrated institutions together into one all-singing, all-dancing venue, but this misses the pioneering point of the Lincoln Center. It is the first gathering of major cultural organizations in the centre of an American city. Yet it has become so much more than that, operating as the artistic epicentre for the country (if not, the world). As an essential part of the cultural fabric of New York City, it is the go-to destination to see the best ballet, the best opera, or the best orchestral concerts all conveniently located in one place. It's a smart move for one of the fastest, most dynamic cities in the world, where opera's "exotic and irrational" heart beats at the centre of a rigid grid of streets and lofty edifices.

A trip to The Met, a microcosm of The Big Apple in its purest art form, ought to be on everyone's hotlist of things to do before you die – perhaps a tad dramatic, but nevertheless befitting a traditional operatic ending.

Vanessa Threapleton-Horrocks, adapted from 'Opera-Nation' (2011)

✣ ✣ ✣

Finally, by contrast, and as a reminder of the range of entertainment on offer in the Big Apple, we pop into a baseball game at the famous Yankee Stadium – a game played on 8th September 2001.

Yankee Stadium, the Bronx. The House that Ruth Built, scene of Babe Ruth's greatest triumphs. The huge stadium was packed, the crowd expectant. The Yankees, the biggest sports franchise in America, were going for their fourth consecutive World Series in a row. That would also be a fifth in six years.

He had great seats – field level, on the third-base side. The boys were thrilled. And today, the Yankees were playing the Red Sox.

The Boston Red Sox. The ancient rivalry, so full of passion – and heartbreak if you were a Red Sox fan.

At 1.15 the game began. And for the next three and a quarter hours, Gorham Vandyck Master enjoyed one of the happiest afternoons of his life. The game was wonderful. The crowd roared. He said to hell with dinner and his cholesterol, and ate three hot dogs. The boys assuredly ate more, but he didn't count.

What a game! The Yankees scored seven runs in the sixth inning, and Tino Martinez hit two home runs, to defeat the Red Sox 9 to 2.

'Well boys,' he said, 'that was a game to remember for the rest of our lives.'

Edward Rutherfurd, New York (2009)

Big weather

*New York is not a city that does anything by half –
including weather. From sub-zero, snowy winters to
blistering or steamy summers, residents (and visitors)
must adapt to anything as Nature reminds them that,
despite the primacy of the built environment, she really
calls the tunes. We'll start cold and then warm up ...*

Three Sundays later winter started. The wind was so fierce that
on a certain block of Madison Avenue, where huge buildings
towered over brownstones and tenements and the street tilted
upward at a sharp angle, two parked cars were blown whole

145

across the street. Hardly anyone witnessed this spectacle except the bag ladies who had staked out territories for the night in the dark indentations of grilled and grated storefronts. Newspapers clinging to their chests, they sat back and watched the refuse of the world blow by – mangled umbrellas, lost gloves, a child's tricycle. At the intersection of Broadway and Ninety-sixth Street, most of the mice had died from cold or shock or from having been run over by cars. Caught up in a dust of snow, their carcasses blew down the boulevard, block after block, as if in flight. Philip, in the taxicab with Eliot, found himself, just for a moment, turning to notice the mosaic of bright yellow squares encrusting the horizon of skyscraper spires, and beyond it, the resonant glow of more distant East Side lights, flickering and splintering, as if seen through water. The snow fell before this vision of the city, and Philip imagined that he was inside one of those tiny globed worlds where the air is viscous water, and the bright snowflakes little chips of plastic that fly up when the globe is shaken, then slowly fall back to earth. He looked up at the sky and tried to make out the vast, transparent shell, with its faint hint of reflection. He was thinking, I live in that thing.

David Leavitt, *The Lost Language of Cranes* (1986)

* * *

That was a very white winter. A blizzard on Presidents' Day 2003 brought one of the heaviest snows in the city's history. For a day or two, outdoor motions seemed a kind of mummery and the newspapers broke up the Iraq stories with photos of children tobogganing on Sheep's Meadow. I passed the morning of the holiday in an armchair in my hotel apartment, mesmerised by a snowdrift on the wrought-iron balcony that grew and deepened and monstrously settled against the glass door, not completely melting until mid-March. […]

Snowflakes like coffee grinds blackened the insect screen. Powdered ice, blown up from the window-trough, had gained on the sill and now crept up the glass. I was, it will be understood, afflicted by the solitary's vulnerability to insights, so that when I peered out into the flurry and saw no sign of the Empire State Building, I was assaulted by the notion, arriving in the form of a terrifying stroke of consciousness, that substance – everything of so-called concreteness – was indistinct from its unnameable opposite.

Joseph O'Neill, Netherland (2008)

✻ ✻ ✻

This rare child's-eye view of New York recounts a memory of kindness in extreme conditions.

I knew it was snowing before I opened my eyes. I could hear the sounds of shovels scraping against the sidewalks, and there was that special quiet in the air that comes when the city is heavily blanketed with snow. I ran to the windows in the front room to have a look at the block – my domain. It must have been very early. None of my friends had made it to the street; only janitors were moving about in the knee-deep snow. Relieved that I hadn't missed anything, I became aware that my sisters and brothers were now aware. I had no time to waste. If I hurried, I could be out there before any of my friends.

I dressed myself in an assortment of hand-me-down winter woollens, but there would be no mittens to keep my hands warm. I had lost them earlier in the season. I was in a real dither as to what to put on my feet; my shoes no longer fit into my rubber galoshes. I could wear shoes or galoshes, but not both. I decided to go with two pairs of socks and the galoshes.

As I was buckling them, I felt the presence of someone standing over me. It was my big brother, Lenny. He asked me if I wanted to go ice skating at the indoor rink in Madison Square Garden. I immediately scrapped my other plans. My thirteen-year-old brother was actually asking me, his nine-year-old sister, to go ice-skating with him. Go? Of course I would go.

But where would we get the money? Lenny said it would cost a dollar to get in and rent the skates. Only two obstacles stood between me and going skating with my brother – the blizzard of 1948 and one dollar. The blizzard I could handle – it was the dollar that presented the problem.

The quest began. We returned some milk bottles, asked our mother for a nickel, begged our father for a quarter apiece, collected a penny or two from coat pockets, discovered two coins that had rolled under the beds, and spotted a rare stray dime nestled in a corner of one of the six rooms in our cold-water railroad flat.

Eventually, fortified with a bowl of hot oatmeal and jamming the hard-earned coins into our pockets, we set out on the twenty-block journey – a city mile.

The wind-driven snow clung to every surface. Lenny and I pretended that we were in the Alps as we climbed over the three-foot mounds of snow that had been shovelled to the curbs. It was our world now – a myriad of tiny snowflakes had shut down the city and kept the adults indoors. The skyscrapers were invisible behind a white veil of snow, and we could almost imagine that New York had been scaled down for us. We could walk right down the middle of Third Avenue with no fear of being run over. It was hard to contain our joy, the incredible sense of freedom we felt out there in the snow.

The twelve blocks to Forty-ninth Street weren't difficult, but the long crosstown streets proved to be chilling. The harsh west winds blowing off the Hudson River made it almost impossible to push forward. I could no longer keep up with my brother. My playful imaginings were replaced by the gnawing cold of my feet. My head was uncovered, my mittenless hands were clenched in my pockets, and a few of the clasps on my galoshes had worked loose. I began to complain gently, not wanting to make a nuisance of myself because I was afraid that Lenny wouldn't ask me to go anywhere with him again.

Somewhere near Fifth Avenue, we stopped in a doorway to take refuge. I timidly told Lenny that my clasps were open. Lenny took his bare red hands out of his pockets and bent down to refasten the snow-crusted, icy metal clasps. Ashamed that Lenny had to take care of me, I stared straight ahead and saw the image of a man walking toward us through the chiffon curtain of snow.

I was unable to tell how old he was —all adults seemed the same age to me – but he was tall, thin, and had a gentle, handsome face. He wore no hat. There was a scarf around his neck, and his overcoat, like ours, was caked with snow.

I don't remember if he spoke to me or not. What I do recall is that he kneeled down before me, his face level with mine. I found myself gazing into soft brown eyes, feeling bewildered and mute. When he was gone, I felt his warmth in the soft, wine-coloured scarf that he wrapped tightly around my head.

I don't remember ice skating that day, or how we got home. All my memory holds is the snow, the kindness of a stranger, and my big brother, Lenny.

Juliana Nash, 'Snow' from *True Tales of American Life*
(ed. Paul Auster, 2001)

✳ ✳ ✳

But snow can be fun. A delightful vignette of New York prostitutes having an innocently good time.

They rode down Broadway, blocks lined with Korean fruit-stands and laundromats and newsstands. Men were struggling to cover piles of the Sunday paper with tarpaulins. To Philip's surprise, a few flakes of snow started to fall, then more and more. He remembered coming out of a movie theatre in the East Village when he was a teenager to find that a snowstorm had come and gone while he was inside. The streetlights reflected off the white carpet that seemed so suddenly to have covered the city, creating a light as brilliant as in a skating rink. No cars could pass. Philip had to squint as he walked out into the middle of Third Avenue, where prostitutes in sequinned skirts and fur-trimmed jackets were throwing snowballs at each other. "Come play with us, honey," they shouted to him – a joke, or a sincere invitation, since they had seen what kind of theatre he had come out of. "No thanks," he said. He looked up. The pale night sky seemed to have risen from this brightness like smoke from a white-hot fire.

David Leavitt, *The Lost Language of Cranes* (1986)

❋ ❋ ❋

Lest we try to attribute all recent extremes of weather to climate change, here's evidence that it could be just as bad in the nineteenth century.

At no time in this century has New York experienced a storm like that of March 13. It had rained the preceding Sunday, and the writer working into the dawn, the newspaper vendor at the railroad station, the milkman on his round of the sleeping houses, could hear the whiplash of the wind that had descended on the city against the chimneys, against walls and roofs, as it vented its fury on slate and mortar, shattered windows, demolished porches, clutched and uprooted trees, and howled, as though ambushed, as it fled down the narrow streets. Electric wires, snapping under its impact, sputtered and died. Telegraph lines, which had withstood so many storms, were wrenched from their posts. And when the sun should have appeared, it could not be seen, for like a shrieking, panic-stricken army, with its broken squadrons, gun carriages and infantry, the snow whirled past the darkened windows, without interruption, day and night. Man refused to be vanquished. He came out to defy the storm. [...]

It was impossible to see the sidewalks. Intersections could no longer be distinguished, and one street looked like the next. On Twenty-third Street, one of the busiest thoroughfares, a thoughtful merchant put a sign on a corner-post: "This is 23rd

Street." The snow was knee deep, and the drifts, waist-high. The angry wind nipped at the hands of pedestrians, knifed through their clothing, froze their noses and ears, blinded them, hurled them backward into the slippery snow, its fury making it impossible for them to get to their feet, flung them hatless and groping for support against the walls, or left them to sleep, to sleep forever, under the snow. A shopkeeper, a man in the prime of life, was found buried today, with only a hand sticking from the snow to show where he lay. A messenger boy, as blue as his uniform, was dug out of a white, cool tomb, a fit resting place for his innocent soul, and lifted up in the compassionate arms of his comrades. Another, buried to the neck, sleeps with two red patches on his white cheeks, his eyes a filmy blue. [...]

Night fell over the arctic waste of New York, and terror took over. The postman on his round fell face down, blinded and benumbed, protecting his leather bag with his body. Families trapped in the roofless houses sought madly and in vain to find a way out through the snow-banked doors. When water hydrants lay buried under five feet of snow, a raging fire broke out, lighting up the snowy landscape like the Northern Lights, and swiftly burned three apartment houses to the ground. [...]

The trains and their human cargoes stand snowbound on the tracks. The city is cut off from the rest of the country and no news goes in or out. The rivers are ice, and the courageous cross them on foot; suddenly the ice gives way, and cakes of it float aimlessly with men aboard them; a tug goes out to rescue them, skirting the ice cake, nosing it toward the bank, edging it to a nearby dock. They are saved. What a cheer goes up from both sides of the river! There are also cheers as the fireman passes, the policeman, and the brave postman. What can have happened to the trains that never arrive? The railroad companies, with admirable despatch, send out food and coal, hauled by their most powerful engines. What of those at sea? How many bodies lie buried under the snow?

Like a routed army that unexpectedly turns on it vanquisher, the snow had come in the night and covered the proud city with death.

José Martí, in *La Nación* (1888)

❋ ❋ ❋

Like many waterside cities, New York can also be subject to thick fogs …

New York has a special interest for me when it is wrapped in fog. Then it behaves very much like a blind person. I once crossed from Jersey City to Manhattan in a dense fog. The ferry-boat felt its way cautiously through the river traffic. More timid than a blind man, its horn brayed incessantly. Fog-bound, surrounded by menacing, unseen craft and dangers, it halted every now and then as a blind man halts at a crowded thoroughfare crossing, tapping his cane, tense and anxious.

Helen Keller, *Midstream: My Later Life* (1929)

❋ ❋ ❋

The transition to summer …

Those early summer afternoons. Hot smells rising from the streets. Even at five, sunshine caught the high-rise windows and burned their edges. Boys played ball again on the public courts; fat young men, glad to be out of the office early, took over the softball fields. Air-conditioning units dripped off the sides of apartment blocks. Walking across town, she felt the dirty cool flecks against her cheek, as many, perhaps, as a wet hand shakes loose after washing. The cherry trees on 82nd Street scattered bloom; confetti aftermaths. Petals wrinkled in the heat, then turned grey with pavement dirt. The days grew longer, stretched on loose elastic that had lost its snap. The rich packed up to leave Manhattan to the poor.

Benjamin Markovits, *Either Side of Winter* (2005)

* * *

And then the heat's full on ...

It was one of those washed-out New York days of deadening, grey heat. All along the avenue, droning AC units were dripping condensation on to the baked sidewalk. High over-head, the pale sun wobbled and fizzed in a milky sky, seemingly too weak and soluble an entity to be a plausible source of the monstrous temperature.

Zoë Heller, *The Believers* (2008)

* * *

By nine in the morning the fake, country-wet freshness that somehow seeped in overnight evaporated like the tail end of a sweet dream. Mirage-grey at the bottom of their granite canyons, the hot streets wavered in the sun, the car tops sizzled and glittered, and the dry, cindery dust blew into my eyes and down my throat.

Sylvia Plath, *The Bell Jar* (1963)

* * *

The extremity of the heat just makes some people laugh!

I came down the steps of the Ashbery that morning and burst out laughing at the heat. New York can't be serious about this. I have read, or television has told me, about parts of space where the manmade boomerangs fly. It's hot out there, several million degrees Fahrenheit. Psychopathic heat. In New York, in July, the heat is psychopathic. On bucking Broadway the cabs all bitched and beefed, ferrying robots, bad dogs, uptown, downtown. I grabbed my trap and joined the shunt.

New York is a jungle. You could go further and say that New York is a jungle. New York *is a jungle*. Beneath the columns of the old rain forest, made of melting macadam, the mean

Limpopo of swamped Ninth Avenue bears an angry argosy of crocs and dragons, tiger fish, noise machines, sweating rain-makers. On the corners stand witchdoctors and headhunters, babbling voodoo-men – the natives, the jungle-smart natives. And at night, under the equatorial overgrowth and heat-holding cloud cover, you hear the ragged parrot-hoot and monkeysqueak of the sirens, and then fires flower to ward off monsters. Careful: the streets are sprung with pits and nets and traps. Hire a guide. Pack your snake-bite gook and your blow-dart serum. Take it seriously. You have to get a bit jungle-wise.

Martin Amis, *Money* (1984)

* * *

The heat that could last on into September, and even October ... though by evening there is a little relief.

It was already October but Manhattan was still baking in the heat of an Indian summer. At that time of the evening, however, the air was edged with cooler currents. Everything was in shadow, the harsh angles of the buildings and the geometry of the grid all softened by the blue wash of nightfall. And yet on Times Square, the night was ablaze. The electric illuminations, the flashing bulbs of the Petticoat Girl and the Corticelli Kitty signs, the theatre hoardings, the cinema kiosks and the moving headlamps of dozens of taxicabs would all burn until long after closing time. As usual, the streets were choked up with people from out of town who had come to gawp at the lights and to spend their savings in the Irish bars and the overpriced restaurants that lined the square. In all that joviality, in all that hilarity, in all that extravagance, it was hard to remember that in Europe a war was being fought.

Monroe headed south down Broadway, past the Flatiron Building on Fifth Avenue and onwards to West Twenty-Third Street. Here, the rush-hour traffic, the tramcars and the elevated trains, the horse-drawn cabs and the private cars, had started to thin out. A couple of booths lit by strings of bare electric bulbs sold pretzels and chestnuts on the corner. Groups of construction workers, their eyes dizzy with height and too much coffee, crouched in doorways and waited for their lift home. A white horse pulled a cart towards the Bowery, its load of seltzer water bottles clanking gently in their wooden crates.

Skirting the edge of Chinatown, he strode towards the Court House and up the ramp of the Brooklyn Bridge. The wide wooden walkway for pedestrians and bicycles rose above the tracks of the electric tramcars and the road until it hung suspended above four lanes of traffic. Most of the office workers and clerks who lived in lodgings in Fort Greene or Carroll Park clocked off at five sharp and had crossed the bridge a couple of hours before, and so he was almost alone as he paced towards the Brooklyn side, his hat pushed down against the wind.

Beatrice Colin, The Songwriter (2010)

Happy holidays

'Happy holidays' is an expression usually reserved for the Christmas season, but here we take the liberty of using it to picture New York in various seasonal celebrations and simply on holiday. First, Alan Bennett on Hallowe'en.

31 October, New York. Upgraded to first on American Airlines, I am early down to Immigration, to be met by a large emerald-green bird, fully feathered and with an orange beak. It flaps its wings and motions me onwards. I take the creature, just discernible as a middle-aged woman, to be a loony and, always nervous at Immigration, remain firmly behind the yellow line. The bird gets extremely agitated, flaps both its wings and indicates that I should proceed through one of the few gates that are manned. I now realise it's Halloween, though the festive spirit doesn't extend to the guy in the booth, who is mean-faced, unwelcoming and possibly more pissed off than he usually is because he has had a whole day in the company of this demented barnyard fowl, which is now clucking up and down the waiting line of jaded travellers, all of them as mystified as I was. Still, compared with others I see later that evening in New York she's a fairly low-level eccentric; there's a man with a pan on his head, another dressed in (or as) a condom, hand in hand with two of the sperms he has presumably frustrated. None of them, though, seems much in party mood, the festivity almost an obligation.

Alan Bennett, *Untold Stories* (2005)

✳ ✳ ✳

Nigerian writer Teju Cole finds himself caught up in a popular annual collective event.

One Sunday morning in November, after a trek through the relatively quiet streets of the Upper West Side, I arrived at the large, sun-brightened plaza at Columbus Circle. The area had changed recently. It had become a more commercial and tourist destination thanks to the pair of buildings erected for the Time Warner corporation on the site. The buildings, constructed at great speed, had just opened, and were filled with shops selling tailored shirts, designer suits, jewellery, appliances for the gourmet cook, handmade leather accessories, and imported decorative items. On the upper floors were some of the costliest restaurants in the city, advertising truffles, caviar, Kobe beef, and pricey "tasting menus." Above the restaurants were apartments that included the most expensive residence in the city. Curiosity had brought me into the shops on the ground level once or twice before, but the cost of the items, and what I perceived as the generally snobbish atmosphere, had kept me from returning until that Sunday morning.

It was the day of the New York marathon. I hadn't known. I was taken aback to see the round plaza in front of the glass towers filled with people, a massive, expectant throng setting itself into place close to the marathon's finish line. The crowd lined the street away from the plaza toward the east. Nearer the west there was a bandstand, on which two men with guitars were tuning up, calling and responding to the silvery notes on each other's amplified instruments. Banners, signs, posters, flags, and streamers of all kinds flapped in the wind, and mounted police on blindered horses regulated the crowd with cordons, whistles, and hand movements. The cops were in dark blue and wore sunshades. The crowd was brightly attired, and looking at all that green, red, yellow, and white synthetic material in the sun hurt the eyes. To escape the din, which seemed to be mounting, I decided to go into the shopping centre. In addition to the Armani and Hugo Boss shops, there was a bookshop on the second floor. In there, I thought, I might catch some quiet and drink a cup of coffee before heading back home. But the entrance was full of the crowd overflow from the street, and cordons made it impossible to get into the towers.

Teju Cole, *Open City* (2011)

✳ ✳ ✳

One of the biggest celebrations of the year: Thanksgiving. The traditional parade, sponsored by the great Macy's department store, is one of 'the' not-to-be-missed events of the New York calendar. The arrival of Santa Claus at the finale of the parade marks the official start of the Christmas season.

Macy's Thanksgiving Day Parade, which started as a pure publicity display, had become one of the great civic events of the year; often a million people watched its progress from Central Park West to Herald Square, four hundred clowns pranced all the way, and its gigantic blow-up elephants and Mickey Mouses floated above the streets like heroic trophies in a triumph.

Jan Morris, *Manhattan '45* (1987 / 2011)

❋ ❋ ❋

And the characteristically humorous take on events from Todd McEwen ...

The city muffled with holiday [...] No volume of cars set the East Side a-vibrating today, hiding as the celebrants were or would be on the Taconic Parkway, in drifts of grandmothers and food, their occupants inside, pounding against the glass, so lately alive. Families.

Thanksgiving is cruel and can strike without warning, said MacK. – Plizz give generous, said Isidor.

Here in the Far East, thin snow turning to ice on the street and Izzy started swearing. – F***ing cold, man. I can't believe I have to go out and get this turkey, to *have* turkey, which I don't even want. I hate Thanksgiving. Do you realize that no one realizes it's all about eating shit? How does coprophagia honour the *Pilgrims*? Hah? How does my eating the most horrible food, food from *England,* which I don't want, memorialize their f***ing sacrifice, whatever it was? Why am I supposed to be thankful that *they ate shit?* – Because Indians? Said MacK – I don't know.

Todd McEwen, *Who Sleeps With Katz* (2003)

❋ ❋ ❋

The start of New York's (multi-cultural) Christmas ...

December came. [...] The super assembled the aluminium Christmas tree, also set out a plastic menorah, also hung a sign that said *Happy Holidays,* gold-trimmed red letters strung together above the lobby mirror. Tree salesmen brought in pines from New England, and the needles perfumed Upper Broadway.

Gabriel Brownstein, 'The Dead Fiddler, 5E'
in *The Curious Case of Benjamin Button, Apt. 3W* (2003)

* * *

The day after Thanksgiving is a nightmare to define in city terms. A few people are allowed to sleep in, but most must work, must act like they didn't jiggle their endorphins the day before and cloud the mind with sport – they've got to get to the office before *THE SHOPPING* starts. [...]

The snow had left the streets mostly but it slung to awnings and roofs and threw enough of the light of a pretty winter day into the bus to lighten the feeling of doom. Izzy and Mary-Ann huddled, Iz in his overcoat-as-battle-tank posture, *thrust into the masses* at the apocalyptic hour of 10.45 am. Behind the driver sat the mother of the worst-behaved kids in New York, they're screaming, they're yelling, jumping up and down on the seats, the mother is very tired, with bags under her eyes from Hell – you can imagine what Thanksgiving had been like for her – no, you couldn't – it was probably all over the walls from cranberries, from stuffing – she had a prematurely sallow face, a face not from New York – but you could tell she thought she was probably going to die here, maybe today. The piercing screams and craven misbehaviour of these children were annoying everyone, who of course had left their houses in the best of holiday spirits – if *that* isn't enough to make you vomit – Christmas begins today – hooray – particularly the driver, who found himself the captain of a bus that couldn't move, in traffic that was becoming monumental – his bus was *failing to live up to its only purpose*, which was to go back and forth and back and forth on 86th Street driving him insane in a few short years. They were totally bogged in front of Gimbel's, where a Saint Nicholas rang a bell, which you could hear above everything, the insidious nasty high and possibly electrically amplified note of the impending holiday, even in the bus with its stuck windows and thumping heater and the engine which might only *idle* ever again. In her desperate sallowness the young mother grabbed her son's head and twisted it around so he was looking at Gimbel's – or traffic – *he* didn't know. – Look, there's Santa, she said (the Santa might have formed part of a prayer for release from her agony), Santa! Wave to Santa. God *damn* if this doesn't still work, as MacK observed, and saw that Izzy saw too – *Santa* and kids' mouths drop open, their movements become drugged ... – *Santa!* Said the boy to his sister, and they suddenly began banging as hard as they could on the flabby plexiglas windows of the poor old bus, *screaming* SANTAAA! SANTAAA! HI SANTAAA!, which was an even greater violation of everyone's civil liberties – and after two minutes of this *f***ing* daemonium during which the bus suffered two changes of the Lexington Avenue stop-light without being allowed to move an inch, the driver turned in his seat and spat at the boy: – *There's no such thing as Santa Claus*, at which the entire bus broke into HEART-WARMING APPLAUSE. [...]

Isidor was disgusted to find a crowd gathered around a Santa on the corner of 49th. But then delighted to see *Santa was in chains* and the crowd enjoying it too! This was a real bonus – the day after Thanksgiving and New York was already giving it to Santa. But then depressed again to find it was a protest – the *I.L.G.W.U.*, 'Santa of the Sweat Shops'. As they walked east Iz fondly remembered the Hunchback of Notre Dame on his little turntable of humiliation – had to admit Santa looked awfully good in such a pose – it set him up emotionally for weeks. EXEUNT MIDTOWN OMNES, after Santa is led away.

Todd McEwen, *Who Sleeps With Katz* (2003)

✳ ✳ ✳

Alistair Cooke gives a lovely image of Park Avenue
(tastefully) decked out for Christmas.

The curious thing about a city that boasts extravagantly about its
best features, as well as some of its worst, is that there is a never-
mentioned little miracle in New York City. It is the railed-off plots
of grass that for almost three miles run down the middle of Park
Avenue and divide the uptown and downtown traffic. Along this
whole stretch (fifty-four blocks from 96th to 42nd Street), what is
a constant delight and surprise is the regularly changing character
of these more than fifty little gardens. And they're not so little:
each, one city block long and about fifteen feet wide.

You drive down this avenue one season of the year through a
great ripple of crocuses. Another time, tulips from here to infinity.
Sometimes you notice that at each end of each garden there is a
new young tree, a hundred or so of them from the 96th Street
entrance down to where the Avenue ends at Grand Central Station.
Or maybe next time, they are locusts or London plane trees. At
Christmas time, as now, they've been replaced by small firs.

I suppose we take it so easily for granted (and thousands
of the true city types never notice the changes at all) because
the very large workforce that performs these magical transfor-
mations works by night and by stealth. In fifty years of living
round the corner from this long divide of Park Avenue I have
never seen any of them at their remarkable labour of creating,
along three miles, complete variations of miniature landscapes
about, it seems, once every few weeks.

I know they're at it, because I once tactfully guessed at the
fortune it requires to employ them and to maintain this city
perquisite. I happened to know the possessor of the fortune,
a lady named Mary Lasker (heiress of an advertising multi-
millionaire, a self-effacing, absolutely non-socialite doer of
many unadvertised good works of which the Park Avenue

divider is the only conspicuous one). At Christmas time, especially, it makes me think again, with gratitude, of the late Mary Lasker. For now each tree, a hundred or so, is lit at twilight.

By Mrs Lasker's request, and, thank God, this confirming dictate of the Park Avenue property owners, the trees are not gaily decorated with red bulbs and green bulbs and purple bulbs and yellow bulbs – illuminations that make so many city squares and streets look like amusement arcades gone berserk. Each of the Park Avenue firs is decorated with about five hundred tiny oyster-white bulbs. So at twilight, you look down from the small eminence of 96th Street at this three-mile stretch of small, small fountains of light. All the way down, the only colours are the alternating reds and greens of the traffic lights at the fifty-odd intersections.

Alistair Cooke, *Letter From America* (24 December 1999)

❋ ❋ ❋

One of the pleasures of the Christmas season in New York are the opportunities for ice-skating, most popularly in Central Park or at the Rockefeller Center.

On New Year's Day the four of them went ice skating in Central Park; the thaw had set in again, and the ice puddled over – there weren't many people about. The perfect unreflecting snow had melted into browns and gleams, a dispiriting lapse from pristinity.

Benjamin Markovits, *Either Side of Winter* (2005)

❋ ❋ ❋

Always great festivities for the 4th July, of course – this diary entry, recording an occasion when they had to be cancelled, gives the flavour by describing what is not going to happen.

(1832) WEDNESDAY, JULY 4 It is a lovely day, but very different from all the previous anniversaries of independence. The alarm about the cholera has prevented all the usual

jollification under the public authority. There are no booths in Broadway, the parade which was ordered here has been countermanded, no corporation dinner, and no ringing of bells. Some troops are marching about the street, "upon their own hook," I suppose. Most of the stores are closed, and there is a pretty smart cannonade of crackers by the boys, but it is not a regular Fourth of July. The Board of Health reports to-day twenty new cases and eleven deaths since noon yesterday. The disease is here in all its violence and will increase. God grant that its ravages may be confined, and its visit short!

Philip Hone, *Diary* (1832)

✻ ✻ ✻

When New Yorkers want a bit of traditional summer fun, there's always Coney Island. But here's a visiting Russian writer not quite in the mood for enjoying the place.

This is Coney Island.

On Monday the metropolitan newspapers triumphantly announce:

"Three Hundred Thousand People in Coney Island Yesterday.
Twenty-three Children Lost."

"There's something doing there," the reader thinks.

First a long ride by trolley thru Brooklyn and Long Island amid the dust and noise of the streets. Then the gaze is met by the sight of dazzling, magnificent Coney Island. From the very first moment of arrival at this city of fire, the eye is blinded. It is assailed by thousands of cold, white sparks, and for a long time can distinguish nothing in the scintillating dust round about. Everything whirls and dazzles, and blends into a tempestuous ferment of fiery foam. The visitor is stunned; his consciousness is withered by the intense gleam; his thoughts are routed from his mind; he becomes a particle in the crowd. People wander about in the flashing, blinding fire intoxicated and devoid of will. A dull-white mist penetrates their brains, greedy expectation envelopes their souls. Dazed by the brilliancy the throngs wind about like dark bands in the surging sea of light, pressed upon all sides by the black bournes of night.

Everywhere electric bulbs shed their cold, garish gleam. They shine on posts and walls, on window casings and cornices; they stretch in an even line along the high tubes of the power-house; they burn on all the roofs, and prick the eye with the sharp needles of their dead, indifferent sparkle. The people screw up their eyes, and smiling disconcertedly crawl along the ground like the heavy line of a tangled chain.

A man must make a great effort not to lose himself in the crowd, not to be overwhelmed by his amazement – an amazement in which there is neither transport nor joy. But if he succeeds in individualizing himself, he finds that these millions of fires produce a dismal, all-revealing light. Though they hint at the possibility of beauty, they every-where discover a dull, gloomy ugliness. The city, magic and fantastic from afar, now appears an absurd jumble of straight lines of wood, a cheap, hastily constructed toy-house for the amusement of children. [...]

The amusements are without number. There on the summit of an iron tower two long white wings rock slowly up and down. At the end of each wing hang cages, and in these cages are people. When one of the wings rises heavily toward the sky the faces of the occupants of the cages grow sadly serious. They all look in round-eyed silence at the ground receding from them. In the cages of the other wing, then carefully descending, the faces of the people are radiant with smiles. Joyous screams are heard, which strangely remind one of the merry yelp of a puppy let to the floor after he has been held up in the air by the scuff of his neck.

Boats fly in the air around the top of another tower, a third keeps turning about and impels some sort of iron balloon, a fourth, a fifth – they all move and blaze and call with the mute shouts of cold fire. Everything rocks and roars and bellows and turns the heads of the people. [...]

Inside the buildings the people are also seeking pleasure, and here, too, all look serious. The amusement offered is educational. The people are shown hell, with all the terrors and punishments that await those who have transgressed the sacred laws created for them.

Hell is constructed of papier maché, and painted dark red. Everything in it is on fire – paper fire – and it is filled with the thick, dirty odour of grease. Hell is very badly done. It would arouse disgust in a man of even modest demands. It is represented by a cave with stones thrown together in chaotic masses. The cave is penetrated by a reddish darkness. On one of the stones sits Satan, clothed in red. Grimaces distort his lean, brown face. He rubs his hands contentedly, as a man who is doing a good business. He must be very uncomfortable on his perch, a paper stone, which cracks and rocks. But he pretends not to notice his discomfort, and looks down at the evil demons busying themselves with the sinners.

A girl is there who has just bought a new hat. She is trying it on before a mirror, happy and contented. But a pair of little fiends, apparently very greedy, steal up behind her and seize her under the armpits. She screams, but it is too late. The demons put her into a long, smooth trough, which descends tightly into a pit in the middle of the cave. From the pit issue a grey vapour and tongues of fire made of red paper. The girl, with her mirror and her new hat, goes down into the pit, lying on her back in the trough.

A young man has drunk a glass of whisky. Instantly the devils clutch him, and down he goes thru that same hole in the floor of the platform.

The atmosphere in hell is stifling. The demons are insignificant looking and feeble. Apparently they are greatly exhausted by their work and irritated by its sameness and evident futility.

Maxim Gorky, 'Boredom' (1907)

Big yellow taxis etc

Negotiating one's way around an unfamiliar place can be an anxiety-inducing experience unless armed with the appropriate guides and information. Here we don't aim to tell you how to do it but to give some of the flavours of the city's transport systems – starting with the distinctive New York 'big yellow taxi' (a nod towards the Joni Mitchell song of that name).

The taxi was as big as a locomotive and painted a loud yellow like a German mailbox. Purple lights were flashing on its roof, similar to the watchful, flashing eyes of the police cars, and for a while I had the sensation of being a distinguished visitor who is supposed to be escorted to his destination untroubled by anybody or anything. The upholstery of the car was hard, and its exposed steel floor was dirty; the passenger was being offered transportation, but nothing more. The driver received airborne messages continually, incessantly, repeatedly: invisible people were talking to him, weighing him down, torturing him, hounding him. Now and then the man replied to these voices of absent air ghosts; he spoke sullenly and irritably toward the windshield, swallowing his syllables in a demonstrably economical manner, yet I couldn't understand a single word of his defence. Perhaps he was merely telling his big brother that he was driving a greenhorn to his hotel.

A fire truck roared past, flaming red with a shrill scream of siren. Just as I thought! I could already see a skyscraper burning, Broadway ablaze, already I was reading the headlines in all the papers of the world. Powerful catastrophes appeared to hang in the air here. How did New York smell? Here it still reeked of the sea, of ships, I could make out a whiff of the Netherlands, I detected the colony of New Amsterdam. But how did the continent smell? That only became apparent with the evening wind from the land: a smell of grass, of a blooming or withered prairie, of clean-mowed lawns circling the houses of Americans. Yet the city itself also smelled like overheated steam, like the fluffy, white clouds that continually pushed through the road surface, hovering under the tires of automobiles, wrapping pedestrians' legs in mist and making them tread on clouds like allegorical figures. Later it was explained to me that this steam is emitted from huge heating systems, but at first glance New York seemed to be rising up from volcanic soil, with the asphalt and sidewalks and brickwork preventing a dangerous eruption.

What is more, the street that we were driving along didn't fit the idea of a major world city. The street was pretending, playing at being Old Amsterdam, it was cosy: all kinds of cats and caged birds and mongrel dogs were looking out of the dusty-friendly windows, little stores offered all sorts of greenery, old junk, and cheap groceries for sale. People were moving along the sidewalks, people were at home here, people in slippers. Even in New York there was provincialism and the pride of a city district, like in Paris or London. There was neighbourhood gossiping like in old Berlin, no hurry, none of that American tempo which is a totally false, European conception. Yet the hunkering down in front of one's house was new and strangely American to me – that sustained, hours-long sitting around by women, children, and apparently unoccupied men on the iron or wooden steps that lead up to small porches or twine around the houses as fire escapes.

But the buildings soon grew larger, as I had expected and as shown in films, picture books, and dreams. The street became a ravine, we drove deep down along the floor of a grey canyon, and the sky above was an endlessly distant, very narrow, yet cheerful blue stripe.

Wolfgang Koeppen, *Amerikafahrt* ('American Journey', 1959)

translated by Susan Thorne

✳ ✳ ✳

Aaron's knowledge was wide, especially about England (he had even heard of John Major), but it didn't extend to the geography of New York City. He had a lot of trouble finding the Algonquin Hotel, even though it could hardly be better known and is centrally located in Midtown Manhattan. But New York taxi drivers are notorious for their ability to lose their way in a city laid out according to an almost childishly simple plan. Aaron was one of 32,000 drivers of what are called 'livery cars', the kind of taxis, like London's minicabs, that can only be hired by pre-arrangement. New York also had more than eleven thousand of the famous yellow cabs which were allowed to pick up fares on the streets. In addition, there were countless unlicensed cabs plying their trade illegally, beyond the control of the New York City Taxi and Limousine Commission.

My brother John once told me with an air of great authority that the average waiting time for a New York taxi was two and a half minutes. This could not have been true. In the rush hour or in the rain, it was just as difficult to find a cab in New York as it was in London. But at quiet times of day the taxis came swaying and jostling down the avenues like shoals of fish, swerving violently towards the kerb at the smallest suggestion of a raised hand. Then, unlike the complacent taxi drivers of London, they would roar off as fast as they could in the approximate direction of where you wanted to go.

What most New York taxi drivers seemed to lack, with the notable exception of Aaron, was the slightest pride in their work. One told me once that he wasn't really a taxi driver but a comedy trumpeter. He only drove a taxi because there was so little work nowadays for comedy trumpeters. A comedy trumpeter, he explained, was someone who could produce funny noises from his trumpet and make balloons come out of it and burst. While London taxi drivers were conceited to a fault, those of New York were gloomily aware of being near to the bottom of the social heap. Because it was easy to obtain a badge – you only had to be over nineteen, possess a clean driving licence, and pass a simple proficiency test in English – a large percentage of New York taxi drivers were new immigrants to the United States. [...]

The lot of New York taxi drivers was generally not a happy one. Fares were held low, so that they had to work very hard to earn a living wage, and theirs was one of the most dangerous jobs in America. In London, if anybody was ever frightened in a cab, it was usually the passenger. In New York, it was the other way round. Forty-five New York taxi drivers were murdered in 1992, and a similar number in 1993. The National Institute of Occupational Safety reported that taxi drivers were more likely to get killed on the job than workers in any other American industry. [...]

One Tuesday, in October 1993, thousands of taxi drivers brought the city to a standstill during the evening rush hour by driving at snail's pace up Broadway. They were demonstrating for greater protection and the right to refuse fares. The Taxi Commission issued a statement deploring the murders, but implying that they were inevitable. In the cab business, it said, 'dangerous conditions are inherent because the driver is carrying money in the car and transporting persons unknown to him'. New York City's then Police Commissioner, Raymond Kelly, made the same point even more succinctly. 'Cabs are like mobile cash machines,' he said.

The protest was unsuccessful because the Taxi Commission continued to insist that taxi drivers should never refuse a fare, but it published a list of proposed new safety precautions: special external lights which could be made to flash if there was trouble inside, obligatory bullet-proof glass divisions between passenger and driver, and 'speakerphones' which at the press of a button would link drivers instantly to the police. The New York Police Department had meanwhile set up a special protection unit of undercover officers to follow yellow cabs and livery drivers and sometimes even pose as taxi drivers themselves. Most of the murders, though, were at the bottom end of the business, especially among the drivers of unlicensed cabs. Aaron's chances of survival were pretty good.

Alexander Chancellor, *Some Times in America* (1999)

* * *

Martin Scorsese's classic 1976 film *Taxi Driver* unfolds a nightmare vision in which the dirty boulevard envelops the world. The movie starts inside the cab of Travis Bickle (Robert De Niro). It is late on a summer night as he glides through Times Square. The crowds of people have thinned out, but the signs are still on fire, the colours splash red and blue (*à la* Minnelli), the ambience is melancholy but sublime. The audience feels comfortably enveloped in the classic Times Square landscape, the world first designed by Vincente Minnelli for MGM's *On The Town*. But then he hits the deuce, and it is almost like a crash. Suddenly the street jumps out at him: The colour base turns garish yellow, camera movements speed up and become jagged, the street seems to ooze people, they look almost naked, they snake and shake their bodies provocatively at one another and at the world. It is an explosive paranoid nightmare of the dirty boulevard, a primal vision of the city as a threat, the street as a threat, the crowd as a threat, sex as a threat, other people as a threat. He shakes with rage. "Someday," he says in a voiceover, "a real rain will come and wash all the scum off the streets." We don't understand what has happened to him, but he has turned very abruptly scary, and we have to be glad we're not in his cab.

Marshall Berman, *On The Town* (2006)

❊ ❊ ❊

And New York's roads in general – whether you're in a taxi or a private car …

Canal Street, in lower Manhattan, is the shortest route from an East River crossing to a Hudson River crossing on the island. To the east, Canal Street leads across the Manhattan Bridge, to Brooklyn; to the west, it leads into the Holland Tunnel, to New Jersey. Canal Street is actually an extension of Brooklyn's Flatbush Avenue and of any number of roads in New Jersey laid through the crooked alleys of downtown. The traffic on Canal Street never stops. It is a high-energy current jumping constantly between the poles of Brooklyn and New Jersey. It hates to have its flow pinched in the density of Manhattan, hates to stop at intersections. Along Canal Street, it moans and screams. Worn brake shoes of semi trucks go "Ooohhh nooohhh" at stoplights, and the sound echoes in the canyons of warehouses and Chinatown tenements. People lean on their horns from one end of Canal Street to the other. They'll honk non-stop for minutes at a time, until the horns get tired and out of breath. They'll try different combinations: shave-and-a-haircut, long-long-long, short-short-short-long. Some people have musical car horns; a person purchasing a musical car horn seems to be limited to a choice of four tunes – "La Cucaracha," "Theme from *The Godfather*," "Dixie," and "Hava Nagila." Eventually, the flow of traffic knocks over everything upright along its route – mailboxes, fire hydrants, light poles, signs. Litter, fruit, rats, pigeons, and hats it flattens and pulverises.

Ian Frazier, *Gone to New York* (2005)

✻ ✻ ✻

Townhouses began to appear between Second and Third and then apartment blocks grew taller, grander, after Lexington. She glanced down the long central section of Park Avenue towards the heart of midtown where her father worked. The lines of planted daffodils, in the mild February weather, had just begun to lift their heads, suggesting both method and profusion. Yellow cabs rivalled the flowers, clustering at the lights. A stately, humourless avenue, *sans* shopfronts and pavement stalls.

Benjamin Markovits, *Either Side of Winter* (2005)

✻ ✻ ✻

New York boasts the world's first tunnel designed specifi-cally for road traffic – the Holland Tunnel (nothing to do with the Dutch). The entrance is approached from Canal Street where the traffic starts to descend slowly about three blocks from the river. Holland was a commuter, belonging to the first generation of people driving in to work from the suburbs in cars. Here's a little bit about this remarkable New York engineer.

Clifford Holland was born in 1883, in Somerset, Massachusetts. Among his ancestors were Puritan ministers who came to New England in the 1600s. Holland graduated from the Cambridge

Latin School in 1902, worked his way through Harvard, got a degree there in civil engineering in 1906, and came to New York to work on tunnels. As tunnel engineer with the Public Service Commission, he built four double-tube subway tunnels under the East River that the BMT trains run through. In 1919, partly to relieve traffic congestion downtown, a new agency called the New York and New Jersey Vehicular Tunnel Commission decided to build a tunnel under the Hudson River, from Canal Street to Twelfth Street in Jersey City. They hired Holland as chief engineer to design and build it.

Ian Frazier, *Gone to New York* (2005)

❊ ❊ ❊

Now we take a few trips on New York's subway.

Ding-dang, the doors slid shut. She was on the train.

Her car was filled with a group of wide-eyed, slack-jawed French boys. She sat down and closed her eyes, letting herself be lulled by their pretty-sounding, incomprehensible chatter. At the Grand Street stop, the door to the next car slid open with an angry clang and a scruffy, middle-aged black man stumbled in. The tourist boys stirred anxiously. 'Hello, ladies and gentlemen,' the man said. 'My name is Floyd. I am homeless and I suffer from diabetes. Please don't be nervous. I ain't begging. I am here to entertain you.'

He closed his eyes and let out a long, wordless falsetto note. The song was 'The Lion Sleeps Tonight' – a silly novelty number that Karla had always associated with the oldies radio stations and kitsch. But now, hearing it sung in this dingy subway car, she was struck by its beauty. How simple and true it seemed! How filled with the mystery and sadness of life!

The train suddenly emerged from the tunnel, and the car was filled with daylight. They were crossing the Manhattan Bridge. Out of the window, through a lattice-work of girders and trusses and wire netting, the crowded tip of the island that

175

Karla was leaving rose up before her now, a thicket of verticals, a child's idea of a city. Down below, a toy-size tugboat pressed its way through the pale scum of ice on the river. She thought of Khaled, waiting for her in his apartment, and she willed the train to go faster. If she didn't get there soon, he might disappear, or decide that he didn't want her after all.

Floyd finished his song and began walking up and down the aisle, holding out a crumpled paper bag. 'Ladies and gentlemen, if you enjoyed my musicality, please show your appreciation with a financial donation. Nothing is too little or too large. I take coins, bills, cheques, American Express … '

Zoë Heller, The Believers (2008)

✻ ✻ ✻

Fallow had no physical fear of riding the New York subways. He fancied himself a rugged fellow, and in any case, nothing untoward had ever befallen him in the Underground. No, what he feared – and it amounted to a true fear – was the squalor. Heading down the stairs of the City Hall subway station with all these dark shabby people was like descending, voluntarily, into a dungeon, a very dirty and noisy dungeon. Grimy concrete and black bars were everywhere, cage after cage, level upon level, a delirium seen through black bars in every direction. Every time a train entered or left the station there was an agonized squeal of metal, as if some huge steel skeleton were being pried apart by a lever of incomprehensible power. Why was it that in this gross fat country, with its obscene heaps of wealth and its even more obscene obsession with creature comforts, they were unable to create an Underground as quiet, orderly, presentable, and – well – decent as London's? Because they were childish. So long as it was underground, out of sight, it didn't matter what it was like.

Tom Wolfe, The Bonfire of the Vanities (1987)

✻ ✻ ✻

Our subway is the F train. It runs under our building and shakes the floor. The F is generally a reliable train, but one spring as I walked in the park I saw emergency vehicles gathered by a concrete-sheathed hole in the lawn. Firemen lifted a metal lid from the hole and descended into it. After a while, they reappeared, followed by a few people, then dozens of people, then a whole lot of people – passengers from a disabled F train, climbing one at a time out an exit shaft. On the F, I sometimes see large women in straw hats reading a newspaper called the *Caribbean Sunrise*, and Orthodox Jews bent over Talmudic texts in which the footnotes have footnotes, and groups of teenagers wearing identical red bandanas with identical red plastic baby pacifiers in the corners of their mouths, and female couples in porkpie hats, and young men with the silhouettes of the Manhattan skyline razored into their short side hair from one temple around to the other, and Russian-speaking men with thick wrists and big wristwatches, and a hefty, tall woman with long, straight blond hair who hums and closes her eyes and absently practises cello fingerings on the metal subway pole. As I watched the F train passengers emerge among the grass and trees of Prospect Park, the faces were as varied as usual, but the expressions of indignant surprise were all about the same.

Just past my stop, Seventh Avenue, Manhattan-bound F trains rise from the underground to cross the Gowanus Canal. The train sounds different – lighter, quieter – in the open air. From the elevated tracks, you can see the roofs of many houses stretching back up the hill to Park Slope, and a bumper crop of rooftop graffiti, and neon signs for Eagle Clothes and Kentile Floors, and flat expanses of factory roofs where seagulls stand on one leg around puddles in the sagging spots. There are fuel-storage tanks surrounded by earthen barriers, and slag piles, and conveyor belts leading down to the oil-slicked waters of the canal. On certain days, the sludge at the bottom of the canal causes it to bubble. Two men fleeing the police jumped in the canal a while ago; one made it across, the other quickly dies. When the subway doors open at the Smith-Ninth Street stop, you can see the bay and sometimes smell the ocean breeze. This stretch of elevated is the highest point of the New York subway system. To the south you can see the Verrazano-Narrows Bridge, to the north the World Trade Towers. For just a few moments, the Statue of Liberty appears between passing buildings. Pieces of a neighbourhood – laundry on clotheslines, a standup swimming pool, a plaster saint, a satellite dish, a rectangle of lawn – slide by like quickly dealt cards. Then the train descends again; growing over the wall just before the tunnel is a wisteria bush, which blooms pale blue every May.

Ian Frazier, *Gone to New York* (2005)

✳ ✳ ✳

After Grand Street and Chinatown, the train buckled and burst up out of the ground, the Manhattan Bridge, long girders fashioning *Xs*, *Ms*, *Ws*, and *Ns*, the massive city at night. All the towers in midtown with their windows lit, work going on through dinnertime. We had chugged over Chinatown, and midriver you could see it all: the Brooklyn Docks and tanks, power plants and refineries all busy with electric light.

Gabriel Brownstein, 'The Speedboat' (2003)

✳ ✳ ✳

*But somebody just can't wait to get out of the subway
and into the (relatively) fresh air …*

Faces, hats, hands, newspapers jiggled in the fetid roaring subway car like corn in a popper. The downtown express passed clattering in yellow light, window telescoping window till they overlapped like scales.

"Look George," said Sandbourne to George Baldwin who hung on a strap beside him, "you can see Fitzgerald's contraction."

"I'll be seeing the inside of an undertaking parlour if I don't get out of this subway soon."

"It does you plutocrats good now and then to see how the other half travels ... Maybe it'll make you induce some of your little playmates down at Tammany Hall to stop squabbling and give us wageslaves a little transportation ... cristamighty I could tell em a thing or two ... My idea's for a series of endless moving platforms under Fifth Avenue."

"Did you cook that up when you were in hospital Phil?"

"I cooked a whole lot of things up while I was in hospital."

"Look here lets get out at Grand Central and walk. I cant stand this ... I'm not used to it."

"Sure ... I'll phone Elsie I'll be a little late to dinner ... Not often I get to see you nowadays George ... Gee it's like the old days."

In a tangled clot of men and women, arms, legs, hats aslant on perspiring necks, they were pushed out on the platform. They walked up Lexington Avenue quiet in the claretmisted afterglow.

John Dos Passos, *Manhattan Transfer* (1925)

❋ ❋ ❋

If you're really brave you might join the increasing numbers of New York cyclists. This is not to be recommended for the newcomer and is certainly not for the faint-hearted. But David Byrne records some of his cycling experiences in the city and shows us parts of it we might not otherwise have encountered.

I ride in the Five Boro Bike Tour this morning. Forty-two miles! That sounds like a lot to some people but it only takes a little over three hours. And there are breaks. I thought

179

I'd be more tired than I am, as I usually just ride locally to run errands or to get to work or go out at night. Corny as it might seem, it feels like I am participating in an uplifting civic event. People in Queens, Brooklyn, and Staten Island put signs in their yards and cheer the crowds of bikers as we whiz by, like they do for the runners in the marathon – only in this tour no one is racing. No one is keeping track of who comes in first. [...]

The longest part of the route goes through the waterfront neighbourhoods of Brooklyn and Queens, which gives one the pleasantly skewed impression that the old, nutty industrial city that New York once was still exists. These neighbourhoods are made up of an endless series of little factories that make plastic wrap, cardboard boxes, ex-lax, coat hangers, hairbrushes, and the wooden water tanks on top of every Manhattan residential building. Sure, some neighbourhoods like Williamsburg, which we riders touched the edge of, have filled up with art galleries, cafés, and wonderful bookshops, while other neighbourhoods are all Hasidic or Italian, but mostly the waterfront area is still composed of funky factories. These old structures are a million miles from the industrial parks, high-tech campuses, and corporate headquarters that one sees out west (west being across the Hudson). They are small in scale, and often they are family run. These are the places that make those glue-on reinforcement rings for notebook pages and apple corers that you look at and think, Who thought of that? Who designed that? Someone actually thought that up?

A few days later I bike to East New York (a neighbourhood in Brooklyn). [...]

Getting to this neighbourhood I ride through the various Brooklyn ghettos – Dominican, West Indian, Hasidic, and black. By ghetto I don't mean a poverty-stricken, desolate, or decaying area. I don't necessarily mean that the area is black either. Some areas that might be considered ghettos are lively and flourishing. East New York, however, is pretty dicey. A friend was mugged here recently and forced to go into a bodega and buy a man some infant formula! At its worst the neighbourhood looks like some of the very bleak places I've seen in the former Soviet bloc – derelict housing surrounded by crumbling industrial superstructures. (The elevated subway line looks like it hasn't been painted in decades out here.) These signs of decay and ruin are interspersed with lots of churches, and huge temples relocated into former theatres. [...]

Having viewed enough stimulating squalor I decide to take the more conventionally scenic route home. I head toward the water, which is nearby, and ride along the bike path that follows the Belt Parkway along the Brooklyn waterfront. On my left are the swamps and marshes of Jamaica Bay. It's not quite Nantucket, but it's pretty damn nice – and it's surprising that it's inside the New York City limits. Today is a Saturday, and there are lots of people barbecuing. They have set up in the grassy areas at the side of the highway and even on the median strips. It would be almost lovely if the ugly highway weren't so close.

I stop for scungilli (conch cooked in red sauce) at a place in Sheepshead Bay. There are picnic tables on the sidewalk and a window where one can order clams, oysters, and various kinds of seafood. This neighbourhood is named after the tasty Sheepshead fish, so they say. It was once abundant, but now it's gone from here. It was also known as sea bream.

I'm reminded that the other day I wanted to bike to Long Island City to catch an art show at PS1, but it was the day of the New York City Marathon and the Queensboro Bridge bike lane was closed (for handicapped runners they said, though it was completely empty). So I took the bike on the Roosevelt Island tram instead and rode down by the abandoned lunatic asylum on the south end of that island that sits in the middle of the East River. There was no one around. Spooky. From the tip of the island there's a great view of the UN building and of a tiny rock island filled with cormorants – an odd thing to see in the middle of New York City.

David Byrne, *Bicycle Diaries* (2009)

Village life

New York has long been one of the world's most vibrantly creative places. The part of the city that has become a by-word for the creative life is, of course, Greenwich Village.

Long ago, when New York City was affordable, people who felt they didn't fit into the mainstream could take a chance and head there from wherever they were. Bob Dylan came east from Minnesota in the winter of 1961 and made his way downtown to Greenwich Village. Like countless others before him, he came to shed the constricted definition of his birthplace and the confinement of his past.

Suze Rotolo, *A Freewheelin' Time* (2009)

✳ ✳ ✳

Even before the First World War, 'the Village' was a magnet for creative and alternative 'types' of all kinds. Luc Sante tells the fascinating story of some of them.

Before World War I, the air downtown was loaded with the certainty of approaching utopia. For all the varying levels of seriousness, social consciousness, levity, ambition, and mental stability that were present in Greenwich Village, nearly all the events, publications, meetings and performances were informed by a desire to remake the world. The loosing of chains of convention and the reinvention of life underlay everything from the saturnalia of the magazine balls to the demonstrations in favour of Colorado miners and Paterson millworkers to the varyingly daring poetry of everyone from Edna St. Vincent Millay to Harry Kemp. Two events of 1913 appear as exemplary in this regard. They were both slight, almost unnoticed blips, but despite their evanescence – possibly to a certain extent because of it – they contain the humour and retrospectively visible pathos of the time, the sense of might-have-been that wreathes our image of the freewheeling bohemia. First Ellis O. Jones, an associate editor of *Life* (the pre-Luce humour magazine) and a member of the editorial staff of *The Masses*, sent out a press release proclaiming the establishment of the Republic of Washington Square. The notice was generally treated as a gag, and Don Marquis and Franklin P. Adams took note of the upcoming ceremony in their columns with a requisite deadpan. The police, who had also been invited, failed to chuckle. The revolution was set for eleven o'clock on a Monday morning at, oddly enough, the Central Park Mall, a setting far from Greenwich Village that was both inconvenient and indicative of a certain seriousness on Jones's part. When the appointed hour came, a slight drizzle started; only Jones and a handful of his friends had shown up. The police, however, arrived in massed ranks, with machine guns, ambulances, and black marias, and carted Jones away in one of the latter. He later blamed the rain for the failure of his coup.

A few months later, the Free Republic of Greenwich Village was proclaimed with even less fanfare by Gertude Drick, a transplanted Texan and a pupil of John Sloan. Drick was known to one and all as "Woe" and she passed out black-bordered cards bearing this single word; when asked why, she always replied, "Because woe is me." She discovered a neglected but accessible staircase (now sealed) that led to the top of the Washington Square arch, and on a fall evening led Sloan, Marcel Duchamp, and three actors, Betty Turner, Forrest Mann, and Charles Ellis, up there. They carried Chinese lanterns, red balloons, hot-water bags for sitting on, and supplies of food and wine. Woe read a Greenwich Village declaration of independence, proclaimed the existence of the republic, and everyone fired cap pistols and released the red balloons. The party went on until dawn. In the morning, passersby noticed clusters of red balloons in the neighbourhood trees.

What is notable about these invisible secessions – the one slightly crazed, the other somewhat ironic – is that they actually named the thing that all the inhabitants of Greenwich Village bohemia of that time were aiming for, a revolution in more than just a legislative sense, a free territory untrammelled by convention. Greenwich Village was then very distant from the rest of the country, in manners and mores, in sense of justice, in sense of humour, in sexuality and egalitarianism, a distance that was far greater than anything comparable in the present media-dominated era. Josephine Herbst characterised the time as the "incomparably free-wheeling years before the first World War, when modernism had not lost its connection with revolutionary thinking in all social and ethical fields." Soon, however, came the war, anti-German hysteria, the Red Scare, Prohibition, factional feuds, careerism, money-grubbing, and disillusionment.

Luc Sante, *Low Life* (1991)

* * *

One reason why 'creatives' originally settled in the Village was its cheapness – no longer the case. This is the story of the artistic districts of many cities: a low-rent area attracts artists, and the resulting cultural excitement makes the place 'desirable' ... and expensive. Jan Morris describes some of the characteristics that continued to make the area attractive, despite changes through time.

Many such perimeter people, like Joe Gould, have gravitated to Greenwich Village, the tumble of streets, this way and that, which lay to the west of Washington Square, spilling into Chelsea in the north, and having as its focus the Square itself at the foot of Fifth Avenue. The Village was thought by most New Yorkers to be very pretty – its streets so distinct from the mechanical pattern of the city, its dormered houses small and trim, sometimes with pleasant gardens. Not many Europeans, deposited there without explanation, would give it a second look. Its houses were mostly ordinary really, its streets were cramped rather than intimate, and even Washington Square itself, for all its green foliage, was nothing special by extra-Manhattan standards. Visitors were generally taken to see the private alley of former stables called Washington Mews, many of which were inhabited by famous people, but to alien eyes even they looked uninvitingly poky.

Old hands never tired of saying that Greenwich Village had been tamed. In the years of Depression and Prohibition it had proliferated with political activists, profoundly concerned writers and artists, rebels and originals. In 1945 it had become, they said, positively dull by contrast. [...]

But newcomers found it wild and marvellous still. To Americans from the interior it was a dream of liberty and unconvention, to Europeans it possessed an air of bohemia mostly lost in their own ravaged or war-straitened cities. It still *felt* separate from the rest of Manhattan, away down there where the grid of the city failed. It had old pockets of Italian settlement, but it was generally multi-ethnic, or un-ethnic, and its proximity to the Hudson River piers – one of the busiest ferry stations was at the end of Christopher Street – gave it a tang of Sailortown. If it was perhaps less colourfully outrageous than it had been, it was still the most generally easygoing part of town, where nonconformists of every kind, Trotskyists, homosexuals, atonal composers, sniffers of cocaine, could pursue their preferences without disapproval or interference. [...]

If the midtown set went slumming in Harlem, they often went strolling in Greenwich Village, preferably after dinner on summer evenings, when the community was in the full blast of its exhibitionism, debating furiously on park benches, sitting backwards on sidewalk café chairs, drawing instant portraits in charcoal, or just meandering itself, up and down the little streets, trying hard not to be taken for tourists.

Jan Morris, *Manhattan '45* (1987/2011)

✳ ✳ ✳

Suze Rotolo's acclaimed memoir provides one of the best pictures of Village life. Here she reflects on the influence of its past upon the area's present desirability as a place both to live in and to visit, and also gives a vivid portrait of Greenwich in the 60s.

The unique qualities of a time or an era are discovered after it has passed. What puts a place on the map is connected to what happened there that was special. Greenwich Village became a destination because of its bohemian history, which encompassed rebellious politics as well as revolutionary art, music, poetry, and prose. It was a community of people and ideas that soldered and welded itself together into odd structures pointing every which way yet maintaining a solid base with common beliefs in the validity of the voices of the outsider and the underdog.

Some denizens went on to fame in their time and beyond, like Edna St. Vincent Millay, e.e. cummings, Willem de Kooning, Allen Ginsberg, and Bob Dylan, who changed music the way Jackson Pollock had changed painting.

With his creation of the Folklore Center, Izzy Young was a cornerstone of the expansive folk culture of the 1960s. Sam Hood ran the Gaslight despite hassles with the mob and a precarious basement locale. Mike Porco, from a dive, made Gerde's Folk City a music mecca. Art D'Lugoff sired the Village Gate, and Joe Cino created a venue in a café on Cornelia Street where he, along with the Living Theatre and others like them, reinterpreted theatre.

They and numerous others had the tenacity and foresight to internalise the old ways and forge new ones. Soon an influx of tourists made it possible for the clubs, experimental galleries, and theatres to survive and thrive; yet the commercialisation made it harder for younger artists to experiment and to develop their skills or to find a following the way the first arrivals had. Everyone started coming to the Village to audition, to play, to paint, and to write, hoping for exposure, fame, and fortune. It got crowded and more competitive. The hustle was out of the closet big-time.

Record company reps went to the clubs and concerts scouting for the next Bob Dylan, resulting in a glut of pale imitators who wrote even paler songs. The surplus of singer-songwriters suffocated folk music, which was slowly dying of ennui. The population of acoustic folkies performing traditional music gradually thinned out, and those who kept at it found a way to survive with dignity, even with fewer and fewer well-paying gigs in the Village and around the country.

Greenwich Village – with its bohemian tradition overtaken by the hep cats of jazz and the Beats and subsequently the hip folk crowd, which evolved into the hippie culture with a psychedelic soundtrack – had become the place to be. But I was gone by then.

Greenwich Village bohemia exists no more. It was the public square of the twentieth century for the outsiders, the mad ones, and the misfits. Today all that remains are the posters, fliers, and signs preserved on the walls as a reminder of that bygone era when rents were cheap and New York replaced Paris as the destination for the creative crowd.

Those who feel they are not part of the mainstream are always somewhere, however. Greenwich Village is a calling. Though it is a concept now priced out of its physical space, as a state of mind, it will never be out of bounds. In the end, like finds like: it doesn't matter whether there is an actual physical neighbourhood or not. A compelling and necessary idea will always find a place to plant itself. The creative spirit finds a way.

[...]

My circle of friends gradually grew over the next few years. Most of them lived farther out in Queens than I did or out on Long Island. Because we went to different high schools, we would arrange to meet in the Square (as Washington Square Park in Greenwich Village was called) to listen to the folk musicians who gathered there to play on Sundays. Folk music was the anti-establishment music, the music of the left. In addition to traditional folk songs there were songs about unions and fighting fascists, about brotherhood, equality, and peace.

Most of us were children of Communists or socialists, red-diaper babies raised on Woody Guthrie, Leadbelly, and Pete

Seeger. We had listened to Oscar Brand's *Folksong Festival* on the radio while still in our cribs. The pop radio stations played ridiculous treacle, the worst of which was a song called "How Much Is That Doggie in the Window?" sung by Patti Page. [...]

The atmosphere in Washington Square Park was lively. Groups of musicians would play and sing anything from old folk songs to bluegrass. Old Italian men from the neighbourhood played their folk music on mandolins. Everyone played around the fountain and people would wander from group to group, listening and maybe singing along. A banjo player gave me an ebony banjo peg and I wore it on a string around my neck for a long time. There were poets reading their poems and political types handing out fliers for Trotskyist, Communist, or anarchist meetings and hawking their newspapers. Children played in the playground while their mothers talked together on the benches. The occasional religious zealot held forth, waving a Bible, haranguing sinners about redemption. Everything overlapped nicely.

Suze Rotolo, A Freewheelin' Time (2009)

✳ ✳ ✳

Suze Rotolo also describes what used to be one of the most famous locations in the village – an Art Deco prison for women. It closed in 1974 to be replaced by a garden.

The jail known as the Women's House of Detention sat on the triangle of land bordered by Sixth Avenue, Ninth Street, and Greenwich Avenue and was very much a part of the local Village scene. The building was a big, hulking edifice that dwarfed the delicacy of the Jefferson Market Courthouse next to it – today a public library.

The House of Detention windows faced Sixth Avenue and Greenwich Avenue. It had a fenced-in exercise yard on the roof from which the inmates would holler out taunts to passersby on the streets below. The jailed women's lovers, pimps, friends, and families, would line up in front of the shops along Greenwich Avenue and bellow up to them at all hours of the day and night. Anyone living in the neighbourhood with a window open to catch an elusive breeze on summer nights never got much sleep.

Suze Rotolo, *A Freewheelin' Time* (2009)

✻ ✻ ✻

A frequent visitor to the Village, Colette Rossant finds it reminiscent of Paris's Left Bank.

New York life fascinated me, and especially Greenwich Village. Very often, after work, I would take the subway, get off at 8th Street station and walk through the Village. It was late June, and along the narrow curving streets the lovely town houses had geraniums in window boxes and flowers everywhere. I spent my afternoons looking at the small boutiques, sat in coffee houses or spent hours at the Sheridan Square book store. On weekends, Jimmy and I would go to listen to jazz or see an avant-garde play. We often went to the first in-the-round theatre in New York, the Circle in the Square Theater. I can still remember how enthralled I was to see Jason Robards in *The Iceman Cometh*, or Truman Capote's *The Grass Harp*. The crowd was young like us, and after the play or concert we would walk to 10th Street to the Ninth Circle for a drink or dinner, or stop on Cornelia Street for a cappuccino at Caffe Cino. It seemed to me that people all around me were adventurous, that they were open to new ideas and very involved. I felt that there was hope, excitement in the air and found the city vibrant and alive. For me the Village was a bit like the Left Bank in Paris; it felt like home.

Colette Rossant, *Madeleines in Manhattan* (2007)

Edmund White – probably best know for A Boy's Own Story *and* The Beautiful Room is Empty *– gives a vivid picture of his day-to-day life in the Village … including a reality-check on some of the youngsters hanging around!*

I was making four hundred dollars a month. Stan's and my apartment cost just a hundred. It was on MacDougal between Bleecker and Houston, in the heart of the old Greenwich Village, right around the corner from the Little Red School House, a bastion of progressive education, and directly across the street from Bob Dylan's apartment, though I never once glimpsed him and didn't quite see the fuss over a man whose singing sounded whiny to me. On the corner was the San Remo, which had until recently been a famous gay bar but was now straight. Here, in the men's toilet, Terry Southern in his novel *Candy* had set an abortion scene. Frank O'Hara, the New York poet, had hung out there. I pictured thin gay men in Brooks Brothers suits, smoking, drinking martinis, their pale faces covered with light hangover sweat, their teeth brown from cigarettes, their bluish white hands shaking.

There was also a coffee shop across MacDougal called the Hip Bagel. *Hip* was for a while crossed out, then later reinstated, as the word itself was condemned for being square, then rescued through a second degree of irony. It had black walls and individual spotlights trained down on booths. In a back booth on the left I would sometimes drink espresso with an oversize girl who swore she was going to be a famous pop singer someday. I'd never heard of a fat singer off the grand opera stage, so I just nodded politely, though I was impressed to hear that she'd already appeared in *The Music Man*. A few years later she emerged as Mama Cass in the Mamas and the Papas, which meant little to me since except for the times it would provide the sound track for my romances I didn't care for pop. […]

The beatnik/hippie revolution was swirling all around me. After work I'd take the subway down and get off at the West Fourth Street stop and walk to our tiny, dirty, roach-trap apartment on MacDougal. On a warm evening my street was so crowded with kids with long hair and burgundy velvet jeans and mirrored vests and filmy shirts with puffy pirate sleeves that few cars would venture down it. It was still an old Italian neighbourhood with little cheap pasta joints down two or three steps from street level (Monte's was our favourite), cafés serving espresso such as the Caffè Reggio, and funeral homes with alabaster urns lit from within by electric bulbs, the stained-glass windows shrouded by closed beige curtains that were never opened. Our neighbours were Italian and spoke to each other every morning in, I guess, a Neapolitan dialect. Out our scrap of back window we could see old Italian wives cranking laundry across the air shaft on pulley-operated lines. We were far from our Midwestern suburban roots. Over that bedrock of the Italian Village was scattered the more recent topsoil of stores offering hookahs and shabby finery and light boxes and paintings that one could make oneself by splashing acrylics on a revolving potter's wheel – the centrifugal force threw the shiny colours out in crazed patterns. The smell of incense and patchouli filled the air.

As I came home in my suit and tie, weaving my way through the motley throngs, skinny kids in fringed leather coats would growl at me, "Go back to the suburbs." Which made me indignant, since I knew they were probably living with their parents in the suburbs and had to sneak out of the house with a paper bag full of their trendy new clothes. They'd change in the back of an unlit bus, leave behind their bourgeois togs in a bus station locker, and traipse down to the Village in their beads and bangles. They were the "plastic hippies", not I!

Edmund White, *City Boy* (2009)

✳ ✳ ✳

A short, acerbic intervention from Todd McEwen on contemporary Chelsea, which blends with the eastern edge of the Villlage.

What is *happening* to Chelsea, said Isidor, look at all this arty garbage, man, I tell you – almost as if to MacK, as if MacK was there – it is Intolerable. Where there was recently a perfectly, respectably, *miserable* coffee shop, with a perfect cup of miserable mud – Iz went there sometimes – there was now a yellow painted GALLERY offering artefacts native to the Gilbert Islands.

Todd McEwen, *Who Sleeps With Katz* (2003)

Celebrity city

*Throughout its history, New York has surely been one of
the most celebrity-heavy of cities. We start with a look
at some of the earliest celebrities associated with the city.*

Before Poe, the artistic life in New York was genteel and respectably
settled into the social order. Washington Irving was the city's first
great literary figure, and the rustic Fenimore Cooper was established in a house on St. Mark's Place. No-one today can identify
Fitz-Greene Halleck, let alone read him, but for a century or more
he was officially recognised as the city's bard, and his bust stands in
Central Park. Halleck and his even more forgotten colleague Joseph
Rodman Drake were the versifiers of the last era of semi-rural
downtown bourgeoisie, and their poesie was sufficiently mediocre
to appeal in later decades to reactionaries of several generations.
Poe, on the other hand, was treated mostly with contempt during
his lifetime, and only intermittently recognised. [...]

After Poe's death, everything seemed to refer back to him and to have been prefigured by him. His spirit was most nearly palpable at Pfaff's, the city's first bona-fide bohemian hangout, opened in a cellar on the west side of Broadway just above Bleeker Street sometime in the early 1850s. [...]

In its heyday Pfaff's was a crowded place, full of talk and argument, full of promising young writers hoping to get published (among them William Dean Howells, whose cool reception there perhaps accounted for his later attitude toward the bohemians), full of exiles (Clemenceau was one, for a while), and full of Whitman. The critic William Winter, a notable enemy of Walt's, wrote in later years of his "eccentric garb of rough blue and grey fabric – his hair and beard grizzled, his keen, steel-blue eyes gazing, with bland tolerance, on the frolicsome lads around him." He also kept his hat on, and unbuttoned his shirt to display his hairy chest. Whitman set the tone for the others, and his enemies became the enemies of all bohemia: Thomas Bailey Aldrich, E. C. Stedman, R. H. Stoddard, Bayard Taylor, all powerful critics in their day, and known only to historians now. Whitman was more interested in expanding the boundaries of bohemia, and invited to Pfaff's his beloved stage drivers, and young doctors from New York Hospital. By that time, in the decade before the Civil War, bohemia was becoming more than a state of mind; it was an actual place, as artists, writers, actors, and pretenders moved into Bleeker, Bond, and Spring Streets, then murky and rather dangerous thoroughfares. Journalists were soon describing the area as full of long-haired artists in garrets, semi-amateur prostitutes, and (a term that had acquired a derisive sense) "ballet dancers". The *Times* was moved to define a bohemian as "an artist or an author whose special aversion is to work."

Luc Sante, *Low Life* (1991)

* * *

Charles Dickens did not think highly of New York (see his account in the 'Good times, bad times' section), but in some quarters the feelings were mutual and one New Yorker at least viewed all the fuss and flurry around this English celebrity with a somewhat jaundiced eye.

(1842) TUESDAY, FEB. 15. The agony is over; the Boz hall, the greatest affair in modern times, the tallest compliment ever paid a little man, the fullest libation ever poured upon the altar of the muses, came off last evening in fine style. Everything answered the public expectation, and no untoward circumstance occurred to make anybody sorry he went.

The theatre was prepared for the occasion with great splendour and taste. The whole area of the stage and pit was floored over and formed an immense saloon. The decorations and paintings were all "Pickwickian." Shields with scenes painted from the several stories of Dickens, the titles of his works on others surrounded with wreaths, the dome formed of flags, and the side walls in fresco, representing the panels of an ancient oaken hall. A small stage was erected at the extreme end opposite the main entrance, before which a curtain was suspended, exhibiting the portly proportions of the immortal Pickwick, his prince of valets, and his bodyguard of choice cronies. This curtain was raised in the intervals between the cotillions and waltzes to disclose a stage on which were exhibited a series of *tableaux vivants*, forming groups of the characters in the most striking incidents of "Pickwick," "Nicholas Nickleby," "Oliver Twist," "The Old Curiosity Shop," "Barnaby Rudge," etc. The company began to assemble at half past seven o'clock, and at nine, when the committee introduced Mr. and Mrs. Dickens, the crowd was immense; a little upward of two thousand tickets were handed in at the door, and, with the members of committees and their parties who came in by back ways, the assembled multitude numbered about two thousand five hundred. Everybody was there, and every lady was dressed well and in good taste, and decorum and good order were preserved during the whole evening. Refreshments were provided in the saloons on the several floors, and in the green room, which was kept for the members of the committees and their families. This branch of the business was farmed out to Downing, the great man of oysters, who received $2,200. On the arrival of the "observed of all observers," a lane was opened through the crowd, through which he and his lady were marched to the upper end, where the committee of reception were stationed. Here I, as chairman of the committee, received him, and made a short speech, after which they joined in the dancing. [...]

The author of the "Pickwick Papers" is a small, bright-eyed, intelligent-looking young fellow, thirty years of age, somewhat of a dandy in his dress, with "rings and things and fine array," brisk in his manner and of a lively conversation. If he does not get his little head turned by all this, I shall wonder at it. Mrs. Dickens is a little, fat, English-looking woman, of an agreeable countenance, and, I should think, a "nice person."

Philip Hone, *Diary* (1842)

✻ ✻ ✻

New York has long relied on its wealthy families to create the architecture and institutions commensurate with a leading world city. Here's a little story about the Astors and the Vanderbilts ...

New York Society in the Gilded Age was essentially the creation of two very rich women, Mrs William B. Astor and Mrs William K. Vanderbilt, and of the titanic clash between them in the 1880s.

Mrs Astor, née Schermerhorn, was highborn; Mrs Vanderbilt, née Smith, was not. The Astors could trace their wealth and lineage to New York's Dutch aristocracy of the eighteenth century. To be sure, the term *aristocracy* in this usage is a bit of a stretch, since Netherlandish fur traders in the New World were not exactly princes in the Old. [...] Nevertheless, by the late nineteenth century, the fabulously moneyed Astors would be received at the court of St. James and would soon have their aristocratic claims confirmed by English titles of nobility, which were far superior to Dutch ones, had there been any Dutch ones.

By contrast, a Vanderbilt was a nobody. Cornelius 'Commodore' Vanderbilt was merely the richest man in America – indeed, the richest man in the world. Being worth a million dollars made one a man of fortune in the mid-nineteenth century; Cornelius Vanderbilt was worth a hundred million when he died in 1877, and his son was worth twice that a decade later. But the Commodore was still a vulgar steamship and rail magnate who owed his wealth to industry, and Mrs Astor would call on neither him nor his relations. [...]

It was thus established that the Vanderbilts were not to be received in the best Manhattan houses. Mrs Astor let it be known that there were only four hundred men and women in all New York City fit to enter a ballroom – that number being, as it happened, the quantity of guests who fit comfortably into Mrs Astor's own ballroom. The Vanderbilts were not among the Four Hundred.

Mrs Vanderbilt was not vindictive, but she was intelligent and indomitable. No penny would be spared to break the Astor ban. Her first measure, achieved with a liberal dose of her husband's largesse, was to procure an invitation to the Patriarchs' Ball. [...]

Her second step was to have her husband build a new house. It would be located on the corner of Fifth Avenue and Fifty-second Street and like no other house yet seen in New York City [...], a white limestone French château in the style of the Loire Valley. [...]

As the mansion neared completion in 1883, Mrs Vanderbilt announced a housewarming party, on which she would eventually spend some $250,000. [...] Dropping hints of sumptuous and unheard-of entertainments, Mrs Vanderbilt issued a total of twelve hundred invitations. Her anticipated ball became the talk of the town.

One especially eager little partygoer happened to be Carrie Astor, Mrs Astor's favourite daughter, who all summer long had been preparing with her friends a Star Quadrille for Mrs Vanderbilt's ball. But of those twelve hundred invitations, not one had gone to Carrie Astor. All Carrie's friends had been invited – they were already excitedly planning the gowns they would wear for their quadrille – but not the tearful Carrie herself. To everyone who would listen, Mrs Vanderbilt expressed sympathy for the poor girl's plight, but how *could* she invite Carrie, the hostess asked the world, when she had never been introduced to the girl's mother?

So it happened that Mrs William Backhouse Astor took to her carriage one afternoon in the winter season of 1883 and had her footman, clad in blue livery, present her engraved card at 660 Fifth Avenue. This gave Mrs Vanderbilt an unprecedented opportunity to snub the great Caroline Astor, an opportunity that would have been irresistible to a less farsighted woman. But Mrs Vanderbilt immediately responded by delivering to the Astor residence an invitation to her ball, as a result of which Carrie was able to attend after all, accompanied by her mother – in a diamond bodice that cost $200,000 – and the rest of Mrs Astor's Four Hundred.

Jed Rubenfeld, *The Interpretation of Murder* (2006)

❋ ❋ ❋

Also vital to the city's development have been its mayors. One of the greatest – great enough to have an airport named after him – was Mayor La Guardia.

He was essentially a modern man, perfectly suited to see political Manhattan through its transition from reckless provincialism to the authority of world supremacy. Not that he was colourless – few mayors of New York had ever been that. [...]

He was the son of an Italian father and a Jewish mother. He married first a Catholic, then a Lutheran, and was himself a lifelong Episcopalian. He was short – 5' 2" – swarthy and thick-set, like a wrestler, and talked in an unexpectedly high-pitched voice. He wore very wide Stetson hats (hence his nickname "The Hat") and very long coats, and he seemed to be all a-fizzle with energy, hot temper, resolution and reformist zeal: a *New Yorker* cartoon of the day showed City Hall itself shaken to its foundations, as by an earthquake, when his Honour arrived in the morning, only settling down to its old composure when he drove away at night. He was a very clever man, an excellent linguist, and widely experienced, having served as a clerk with the U.S. foreign service, as an Army pilot in the First World War (another of his nicknames was "The Major"), as a congressman in Washington and as the national director of civil defence during the War: but he had directed the greater part of his energies to the running of New York.

"Nobody wants me but the people," La Guardia said, and this was possibly true, for politically he was a kind of hybrid. A Republican, he was a New Dealer too, had always been on good terms with Democratic administrations in Washington, and since 1936 had held office with the support of the American Labour Party – "I've never belonged to any political party," he said once, "for more than 15 minutes." Also he was an inflexible fighter of municipal corruption. He had broken the grip of the New York Democratic machine, Tammany Hal, and he it was whose policies had scoured Manhattan of its most blatant gangsters, banned its criminally-organized gambling, cleaned up its theatre, cleared its streets of pedlars and pushcarts, and exposed Gentleman Jim's appalling laxities. Myth said that when La Guardia was originally sworn in as mayor, on December 31, 1933, the very first thing he did was to pick up the telephone and order the arrest of "Lucky Luciano," the most powerful mobster in the city.

"La Guardia's main weakness," remarked the *Daily News* sarcastically of his attack on fruit machines and gaming houses, "has been a Puritan streak ... gambling was a cancer eating out the slimy soul of American manhood, or something like that ... " But the people loved him all the same, forgave his occasional prudishness, admired his long fight against, as he put it, "political riff-raff, chisellers, racketeers, tinhorns." They liked his volatile style and his diligent brand of showmanship: when *The Fire-fighter* was christened, at La Guardia's suggestion, by the fire-man's daughter with the best school record that year, the Mayor himself decreed her dress for the occasion – a white dirndl gown with a red fire cape. They were amused by his frankness: "When I make a mistake," he said in a celebrated *bon mot*, "it's a beaut." They enjoyed his fondness for popular music, especially when he conducted the combined Police and Sanitation Department bands at their annual Carnegie Hall concerts ("Does Hizzonour want any special arrangements, extra lighting perhaps?" "Hell no, just treat me like Toscanini").

Since 1942 the people had also listened in their millions to his Sunday morning broadcast talks direct from City Hall, which covered every subject under the sun, from how to help children with their homework to the best ways of eating fish – "Ladies, I want to ask you a little favour. I want you please to wear your rubbers when you go out in this weather. If you don't wear your rubbers you may slip and hurt yourself ... Now another word about fish." In 1945 there was a strike of newspaper truck drivers, and the children of Manhattan were denied their comics – in those days absolutely essential to the fulfilment of young Americans, La Guardia read them instead over the radio – "Gather around children, and I will tell you about Dick Tracy – Aah, what do we have here? The gardener! Stabbed! ... *but Dick Tracy is on the trail ...* "

In fact New Yorkers would probably remember La Guardia more vividly for his reading of the comics that year than for anything else, but he was really far more than a mere populist. He was, as he said himself, "an inconsiderate, arbitrary, authoritarian, difficult, complicated, intolerant and somewhat theatrical person," but history would recognize him as one of the most original of all American civic administrators. Now he was sixty-two, and had been mayor of New York longer than anyone else. He was suffering from a terminal cancer, and was tired, and thinner than he used to be. His old fury had abated. His ball-like figure no longer bounced with quite the same effervescence from meeting to meeting, appearance to appearance. In the summer of 1945 La Guardia was in the last months of his revolutionary mayorality, and slackening. It was intermission time at City Hall.

Jan Morris, *Manhattan '45* (1987/2011)

✳ ✳ ✳

Another unforgettable mayor was Robert Moses.

There was something else, he realised, that he wanted to convey to the boy. Something deep and important. Beyond the magnificent houses and apartments, the teeming life of the streets, the newspapers, theatres, galleries – the huge business of the place. What he needed Gorham to understand – what his son was heir to – the thing that really mattered – was the New Yorkers' indomitable spirit.

Even the Depression hadn't really brought the city down. Three giants had saved it. FDR, the president of course – and the good old Dutch name of Roosevelt was as New York as could be. It took the guts and daring of a New Yorker, Charlie reckoned, to push the New Deal through. Second, from the early thirties, right through to '45, New York's tiny, feisty Mayor La Guardia – a Republican technically, but a New Dealer all the way – had run the most honest administration the city had ever seen, and championed the poor through all those painful years. Third, and no less dramatic in his own way, that brutal giant Robert Moses.

No one had ever seen public works on the scale Commissioner Moses undertook. Those massive bridges – the Triborough, from Long Island to Manhattan; the beautiful Whitestone, from Long Island to the Bronx. A slew of public parks. Above all, the huge roadways that swept the ever-growing traffic round New York's boroughs. With these titanic projects, Moses had brought countless millions of federal dollars into the city, employing thousands.

Some people said there was a cruelty about Moses and his methods. They said his big Long Island expressways avoided the great estates of the rich, but devastated the homes of the poor; that he only cared about the flow of motor cars, and ignored public transport. They even said the new highways created barriers, physically separating black neighbourhoods from the public parks.

Charlie wasn't sure. New York's public transport was pretty good, he reckoned, and in this new age of the motor car, the city would have come to a standstill without the new roads. The criticism about the parks and the black neighbourhoods might be true, but the layout of the roads was magnificent. When he drove up the West Side's Henry Hudson Parkway, which swept one gloriously along the great river all the way past the George Washington Bridge, Charlie could forgive Moses almost anything.

Edward Rutherfurd, *New York* (2009)

❋ ❋ ❋

At one time, celebrities arriving in New York could be expected to be welcomed by the mayor's official 'greeter'. Writing at the time when John Lindsay was mayor, Alistair Cooke considers the often tricky protocol of dealing with celebrity visitors to the city.

When I first arrived in the United States, one of the novelties that fascinated me was something called a 'greeter'. New York

City had an appointed, indeed a salaried, official known as the town's greeter. His office has by now gone pretty much the way of the town crier, because – whereas they used to take five days to come from Europe, and several hours to sail up the bay – celebrities now whisk in and out of the city as nonchalantly as housewives bustle in and out of a supermarket.

But in those days, New York had a splendid greeter, a man named Grover Whalen, and his job was roughly, or smoothly, equivalent to that of the State Department's chief of protocol. His office was not, I believe, sanctioned by law or even by custom. It was the inspiration of one Mayor Hyland, a man who before he became Mayor had been a tram driver – or, as I was learning to say, a streetcar motorman. Mayor Hyland was what they used to call a rough diamond and at some point he yearned for a smooth diamond who might, on official occasions, put up a front worthy of the grandeur of New York City. Mr Whalen did not let him down. When some person of blinding glamour was sailing into the city – at various times, I remember, it was Queen Marie of Rumania, Lindbergh, Michael Arlen (and, some of you may tenderly recall, Chico Marx masquerading as an Italian aviator) – the great ship came sliding in when the tide was right, and tug boats hooted at it, and fireboats jetted fountains of water by way of salute, and the liner responded with a blast of the last trump. Either on the pier, or down at City Hall, there would be a welcoming committee headed by the wonderful Grover Whalen, a rare bloom amid the surrounding business suits – with his top hat, cutaway, striped trousers, toothbrush moustache, wing collar, grey stock, pearl stickpin and a white carnation in his buttonhole. He would make a mellifluous speech, and the ex-tram driver, or the ex-band leader, or the ex-con man, or whoever was Mayor, would nod and marvel that he had on hand a greeter worthy of the Earl Marshal at the coronation of an English king.

In those days the United States, for all its accession of financial and naval power, was not so obviously the world power it is today. And the city didn't think twice about the political implications of welcoming a distinguished German or a sheikh or a Frenchman or an Italian. There was always a special fuss reserved for the arrival of a Prime Minister of Ireland, a Cardinal from the Vatican or a Mayor of Jerusalem. For, considering the ethnic composition of the voters of New York, a Mayor of New York going to Europe for nothing but a holiday would – as one told me later on – 'naturally make compulsory stops in Dublin, Rome and Tel Aviv'.

Today, it is all changed. New York has grown up in many ways. Mayor John Lindsay needs no social stand-in, being himself at once as gorgeous as Apollo and the very epitome of Eastern Establishment grace and confidence. But today, also, the Mayor and his staff must scrutinise very cagily the list of important people who are coming on state visits to the United States. For though they may fly in the first place to Washington, if they are political grandees they usually indicate that they would like to come to New York, and the city is required to arrange a banquet for them. In fact, the Mayor of New York sometimes finds himself on a more sensitive spot than the President of the United States. It is grudgingly admitted on all sides that President Nixon, by virtue of his office, cannot rudely ignore any head of state who chooses to come here, although there are times when a head of state, or a head of government, is quietly informed that the only welcome he is likely to get is a Bronx cheer. Plainly, the President cannot sacrifice common courtesy to some purely regional prejudice.

But the Mayor of New York is not, like the Lord Mayor of London, an anonymous figurehead. He is, after the President, the second most important executive in the country. He is the administrative head of the country's biggest city. He is also a practising politician and the chief citizen of a city that crackles at all times with political prejudice. There are in New York City resident colonies of almost any country and any religion that cares to send along a ruler or a delegate or a holy man. There are not too many Arabs in New York, but there are more Jews than there are in Tel Aviv. And on St Patrick's Day more Irish, it appears, than in the whole of Ireland. There was an awful to-do a few years ago about the state visit of an Arab king. When the Mayor let it be known that he would welcome the king in a cool correct way, there was such an uproar that the monarch confined himself to Washington.

Alistair Cooke, *Letter From America* (1 March 1970)

✽ ✽ ✽

In Middagh Street, near the Brooklyn end of the Brooklyn Bridge, there once stood a house inhabited by such an unlikely collection of celebrities that it inspired Sherrill Tippins to write a whole fascinating book on it – February House.

Most intriguing to me, however, were the references to a house that once stood at 7 Middagh Street (pronounced *mid*-daw), a short, narrow lane at the neighbourhood's northwestern tip overlooking the former dockyards and, beyond, New York Harbour. The house had been rented, one neighbour told me, by a group of well-known young poets, novelists, composers, and artists the year before America entered World War II. Aware that enormous devastation lay ahead and determined to continue contributing to the culture as long as possible, they had created an environment for themselves to support and stimulate, inspire and protect – just a few blocks from where I lived.

When I learned that these residents included the poet W.H. Auden, the novelist Carson McCullers, the composer Benjamin Britten, Paul and Jane Bowles, and, of all people, the burlesque artist Gypsy Rose Lee – all under thirty-five but already near the apex of their careers – my interest was piqued even further.

207

In a pictorial survey of Brooklyn's history, I found a photograph of the house – a small, shabby brick and brownstone
structure with elaborate Tudor trim. The man who had signed
the lease and organized this experiment in communal living
turned out to have been George Davis, a fiction editor at *Harper's Bazaar* who had single-handedly revolutionized the role
played by popular magazines in bringing serious literature and
avant-garde ideas to the American masses. Davis was known
for his attraction to the eccentric in culture, in entertainment,
and in his choice of friends. With his encouragement, nights
at the Middagh Street house became a fevered year-long party
in which New York's artistic elite (Aaron Copland, George
Balanchine, Louis Untermeyer, Janet Flanner, and Louise Dahl-
Wolfe, among others) mingled with a flood of émigrés fleeing
Nazi-occupied Europe, including the composer Kurt Weill and
the singer Lotte Lenya, the artist Salvador Dali and his wife,
Gala, and the entire brilliant family of the Nobel Prize-winning
novelist Thomas Mann. Days, however, were dedicated to their
work – writing, composing, painting, and otherwise seeking
new answers, new approaches to life in a collapsing world.

By the winter of 1940–41, 7 Middagh – called "the February
House" by the diarist Anaïs Nin because so many of its residents had been born in that month – had developed a reputation as the greatest artistic salon of the decade. Denis de
Rougemont, the author of *Love in the Western World*, claimed
that "all that was new in America in music, painting, or
choreography emanated from that house, the only centre of
thought and art that I found in any large city in the country."
Throughout the months of that suspenseful season, as Hitler's
armies tightened their hold on Europe and killed or wounded
thousands of British citizens in bombing raids, Thomas Mann's
son Klaus laboured in the Middagh Street dining room, assem-
bling essays, poems, short stories, and reviews for *Decision*, a
monthly "review of free culture," while upstairs in the parlour,

the British émigrés Benjamin Britten and W.H. Auden worked together on an "American" opera that would express their hopes for and misgivings about their adopted country. On the third floor, McCullers agonized over the opening paragraphs of *The Member of the Wedding*, while in the room next door George Davis coached Gypsy on her own project, a comic burlesque mystery novel called *The G-String Murders*. Bowles, then a composer, wrote a ballet score in the cellar while his wife, Jane, did Auden's typing and wrote her own novel, *Two Serious Ladies*. Oliver Smith, destined to become one of Broadway's most prolific set designers and producers but then a destitute twenty-two-year-old, washed the dishes, tended the furnace, and, like many "youngest children," took on the role of family peacemaker. Auden, one of the greatest poets of his generation, served as housemaster to this lively household – which at one point included several circus performers and a chimpanzee – collecting the rent, dispensing romantic advice, playing word games with his housemates, and strictly enforcing nighttime curfews – all while laying the groundwork for some of the most courageous and original work of his career.

Perhaps inevitably, the intensity of life at 7 Middagh and the pressures created by the war in Europe led to physical and emotional breakdowns, domestic disputes, and creative crises. Even as the residents succumbed to the pressure of the times, so too did the United States. The attack on Pearl Harbour, on December 7, 1941, provoked America's entry into the fiercest and most destructive war in history – a six-year conflagration that killed fifty-five million people before it ended. As the artists of 7 Middagh Street had expected, they were scattered in all directions by these events. Some enlisted as soldiers. Other used their skills to create propaganda, conduct surveys, or entertain the troops. And, in the sweeping changes that took place over the half-decade, 7 Middagh Street disappeared, torn down to make way for the construction of the Brooklyn-Queens

Expressway. Today, nothing remains but an unmarked stretch of sidewalk, a wire fence, and a precipitous drop to the lands of traffic speeding from one borough to the next.

What does remain is the work these artists created. The final parts of Auden's book *The Double Man,* his poems "The Dark Years," "If I Could Tell you," "In Sickness and in Health," and the brilliant and innovative oratorio *For the Time Being,* were all completed during or inspired by the year at 7 Middagh. The twenty-seven-year-old Benjamin Britten gained both the artistic experience and the emotional growth necessary to create his first great opera, *Peter Grimes,* Carson McCuller's two final masterpieces, *The Member of the Wedding* and *The Ballad of the Sad Café,* were born in Brooklyn. Auden's support helped Jane Bowles take the first necessary steps toward completing her only novel, while Paul Bowles's jealousy over their relationship spurred him toward the writing of fiction for which he is now largely known. Even Gypsy's *G-String Murders,* written with the help of her admiring housemates, became a 1941 bestseller, establishing her reputation, not just as a stripper who could write, but as a writer who also knew how to keep an audience entranced.

Frequently, I go out of my way to pass the dead-end street where the house once stood, just to remind myself that these extraordinary artists actually occupied the space I do now – living together, arguing, laughing, creating, and using their imaginations to increase others' awareness of the issues and choices laid bare in that horrible, horrifying time. *If we don't act now, when will we?* they asked themselves in choosing this shared creative life, *If we don't use our talents to find a new way of life, who will?*

How this houseful of geniuses answered those questions is the story my elderly neighbours wanted me to hear. But the questions themselves are what keep me coming back, dreaming of the house at 7 Middagh.

Sherill Tippins, *February House* (2005)

✣ ✣ ✣

The Chelsea hotel is virtually synonymous with celebrity. Stephen Clarke and Joseph O'Neill take us inside.

The Chelsea loomed above me like a blood-red gothic mansion. I'd heard about the hotel where Hendrix used to stay and where Sid Vicious allegedly knifed his girlfriend to death, but I didn't expect it to be quite this forbidding.

The shops on the ground floor of the building seemed to hint at the eccentric activities within – a vintage guitar shop, an acupuncturist, a tattoo parlour, and, bizarrely, a fishing-tackle store.

On plaques by the hotel entrance there were quotes by or about some of the famous literary residents. One read: 'Dylan Thomas sailed out of here to die.' Very reassuring.

In the lobby, the first thing I saw was a fat lady hanging from the ceiling on a swing. She was not one of the eccentric gusts but an almost-lifesize sculpture. The whole lobby was an art gallery, its lurid yellow walls hung with modern portraits and abstract splashes. Adding a period touch was a pair of gothic urns on a mantelpiece, implying perhaps that being dead didn't exclude you from hanging out at the Chelsea.

Stephen Clarke, *Merde Happens* (2007)

✣ ✣ ✣

Not counting the lobby, the Chelsea Hotel had ten floors. Each was served by a dim hallway that ran from an airshaft on one side to, on my floor, a door with a yellowing pane of frosted glass that suggested the ulterior presence of a private detective rather than, as was actually the case, a fire escape. The floors were linked by a baronial staircase, which by virtue of the deep rectangular void at its centre had the effect of installing a precipice at the heart of the building. On all the walls was displayed the vaguely alarming artwork of tenants past and present. The finest and most valuable examples were reserved for the lobby: I shall never forget the pink, plump girl on a swing who hovered above the reception area gladly awaiting a push towards West 23rd Street. Occasionally one overheard by-the-night visitors – transients, as the management called them – commenting on how spooky they found it all, and there was a story that the hotel dead were secretly removed from their rooms in the middle of the night. But for me, returning from the office or from quick trips to Omaha, Oklahoma City, Cincinnati – Timbuktus from my New Yorker's vantage point – there was nothing eerie about the building or the community that was established in it. Over half the rooms were occupied by long-term residents who by their furtiveness and ornamental diversity reminded me of the population of the aquarium I'd kept as a child, a murky tank in which cheap fish hesitated in weeds and an artificial starfish made a firmament of the gravel.

Joseph O'Neill, Netherland (2008)

✳ ✳ ✳

Another hotel frequented by celebrities is the Barbizon, on the Upper East Side (140 East 63rd Street). Once for women only, it began admitting men in 1981, became the Melrose Hotel in 2002, was restructured as a condominium in 2005 and renamed Barbizon 63.

The Barbizon Hotel, originally the Barbizon Hotel for Women, used to be a place in which the daughters of the provincial rich would be forced to stay when they went to live in New York. Sylvia Plath, who lived there for a month in 1953, renamed it the Amazon in her novel *The Bell Jar* and said it was for parents 'who wanted to be sure their daughters would be living where men couldn't get at them and deceive them'. Grace Kelly, Liza Minnelli and Joan Crawford had all stayed there in their time. Several years before I was there it had been restored and reopened as a hotel for both sexes, but it retained an atmosphere of quiet respectability and still had many single women among its guests.

It was a delightful, romantic brick building of 1927, with exuberant stone Gothic excrescences. I had two small corner rooms on the sixteenth floor with fine views in two directions, and I had only to cross the road to take the subway direct to 42nd Street and the *New Yorker*'s offices, a ride of about fifteen minutes.

Alexander Chancellor, *Some Times in America* (1999)

✳ ✳ ✳

But New York is nothing if not varied: anyone from the most abstruse European philosopher to Gypsy Rose Lee is on the New Yorker's celebrity menu.

Certainly, Gypsy was an original. Long-legged, radiantly healthy, and remarkably self-possessed, she lacked the blond-bombshell looks that were popular in Hollywood but had a powerful, statuesque beauty all her own. Small-breasted and large-hipped, she designed and often sewed her own costumes to emphasise the long neck, elegant profile, and creamy, glowing skin that her public had grown to love. Her auburn hair, too flyaway to be worn loose, was usually arranged in an elaborate coiffure, and her signature six-inch heels added glamour to her five-foot-nine-inch frame. But her greatest charm lay, George felt, in the athletic, almost tomboyish stride that belied these ladylike accoutrements – a holdover, perhaps, from a childhood spent playing the male part opposite her prettier younger sister in vaudeville. In every way – from her sophisticated manner of handling the ogling crowds to her half-joking, almost British-sounding contralto with carefully pronounced French phrases (punctuated occasionally with an American curse or two) – Gypsy gave the impression of a smart, ambitious, self-made young woman with a well-developed sense of humour. [...]

Although only twenty-six (or perhaps twenty-nine – due to her mother's habit of forging her children's birth certificates,

Gypsy could never be sure of her age), she was enjoying the highest peak yet in an extraordinary career. That summer she had starred in *The Streets of Paris*, a wildly popular revue at the New York World's Fair. [...] With that success behind her, Gypsy was now appearing on Broadway opposite Bert Lahr in the Cole Porter musical *Du Barry Was a Lady* when not posing for photographs for *Harper's Bazaar*, attending parties on Park Avenue, or otherwise getting her name mentioned in New York's gossip columns. Over the past decade, such activities had helped expand Gypsy's fame as a performer from the tawdry, post-vaudeville strip club circuit of the Depression to the classier burlesque "opera houses" of New York, Chicago, and other large cities and finally to the more legitimate stages of Broadway, Hollywood, and the World's Fair.

Sherrill Tippins, *February House* (2005)

❊ ❊ ❊

One of the greatest American publications is, of course, the weekly magazine The New Yorker, *founded by Harold Ross in 1925. Its mixture of the humorous with the serious, along with its publishing of short stories by some of the greatest names in twentieth- and twenty-first-century literature, ensure it remains a vital reflection of the intellectual and cultural life of the city. In this abridged excerpt from* The Years with Ross, *humourist and* New Yorker *writer-cartoonist, James Thurber, remembers the magazine's founder and long-time editor.*

Harold Ross died December 6, 1951, exactly one month after his fifty-ninth birthday. In November of the following year the *New Yorker* entertained the editors of *Punch* and some of its outstanding artists and writers. I was in Bermuda and missed the party, but weeks later met Rowland Emett for lunch at the

Algonquin. 'I'm sorry you didn't get to meet Ross,' I began as we sat down. 'Oh, but I did,' he said. 'He was all over the place. Nobody talked about anybody else.'

Ross is still all over the place for many of us, vitally stalking the corridors of our lives, disturbed and disturbing, fretting, stimulating, more evident in death than the living presence of ordinary men. A photograph of him, full face, almost alive with a sense of contained restlessness, hangs on a wall outside his old office. I am sure he had just said to the photographer, 'I haven't got time for this.' That's what he said, impatiently, to anyone – doctor, lawyer, taxman – who interrupted, even momentarily, the stream of his dedicated energy. Unless a meeting, conference, or consultation touched somehow upon the working of his magazine, he began mentally pacing.

I first met Harold Ross in February 1927, when his weekly was just two years old. He was thirty-four and I was thirty-two. The *New Yorker* had printed a few small pieces of mine, and a brief note from Ross had asked me to stop in and see him some day when my job as a reporter for the New York *Evening Post* chanced to take me uptown. Since I was getting only forty dollars a week and wanted to work for the *New Yorker*, I showed up at his office the next day. Our meeting was to become for me the first of a thousand vibrant memories of this exhilarating and exasperating man. [...]

I had caught glimpses of him at the theatre and at the Algonquin and, like everybody else, was familiar with the mobile face that constantly changed expression, the carrying voice, the eloquent large-fingered hands that were never in repose, but kept darting this way and that to emphasize his points or running through the thatch of hair that stood straight up until Ina Claire said she would like to take her shoes off and walk through it. That got into the gossip columns and Ross promptly had his barber flatten down the pompadour. [...]

Ross was, at first view, oddly disappointing. No one, I think, would have picked him out of a line-up as the editor of the *New Yorker*. Even in a dinner jacket he looked loosely informal, like a carelessly carried umbrella. He was meticulous to the point of obsession about the appearance of his magazine, but he gave no thought to himself. He was usually dressed in a dark suit, with a plain dark tie, as if for protective coloration. In the spring of 1927 he came to work in a black hat so unbecoming that his secretary, Elsie Dick, went out and bought him another one. 'What became of my hat?' he demanded later. 'I threw it away,' said Miss Dick. 'It was awful.' He wore the new one without argument. Miss Dick, then in her early twenties, was a calm, quiet girl, never ruffled by Ross's moods. She was one of the few persons to whom he ever gave a photograph of himself. On it he wrote, 'For Miss Dick, to whom I owe practically everything.' She could spell, never sang, whistled, or hummed, knew how to fend off unwanted visitors, and had an intuitive sense of when the coast was clear so that he could go down in the elevator alone and not have to talk to anybody, and these things were practically everything.

In those early years the magazine occupied a floor in the same building as the *Saturday Review of Literature* on West 45th Street. Christopher Morley often rode in the elevator, a tweedy man, smelling of pipe tobacco and books, unmistakably a literary figure. I don't know that Ross ever met him. 'I know too many people,' he used to say. The editor of the *New Yorker*, wearing no mark of his trade, strove to be inconspicuous, and liked to get to his office in the morning, if possible, without being recognized and greeted. [...]

By the spring of 1928 Ross's young *New Yorker* was safely past financial and other shoals that had menaced its launching, skies were clearing, the glass was rising, and everybody felt secure except the skipper of the ship. From the first day I met him till the last time I saw him, Ross was like a sleepless, apprehensive sea captain pacing the bridge, expecting any minute to run aground, collide with something nameless in a sudden fog, or find his vessel abandoned and adrift, like the *Mary Celeste*. When, at the age of thirty-two, Ross had got his magazine afloat with the aid of Raoul Fleischmann and a handful of associates, the proudest thing he had behind him was his editorship of the *Stars and Stripes* in Paris from 1917 to 1919.

James Thurber, The Years With Ross (1959)

❊ ❊ ❊

Visiting celebrity Alan Bennett remembers encountering an even bigger celebrity …

The purpose of this very much flying visit, paid for by Random House, is to do a five-minute 'segment' on the *Today* show, the book club of which has selected (or had selected for them) *The Lady in the Van* and *The Clothes They Stood Up In* as their this month's read. It's actually the choice of Helen Fielding, whom I'd imagined utterly metropolitan but turns out to be from Morley, though now living in Los Angeles presumably on the proceeds of her two bestsellers. After the segment we have tea in the Pierre and talk about Leeds, and I walk down the corridor where forty years ago Dudley Moore and I saw Stravinsky.

Alan Bennett, Untold Stories (2005)

❊ ❊ ❊

Freud's arrival in New York is described earlier. Here he is again.

Freud arrived in New York on the Lloyd liner *George Washington*. He was accompanied by his disciples Jung and Ferenczi, both some years his junior. They were met at the dock by two more younger Freudians, Drs. Ernest Jones and A.A. Brill. The entire party dined at Hammerstein's Roof Garden. There were potted palms. A piano violin duo played Liszt's *Hungarian Rhapsody*. Everyone talked around Freud, glancing at him continuously to gauge his mood. He ate cup custard. Brill and Jones undertook to play host for the visit. In the days following they showed Freud Central Park, the Metropolitan Museum and Chinatown. Catlike Chinamen gazed at them out of dark shops. There were glass cabinets filled with litchi nuts. The party went to one of the silent films so popular in stores and nickelodeons around the city. White smoke rose from the barrels of rifles and men wearing lipstick and rouge fell backwards clutching their chest. At least, Freud thought, it is silent. What oppressed him about the New World was its noise. The terrible clatter of horses and wagons, the clanking and screeching of streetcars, the horns of automobiles. At the wheel of an open Marmon, Brill drove the Freudians around Manhattan. At one point, on Fifth Avenue, Freud felt as if he was being observed; raising his eyes he found some children staring down at him from the top of a double-decker bus.

Brill drove the party down to the Lower East Side with its Yiddish theatres and pushcarts and elevated trains. The fearsome elevated rumbled past the windows of tenements in which people were expected to live. The windows shook, the very buildings shook. Freud had to relieve himself and nobody seemed to be able to tell him where a public facility could be found. They all had to enter a dairy restaurant and order sour cream with vegetables so that Freud could go to the bathroom. Later, back in the car, they pulled up to a corner to watch a street artist at work, an old man who with nothing but a scissors and paper made miniature silhouette portraits for a few cents. Standing for her portrait was a beautiful well-dressed woman. The excitable Ferenczi, masking his admiration for the woman's good looks, declared to his colleagues in the car his happiness at finding the ancient art of silhouette flourishing on the streets of the New World. Freud, clamping his teeth on his cigar, said nothing.

E.L. Doctorow, *Ragtime* (1976)

✻ ✻ ✻

This brief extract gives a moving picture of the great Spanish poet and playwright Federico García Lorca alone in the city at night, no doubt gathering inspiration for his New York poems.

Late at night, after the rumble of traffic had died down and the summer air had cooled, Lorca often took to the streets by himself. Sometimes he strayed to the waterfront or to the Brooklyn Bridge, where he and Sofia Megwinoff occasionally strolled by day. The site entranced him as it did Hart Crane. Standing alone on the bridge, high above the East river, he could see the formidable gray silhouette of Wall Street to the south, and beyond it – a pinpoint in the inky bay – the Statue of Liberty. Behind him, to the north, the huge granite towers of midtown Manhattan rose into the night. He remained on the bridge, absorbed in his thoughts, a minuscule human figure dwarfed by the huge American metropolis. Returning uptown to Columbia in the dark hours of early morning, he sometimes picked up a pencil or a pen, and in the quiet of his room tried to record his impressions.

Leslie Stainton, *Lorca: A Dream of Life* (1999)

✻ ✻ ✻

And, as a contrast, another kind of celebrity ... one who, for some, really was the voice of New York.

New York homegirl Ethel Merman, née Zimmerman, is one of Times Girl's most flamboyant descendants. She made a Broadway career that started in the Depression and ran into the 1970s. Unlike many other divas who used Broadway as a springboard to Hollywood, she seems never to have been comfortable outside the theatre's eight-days-a-week routine, and never at home outside New York. This made card-carrying New Yorkers like my parents especially fond of her: as New York became increasingly isolated and embattled, she was *our* voice.

Marshall Berman, *On the Town* (2006)

New Yorkers

Finally, what's it like to be a New Yorker? – either temporary or permanent. First, some possible down-sides.

On Second Avenue the springtime scraping of roller skates was heard on hollow, brittle sidewalks, a soothing harshness. Turning from the new New York of massed apartments into the older New York of brownstone and wrought-iron, Sammler saw through large black circles in a fence daffodils and tulips, the mouths of these flowers open and glowing, but on the pure yellow the fallout of soot already was sprinkled. You might in this city become a flower-washer. There

221

was an additional business opportunity for Wallace and Feffer.

He walked once around Stuyvesant Park, an ellipse within a square with the statue of the peg-legged Dutchman, corners bristling with bushes. [...]

Sammler had learned to be careful on public paths in New York, invariably dog-fouled. Within the iron-railed plots the green lights of the grass were all but put out, burned by animal excrements. The sycamores, blemished bark, but very nice, brown and white, getting ready to cough up leaves.

Saul Bellow, *Mr Sammler's Planet* (1970)

✳ ✳ ✳

Noise in New York is not something most people feel comfortable complaining about. There is plenty that is acceptable to complain about in Manhattan – and the other boroughs – but to complain about noise is a bit like a climber on Mount Everest whining that there's not enough oxygen. If you need oxygen, why the hell did you decide to climb Mount Everest in the first place? And if you can't deal with the noise, you shouldn't be in New York.

The other problem is, the levels of noise are not universal. I mean, if a person has a great loft near the Holland Tunnel, but it's noisy from traffic, tough. You have a great loft, so shut up. We live in Brooklyn, on top of a hill, on top of a building on top of a hill, with great views: people come to visit and they say, 'Oh, it's so quiet.' It is quiet, except at certain times of day when airplanes are coming in to land at JFK, when I have to go out on to the terrace to make sure they are not going to crash into my apartment. So it's not really acceptable for me to say, 'Oh no, it's not quiet here – we have noise between seven and nine, when jetplanes come in.' Nobody's going to care – after all, they don't have that jetplane landing problem. [...]

I once lived in the meat market district – this was years ago, before the area became fashionable – and between the transvestite prostitutes, who retired to sleep each night on a loading dock directly across from my window, five floors below, where they held a slumber party complete with loud cassettes playing dance music and lots of giggles, gossip and makeup sessions – and the delivery of meat, on huge trucks, starting at about five a.m. – it was a noisy place. How was I going to complain about it, though? What could I say? That the meat being delivered made it impossible to sleep? Who, really, was going to care?

Tama Janowitz, *Area Code 212* (2002)

✳ ✳ ✳

Fictional New Yorker Mr Sammler may have an eye for the dirt and human smells, but he's also alive to the sweetness of spring in the city.

The sun shone as if there were no death. For a full minute, while the bus approached, squirting air, it was like that. Then Mr. Sammler got on, moving like a good citizen toward the rear, hoping he would not be pushed past the back door, for he had only fifteen blocks to go, and there was a thick crowd. The usual smell of long-seated bottoms, of sour shoes, of tobacco muck, of stogies, cologne, face powder. And yet along the river, early spring, the first khaki – a few weeks of sun, of heat, and Manhattan would (briefly) join the North American continent in a day of old-time green, the plush luxury, the polish of the season, shining, nitid, the dogwood white, pink, blooming crabapple. Then people's feet would swell with the warmth, and at Rockefeller Center strollers would sit on the polished stone slabs beside the planted tulips and tritons and the water, all in a spirit of pregnancy. Human creatures under the warm shadows of skyscrapers feeling the heavy pleasure of their nature, and yielding.

Saul Bellow, *Mr. Sammler's Planet* (1970)

❋ ❋ ❋

After describing his arrival, Alexander Chancellor describes a first encounter with a New York resident.

Europeans arriving in New York no longer get their first sight of Manhattan from the sea. They now alight at Kennedy Airport and are plunged into a mass of frantic, bustling humanity. The scene is in sharp contrast to London Airport, where departing passengers display all the urgency of cows entering a milking parlour. The drive through Queens along the Van Wyck Expressway and Grand Central Parkway feels rather frightening when you do it for the first time. On each side of the swaying streams of traffic are miles of shabby housing, exuding menace.

Then, as you approach the Triborough Bridge, great clusters of skyscrapers loom into view from across the East River, and the heart leaps. It is a sight comparable only to Venice in its improbable beauty. That has been said before, of course. In fact, there have been so many attempts by visitors to sum up New York – how the air is electric, how the light is brilliant, how it looks like a giant asparagus bed – that I will try to be sparing with them. Europeans, as the late *New Yorker* writer Brendan Gill has pointed out, feel 'strongly inclined to tell us what America is like', and that is especially true of New York, which seems to invite simple generalisations.

Laura Waugh, the wife of the writer Evelyn, was mocked by her family for the rest of her life after telling them that New York struck her as 'like a cocktail – exciting!' That is the usual impression, but the great Irish journalist Claud Cockburn wrote in his autobiography, *In Time of Trouble* (Rupert Hart-Davis, 1957), that, on the contrary, New York was remarkable for the leisurely quality of its life. 'Voyagers have a note in their books to the effect that in America what you have is "tempo and hustle",' he wrote. 'But in reality the tempo of New York on a day of business is like the tempo of Brighton on a day of holiday.'

In any case, getting across the Triborough Bridge and on to the island of Manhattan is a moment of relief and exhilaration. Once surrounded by water, you feel as secure at the citizen of a fortified medieval town. You have entered a circumscribed, finite world, a teeming colony of ants who know and care about nothing beyond themselves. While London spreads out like a great ink blot across south-east England, Manhattan is neatly confined to its island, on which it can grow only upwards. In a country as enormous as the United States there is something a little comic, as well as exciting, in the spectacle of so many people battling over so little space.

Arriving in New York on a sunny afternoon in March 1974, I checked in at an old-fashioned midtown hotel and then went straight out on to Fifth Avenue to find a packet of English cigarettes. I hadn't walked very far when I was suddenly addressed by a voice from the crowd. 'What's the matter with you, for Christ's sake?' it said. 'Why the hell do you look so glum?' I looked up from the sidewalk and saw a pretty girl grinning at me. 'This is the first sun we've had this year!' she said reproachfully.

I said I was very sorry, had just arrived from England, and would make a point of looking less glum in future. This was my first encounter with American positive thinking and with another perplexing phenomenon – the fact that Americans never appear to be shy. Americans look you steadily in the eye and do not blink. If you ask them how they are, they are always very well and greatly enjoying whatever it is they are doing.

Alexander Chancellor, *Some Times in America* (1999)

What some people feel as the great 'buzz' of a vibrant, demanding city, one-time New Yorker (and frequent returner) novelist John Updike experiences as something more negative: an exhausting living Hell!

Always, as one arrives, there is the old acceleration of the pulse – the mountainous grey skyline glimpsed from the Triboro Bridge, the cheerful games of basketball and handball being played on the recreational asphalt beside the FDR Drive, the startling, steamy, rain-splotched intimacy of the side streets where one's taxi slows to a crawl, the careless flung beauty of the pedestrians clumped at the street corners. So many faces, costumes, packages, errands! So many preoccupations, hopes, passions, lives in progress! So much human stuff, clustering and streaming with a languid colourful impatience like the pheromone-coded mass manoeuvres of bees!

But soon the faces and their individual expressions merge and vanish under a dulling insistent pressure, the thrum and push of congestion. As ever more office buildings are heaped upon the East Fifties – the hugest of them, the slant-topped white Citicorp building, clearly about to fall off its stilts onto your head – and an ever-greater number of impromptu merchants spread their dubiously legal wares on the sidewalks, even pedestrian traffic jams. One is tripped, hassled, detoured. Buskers and beggars cram every available niche. The sidewalks and subway platforms, generously designed in the last century, have been overwhelmed on both the minor and major entrepreneurial scales. The Manhattan grid, that fine old machine for living, now sticks and grinds at every intersection, and the discreet brownstones of the side streets look down upon a clogged nightmare of perpetual reconstruction and insolent double parking. Even a sunny day feels like a tornado of confusion one is hurrying to get out of, into the sanctum of the hotel room, the office, the friendly apartment. New York is a city with virtually no habitable public space – only private spaces expensively maintained within the general disaster. While popular journalism focuses on the possible collapse of Los Angeles and San Francisco into chasms opened by earthquakes, here on the East Coast, on its oblong of solid granite, the country's greatest city is sinking into the chasm of itself.

Hardened New Yorkers will sniff, What else is new? Their metropolis has been a kind of vigorous hell since the days of the Five Points and the immigrant-packed Lower East Side. Its vitality and glamour are ironically rooted in merciless skirmish and inconvenient teeming; a leering familiarity with crowdedness and menace is the local badge of citizenship, and the city's constant moral instruction features just this piquant proximity of rich and poor. [...]

My complaint, as an exile who once loved New York and who likes to return a half-dozen times a year, is not that it plays host to extremes of the human condition: there is grandeur in that, and necessity. For the Korean grocer and the Ukrainian taxi-driver, the apparent turmoil holds out opportunity and hope. The chaos is not quite complete; food is trucked in through the tunnels and purveyed in epic daily amounts, Bloomingdale's brightly peddles kitchen wares to young couples who have somehow found an apartment they can afford, the museums continue to expand, Central Park still offers patches of grass for a sunbath and a doze in the bosom of humanity. But the price of those delights, in the three decades of my exile, has gone from steep to exorbitant. Archibald MacLeish, toward the end of his long life, told me, "New York used to be a giving place, a place that gave more than it took. Now it takes more than it gives." [...]

Toward the end of each of my by now countless trips to New York, I must still fight a rising panic that I won't be able to get out. The city, like the Soviet Union, has this constant usefulness: it makes you glad you live somewhere else. As in the Soviet Union, nothing is easy: there are lines at the bank and the post office, there is nowhere to park, everything is an exhausting walk away, the restaurant has no tables, the theatre has no seats, and carbon monoxide ubiquitously offers an invitation to succumb. Time has only strengthened my impelling perception of thirty years ago: being in New York takes so much energy as to leave none for any other kind of being.

John Updike, *Odd Jobs* (1991)

* * *

Three short pieces lauding New York as the place where one can be or re-invent oneself.

A huge man sitting next to me on a bus going up Third Avenue asked me if I lived here permanently. When I said that I did, he remarked, 'It is the place to be if you are of "a different stripe".' There are so many different nationalities, so many different income groups, so many different sexes, that the freaks pass unnoticed. People have always imag- ined, or pretended to imagine, that I seek to provoke hostile attention. This is rubbish. What I want is to be accepted by other people without bevelling down my individuality to please them – because if I do that, all the attention, all the friendship, all the hospitality that I receive is really for somebody else of the same name. I want love on my own terms.

Here I have it.

Quentin Crisp, *Resident Alien* (1996)

* * *

One measure of New York's enduring primacy is that it continues to act as a lightning rod for national resentment. When Americans rail against "Washington", they mean the abstraction of federal government, not the District of Columbia. New York is resented as an actual place – for its rudeness, its arrogance, its crowds and dirt, its moral turpitude, and so forth. Global resentment is the highest compliment a city can receive, and by nurturing the notion of the Apple as the national Forbidden Fruit such resentment guarantees not only that ambitious souls of the "If I can make it there, I'd make it anywhere" variety will gravitate toward New York but that the heartland's most culturally rebellious young people will follow. There's no better way of rejecting where you came from, no plainer declaration of an intention to reinvent yourself, than moving to New York; I speak from personal experience.

Jonathan Franzen, *How to be Alone* (2002)

New York gave me a feeling of possibility I'd never gotten in the suburbs, driving home from Lord and Taylor with my mother, say. There, when I'd see people in other cars, I'd know they were on their way home, where their choices would be the same as mine: they could watch TV or read. In New York that summer, especially at dusk, in the Village or in midtown or on the Upper West Side, walking in a crowd of people or looking up at all the lit windows of an office or apartment building, I could feel like there were a thousand ways my life could go.

Melissa Bank, *The Wonder Spot* (2005)

Martin Amis also paints New Yorkers as people 'determined to be themselves'.

So I walked south down bending Broadway. What's all this *mm-hm* shit? I strode through meat-eating genies of subway breath. I heard the ragged hoot of sirens, the whistles of two-wheelers and skateboarders, pogoists, gocarters, windsurfers. I saw the barrelling cars and cabs, shoved on by the power of their horns. I felt all the contention, the democracy, all the italics, in the air. These are people determined to be themselves, whatever, little shame attaching. Urged out from the line of shufflers and idlers, watchers, pavement men, a big blond screamer flailed at the kerb, denouncing all traffic. His hair was that special mad yellow, like an omelette, a rug omelette. As he shadowboxed he loosely babbled of fraud and betrayal, redundancy, eviction. 'It's my money and I want it!' he said. 'I want my money and I want it now!' The city is full of these guys, these guys and dolls who bawl and holler and weep about bad luck all the hours there are.

Martin Amis, Money (1984)

✳ ✳ ✳

New York is a city that values individuality, and even allows the true eccentric to thrive.

Countless citizens of Manhattan considered themselves outside class, outside convention too, and life for such mavericks was greatly eased by the city's fondness for individuality. At its coarsest, this may have been just laissez-faire or no-holds-barred, but in subtler kinds it was an aristocratic recognition of human values. The city had always enjoyed peculiarities of nomenclature and geography – the North River, is its citizens loved to tell out-of-towners, was not in the north, the East River was not a river, Houston Street was inexplicably pronounced Howston and there was a little enclave of Manhattan, Marble Hill, which was not on the island at all, but on the Bronx side of the Harlem River. In just the same way did Manhattan cherish its human exceptions, its show-offs and its oddballs. This was a city of extraordinary people, and it was proud of the fact. All was forgiven a man – well

230

nearly all – if he was extraordinary enough. Venal but entertaining politicians, brutal but colourful gangsters, excruciatingly snobby socialites, preposterously vain performers, all found their way to Manhattan's heart, and the city's law was rich in tales of recluses, exhibitionists and miscellaneous cranks.

For instance a universally welcome figure in Greenwich Village, the more or less literary quarter of town, was the penniless litterateur Joseph Ferdinand Gould, who had been writing for almost as long as anyone could remember a gigantic Oral History of the World. Gould, who was in his fifties, 5' 4" tall and a member of the Harvard class of 1911, used to say that he lived on air, self-esteem, coffee, fried-egg sandwiches and ketchup, and claimed to have translated much of Longfellow into the seagull language. With his ivory cigarette holder, his baggy clothes, his toothless grin, his beard and his bald top, he had been frequenting the bars and cafés of the Village for thirty years and more, and was known to everyone as The Professor.

By 1945 his history, which he was writing in a series of school composition books, is said to have contained at least 9 million long-hand words, and most of it had been deposited for safekeeping, in case of air raids, on a Long Island chicken farm. Nobody however had ever read it, and nobody really knew whether it was genius, gibberish or just mediocrity. Gould was treated with affection anyway. He was given free drinks and meals all over the place, and was invited to all the best Village parties, where at the drop of a hat he would recite some well-known poem in seagull. There was perhaps not another metropolis in the whole world where so apparent a charlatan would have found such generous kindness.[1]

Jan Morris, *Manhattan '45* (1987 / 2011)

---

1 Gould was given a wider and lasting fame by Joseph Mitchell in *McSorley's Wonderful Saloon*. He died in 1957, aged sixty-eight, alas in a hospital for the mentally ill, and what became of his *Oral History* nobody seems to know. Hemingway sent gladioli to his funeral.

* * *

*In a city formed largely from successive waves of
immigration, various ethnic groups have found themselves under pressure from newcomers. Julia Blackburn describes the beginnings of Harlem.*

Although the majority of black Americans lived and worked
in the South, they also had a long connection with New
York. Already by 1771 they made up about one-sixth of the
city's total population. But this number began to decrease
once New York became the destination of hundreds of thousands of immigrants escaping from hunger and persecution
in Europe. Each newly arrived group fought for its share of
territory and power in the city, and throughout the nineteenth
century the black population was driven out of areas where
they had established themselves. They were pressed further
and further to the north. They had to escape from the violence
and intimidation that was brought to bear on them in Soho
and in Greenwich Village, in the Five Points district (which
became Chinatown) and in Little Africa (which was transformed into Little Italy). [...]

By 1905 the first of the more well-to-do black families had
moved into Harlem, occupying the elegant red stone houses
that had been left empty after a slump. They were prepared
to pay higher rents in exchange for the space and dignity
that could be found here, and at first the neighbourhood was
'stable and unified', with blacks and whites living in close
proximity to each other. However, most of the properties in
Harlem were owned by white landlords, who could charge
rents as much as 58 per cent more than the average in the rest
of the city. Of the 12,000 retail stores operating in Harlem in
1930, only 391 were owned by blacks and 172 of them were
groceries.

With the internal migration from the countryside to the city and from the South to the North, Harlem's population increased by 600 per cent between 1910 and 1935. The grand houses in their wide boulevards were transformed into 'filthy, vermin-ridden buildings' as more and more people were crowded into the one area of the city where they were able to live. By the late 1920s there were around 200,000 people crammed into three and a half square miles.[2] The overcrowded houses had become tenement blocks; schools, sanitation and all the basic amenities of life were neglected by the civic authorities, and the death rate was twice as high as in the rest of the city. There was just one hospital, the Harlem General, which was known locally as the Butcher Shop or the Morgue. In 1931 it was providing 273 beds for the entire community.

As well as employment, housing and health problems, there were also the persistent humiliations and social discriminations. In Blumstein's or Koch's, the big Harlem department stores on 125th Street, a black woman was not permitted to try a dress on in the store. The people of Harlem were forbidden to use the toilet facilities in shops or restaurants. Black movie-goers could only sit in the balcony at Loew's Victoria on 125th Street. A black person could not be served at a bar with a white friend.

The tensions in Harlem reached a crisis during the First World War, when many black Americans wondered 'why we fight for democracy abroad when we don't have democracy at home'. A similar crisis came with the onset of the Second World War. James Baldwin, in his essay *The Harlem Ghetto*, spoke of the 'furious bewildered rage' that was taking root throughout these years, as 'all over Harlem, Negro boys and girls are growing into a stunted maturity, trying desperately to find a place to stand; and the wonder is not that so many are ruined, but that so many survive.'

---

2 By 1940 that number had increased to 500,000, still contained within the same area.

But people made the best of what they had, and Harlem in the first decades of the 1900s was full of clubs, ballrooms, speakeasies, hole-in-the-wall joints, whorehouses and reefer pads; all sorts of enclosed paradise worlds where you could forget your troubles for a while, with the help of music and dancing, and sex and liquor, and whatever drugs were available at the time.

For wealthy white New Yorkers, the word Harlem was a 'national synonym for naughtiness', and the 'pleasure-living' would go 'slumming' in search of excitement and entertainment. Some places, like the Cotton Club, maintained strict rules of segregation, while others – and in particular the famous Savoy Ballroom that opened in 1926 – had a mixed clientele.

The Savoy occupied an entire block on Lenox Avenue. You came in via a marble pillared staircase lit by cut-glass chandeliers and stepped out into an orange-and-blue dance hall, which had a revolving stage for a band at either end so that the music never had to stop. Louis Armstrong, Ella Fitzgerald and Cab Calloway were regular performers. Wednesday-night shows were reserved for fraternal organisations, and Thursdays for kitchen maids, who had one free night in the week. Everything was kept very dignified and orderly and, even when Prohibition had been repealed, the Savoy served only ginger beer. One in five of the guests was white and mixed dancing was commonplace.

But the excitement of the 1920s gave way to the Great Depression and, by 1934, half of the black working population in all of the United States was without employment, as opposed to less than a quarter of the white population. Almost half of all families in Harlem were receiving benefit, and because the provision was eight cents a meal for food, and nothing at all if a man of working age was part of the household, it was not uncommon to see whole families foraging in garbage cans in search of scraps to eat.

Julia Blackburn, *With Billie* (2005)

* * *

Jan Morris continues the portrait of Harlem, post-World War II.

You climbed those subway steps, hardly fifteen minutes from Rockefeller Center, and instantly everyone around you was black! It was like another world; but to the surprise of many tourists, in some ways it was a world much like one's own. Not all Harlemites, it turned out, were rioters, slum folk or trumpeters! Most of Harlem was certainly drab and poverty-stricken, but by no means all. There were well-dressed men about, and women of elegance, and businessmen not at all unlike, were it not for their colour, the scurrying middle-rank executives of midtown. There were even quite likely to be, if you strolled up to Van Cortlandt Park on a summer afternoon, courtly West Indians playing cricket. Here were the Harlem River Houses, a much-admired and beautifully-maintained public housing scheme, and here was the excellent Red Rooster restaurant, and here on Seventh Avenue was the Hotel Theresa, not a bad hotel at all, thirteen stories high and steam-heated throughout.

Then book-browsers of any colour would feel themselves at home at Lew Michaux's, which was not only a powerhouse of black thought in New York City, but every aficionado's idea of a proper bookshop. It was a marvellously jumbled place, with books by every black author, biographies of every black celebrity and black newspapers from all over – the Chicago *Defender*, the New York *Age*, the Pittsburgh *Courier*, the *Afro-American* – LYNCH TERROR HITS N.C. TOWN, PROBE ATHENS, ALA., RIOT ... There was an art gallery for black sculptors and painters, sidewalk debates proliferated outside, and in the middle of it all, as likely as not passionately arguing politics with a group of friends, enemies or total strangers, was Michaux himself, the best-known arguer in Harlem. [...]

Some people of great importance lived in this remarkable ghetto (as they already called it). There was Adam Clayton Powell, Jr., for instance, who had succeeded his equally famous father as pastor of the Abyssinian Church. Six feet tall, athletic and wonderfully compelling of presence, he loved cars, wine and night life, married first a showgirl, then a swing pianist, and was already using his pulpit as a rostrum of black emancipation. He was not only a local hero as a champion of all things black, but a national figure as New York's first black congressman. There were young writers like James Baldwin, growing up in Harlem then, and old ones like Langston Hughes famous and revered. There was the distinguished lawyer Thurgood Marshall, and the eminent sociologist W.E.B. Du Bois. The great black sportsmen of the day were grandees of Sugar Hill, from Jack Johnson the first black heavyweight champion of the world to Joe Louis the latest. The diminutive Father Divine was an international celebrity. And most thrillingly of all, of course, for any ordinary visitor to Harlem, one might see in the street, if not too early in the morning, or supping at the Red Rooster if late enough in the afternoon, one of the supreme black performers who still lived up here – Duke Ellington, Ella Fitzgerald, Count Basie, Billie Holiday, "Bojangles" Robinson or Cab Calloway, the aristocrats of Harlem, whose names were known almost everywhere on earth.

Jan Morris, *Manhattan '45* (1987/2011)

❊ ❊ ❊

If Harlem had its own distinctive culture, then so too did other areas of New York, such as Brooklyn. Thomas Wolfe (1900–1938) – not to be confused with novelist Tom Wolfe (born 1931) gives us a dose of the Brooklyn accent and way of doing things.

Dere's no guy livin' dat knows Brooklyn t'roo an' t'roo, because it'd take a guy a lifetime just to find his way aroun' duh f—town.

So like I say, I'm waiti' for my train t' come when I sees dis big guy standin' deh – dis is duh foist I eveh see of him. Well, he's lookin' wild, y'know, an' I can see dat he's had plenty, but still he's holdin' it; he talks good an' is walkin' straight enough. So den, dis big guy steps up to a little guy dat's standin' deh, an' says, "How d'yuh get t' Eighteent Avenoo an' Sixty-sevent' Street?" he says.

"Jesus! Yuh got me, chief," duh little guy says to him. "I ain't been heah long myself. Where is duh place?" he says. "Out in duh Flatbush section somewhere?"

"Nah," duh big guy says. "It's out in Bensonhoist. But I was never deh befoeh. How d'yuh get deh?"

"Jesus," duh little guy says, scratchin' his head, y'know" – yuh could see duh little guy didn't know his way about – "yuh got me, chief. I neveh hoid of it. Do any of youse guys know where it is?" he says to me.

"Sure," I says. "It's out in Bensonhoist. Yuh take duh Fourt' Avenoo express, get off at Fifty-nint Street, change to a Sea beach local deh, get off at Eighteent' Avenoo an' Sixty-toid, an' den walk down foeh blocks. Dat's all yuh got to do," I says.

Thomas Wolfe, *From Death to Morning* (1935)

❋ ❋ ❋

The life of New York's gay community is well documented by Edmund White. Here he remembers what it was like during the city's difficult years of the 1970s.

In the 1970s in New York everyone slept till noon.

It was a grungy, dangerous, bankrupt city without normal services most of the time. The garbage piled up and stank during long strikes of the sanitation workers. A major blackout led to days and days of looting. We gay guys wore whistles around our necks so we could summon help from other gay men when we were attacked on the streets by gangs living in the projects between Greenwich Village and the West Side leather bar.

The upside was that the city was inexpensive, and Manhattan, especially the part of it below Fourteenth Street, was full of young actors-singers-dancers-waiters who made enough money working their restaurant shifts three nights a week to pay for their acting lessons and their cheap rents. Unlike our hometowns back in the Midwest, where the sidewalk was rolled up at six P.M., the delis and coffee shops were open all night and the bars till four in the morning. That whole army of actor-waiters saw their restaurant jobs as just another opportunity for "scene study" ("Who am I tonight? An Austrian aristocrat who's fallen on bad times? A runaway from an incestuous family in the Tennessee Hills? A Swedish gymnast?"). No matter how big their tips were, they managed to drink them away in a bar after the restaurants closed as they talked excitedly about their art and their loves. Everyone smoked all the time, and when you French-kissed someone, it was like rubbing one ashtray against another.

New York seemed either frightening or risible to the rest of the nation. To us, however, it represented the only free port on the entire continent. Only in New York could we walk hand in hand with a member of the same sex. Only in New York could we ignore a rat galloping across our path and head out for a midnight play reading. Artists on the Lower East Side were recycling the most primitive and worthless materials – junk, really.

But there was also a mandarin New York, a place where painters and choreographers and novelists and poets strove to produce serious art of the highest order. This was an elite group of people, scattered throughout the Village and the emerging neighbourhood of Chelsea and the comfortable, kicked-out Upper West Side; in this mandarinate artists and intellectuals still felt connected to the supreme artists of the past, still thought that their work would be the latest instalment in a quasi-divine legacy. [...]

New York, in short, in the seventies was a junkyard with serious artistic aspirations. I remember that one of our friends, the poet Brad Gooch, wanted to introduce us to his lover, who'd become an up-and-coming Hollywood director, but Brad begged him not to tell us that he worked as a director since Hollywood had such low prestige among us. That sort of reticence would be unthinkable today in a New York that has become enslaved by wealth and glitz, but back then people still embraced Ezra Pound's motto, "Beauty is difficult."

Edmund White, *City Boy* (2009)

❊ ❊ ❊

A city the size of New York isn't just made up of artists, writers, financial wizards, celebrities and strug-gling new immigrants. The population is supported by thousands of ordinary workers engaged, for example, in the task of simply getting the city fed. Here's a passing – and vivid – vignette of one such group of workers.

He entered the city at One hundred twenty-fifth Street, under the ultrahigh railroad bridge that crossed the meat wholesalers' area. Sammler had some affection for this intricate bridge and the structural shadows it threw. Reflected in the shine of the meat trucks. The sides of beef and pork, gauze-wrapped, blood-spotted. Things edible would always be respected by a man who had nearly starved to death. The labourers, too, in white smocks, broad and heavy, a thickset personnel, butchers' men. By the river the smell was equivocal. You were not sure whether the rawness came from the tide-water or the blood. And here Sammler once saw a rat he took for a dachshund.

The breeze out of this electric-lighted corner had the fragrance of meat dust. That was sprayed from the band saws that went through frozen fat, through marbled red or icy porphyry, and whizzed through bone. Try to stroll here. The pavements were waxed with fat.

Saul Bellow, *Mr. Sammler's Planet* (1970)

✻ ✻ ✻

But what makes New York 'New York' is, above all, its incredible ethnic and religious mix. Jan Morris and Ian Frazier.

The English writer Cecil Roberts, who had spent the war years in Manhattan, reported that on the five floors of his apartment house there lived an Austrian doctor, a Lithuanian politician, a Dutch artist, a Polish rabbi, a Turkish broadcaster, a cousin of the Shah of Persia, an American-Armenian, a Cuban pianist, an Australian nurse, a Spanish shipping agent and a German-born art dealer.

Jan Morris, *Manhattan '45* (1987 / 2011)

✻ ✻ ✻

The oldest house in Queens – perhaps in the city – is a frame farmhouse built in 1661 by a man who later suffered banishment for letting Quakers meet there. His neighbours in the town of Flushing sent the Dutch governor a remonstrance stating their belief in religious freedom not only for Quakers and other Christians but also for "Jews, Turks, and Egyptians." Today, the house, called the Bowne House, sits on a small patch of lawn between a four-story apartment building and a city playground. The theoretical Jews, Turks, and Egyptians are now real and living nearby, but nearest are the Koreans. Almost all the signs you see in downtown Flushing are in Korean, and the neighbourhood has a Quaker meetinghouse, Korean Buddhist temples, and Korean Catholic and Protestant churches. At the end of the No. 7 Flushing subway line, pamphleteers for a city council person hand you flyers saying that the line is going to hell, while other people hand you fundamentalist Christian tracts saying that you are. Pentecostal churches in storefronts all over Queens have signs in the window advising, for example, "Do nothing you would not like to be doing when Jesus comes," in Spanish and English. A multimillion-dollar Hindu temple, the largest in the city, recently went up in Flushing. Many Hindus, Buddhists, and Sikhs have recently added small celebrations of Christmas to their traditional worship calendars. Groups of Gnostics meet in Queens, and Romanian Baptists, and followers of the guru Sri Chinmoy, who sometimes express their faith by doing enough somersaults to get into the *Guinness Book of World Records*.

Ian Frazier, *Gone to New York* (2005)

❊ ❊ ❊

Everybody, it seems, is here. At grand Army Plaza, I have seen traffic tie-ups caused by Haitians and others rallying in support of President Aristides, and by St. Patrick's Day parades, and by Jews of the Lubavitcher sect celebrating the birthday of their Grand Rebbe with a slow procession of ninety-three motor homes – one for each year of his life. Local taxis have bumper stickers that say 'Allah is Great'; one of the men who made the bomb that blew up the World Trade Center used an apartment just a few blocks from me. When an election is held in Russia, crowds line up to cast ballots at a Russian polling place in Brighton beach. A while ago, I volunteer-taught reading at a public elementary school across the park. One of my students, a girl, was part Puerto Rican, part Greek, and part Welsh.

Ian Frazier, *Gone to New York* (2005)

✻ ✻ ✻

*And a final piece from E. L. Doctorow celebrating the
infinite variety of the people you will meet if you go
to that amazing, seething, complex, enchanting city –
New York.*

Here in the neighbourhood of St. Tim's, lots of people just getting
by. On the corner, young T-shirted girl, braless, tight cutoffs, she
is running in place with her Walkman. Gray-haired over-the-hill
bohemian, a rummy, he affects a ponytail. Squat, short Latina,
steatopygous. Stooped old man in house slippers, Yankees cap,
filthy pants held up by a rope. Young black man crossing against
the traffic, glaring, imperious, making his statement.

East Village generally still the six-storey height of the nineteenth
century. The city is supposed to deconstruct and remake itself
every five minutes. Maybe midtown, but except for the Verrazano
Bridge, the infrastructure was in place by the late thirties. The last
of the major subway lines was built in the twenties. All the bridges,
tunnels, and most of the roads and parkways, improved or unim-
proved, were done by the Second World War. And everywhere you
look the nineteenth is still here – the Village, East and West, the
Lower East Side, Brooklyn Bridge, Central Park, the row houses
in Harlem, the iron-fronts in Soho …

The city grid was laid out in the 1840s, so despite all we still
live with the decisions of the dead. We walk the streets where
generations have trod have trod have trod.

But, Jesus, you're out of town a couple of days and it's hyper-
shock. Fire sirens. Police-car hoots. Ritual pneumatic drilling
on the avenues. The runners in their running shorts, the Roll-
erblades, the messengers. Hissing bus doors. Sidewalk pileups
for the stars at their screenings. All the restaurants booked.
Babies tumbling out of the maternity wards. Building facades
falling into the streets. Bursting water mains. Cop crime. Every
day a cop shoots a black kid, choke-holds a perp, a bunch of

them bust into the wrong apartment, wreck the place, cuff the women and children. Cover-ups by the Department, mayor making excuses.

New York New York, capital of literature, the arts, social pretension, subway tunnel condos. Napoleonic real estate mongers, grandiose rag merchants. Self-important sports-writers. Statesmen retired in Sutton Place to rewrite their lamentable achievements ... New York, the capital of people who make immense amounts of money without working. The capital of people who work all their lives and end up broke and grey. New York is the capital of boroughs of vast neighbour-hoods of nameless drab apartment houses where genius is born every day.

It is the capital of all music. It is the capital of exhausted trees.

The migrant wretched of the world, they think if they can just get here, they can get a foothold. Run a newsstand, a bodega, drive a cab, peddle. Janitor, security guard, run numbers, deal, whatever it takes. You want to tell them this is no place for poor people. The racial fault line going through the heartland goes through our heart. We're colour-coded ethnic and social enclavists, multiculturally suspicious, and verbally aggressive, as if the city as an idea is too much to bear even by the people who live in it.

But I can stop on any corner at the intersection of two busy streets, and before me are thousands of lives headed in all four directions, uptown downtown east and west, on foot, on bikes, on in-line skate, in buses, strollers, cars, trucks, with the subway rumble underneath my feet ... and how can I not know I am momentarily part of the most spectacular phenomenon in the unnatural world? There is a species recognition we will never acknowledge. A primatial over-soul. For all the wariness or indifference with which we negotiate our public spaces, we rely on the masses around us to delineate ourselves. The city may begin from a marketplace, a trading post, the confluence of waters, but it secretly depends on the human need to walk among strangers.

And so each of the passersby on this corner, every scruffy, oversize, undersize, weird, fat, or bony or limping or muttering or foreign-looking, or green-haired punk-strutting, threatening, crazy, angry, inconsolable person I see ... is a New Yorker.

E.L. Doctorow, *City of God* (2000)

Selective Index

Names marked with * indicate a writer whose work is excerpted in the text.

Acknowledgements

Oxygen Books would like to thank the many people who have supported *city-pick NEW YORK* with their enthusiasm, professional help, ideas for texts to include, and generosity. Among them we would like to mention particularly the permissions personnel in the many publishers and agencies we have dealt with, along with Andrew Furlow, Mikka Haugaard, Graham Main, Wendy Sanford, Josie Smeed, Tim Stanley – and not forgetting Eduardo Reyes for his lovely illustrations, and the team at Shenfield Discount Cycles for keeping our transport fleet on the road.

Amis, Martin *Money* ©1984, published by Vintage Books. Reprinted by permission of the Random House Group Ltd., and the Wylie Agency.

Auster, Paul *City of Glass (The New York Trilogy)* © Paul Auster 1985. Reprinted by permission of Faber and Faber Ltd.

Bank, Melissa *The Wonder Spot* © 2005. Reprinted by permission of Penguin Books.

Becker, Jurek *Nach der ersten Zukunft* © Suhrkamp Verlag Frankfurt am Main 1980. Translation © Susan Thorne 2011. translated and printed with permission of Suhrkamp Verlag Berlin.

Bellow, Saul *Mr Sammler's Planet* © 1970. Reprinted by permission of Penguin Books.

Bennett, Alan *Untold Stories* © 2005. Reprinted by permission of Faber and Faber Ltd.

Berman, Marshall *On the Town* © 2006, 2009. Reprinted by permission of Georges Borchardt, Inc., on behalf of the author.

Blackburn, Julia *With Billie* 2005 published by Vintage Books. Reprinted by permission of the Random House Group Ltd., and by permission of the author c/o Rogers, Coleridge & White Ltd., 20 Powis Mews, London W11 1JN.

Block, Lawrence *Small Town* 2003 Reprinted by permission of the Orion Publishing Group Ltd.

Brownstein, Gabriel *The Curious Case of Benjamin Button, Apt. 3W* 2003. Reprinted by permission of Bloomsbury Publishing Plc.

Byrne, David *Bicycle Diaries* 2009 © Todo Mundo Ltd, 2009. Reprinted by permission of Faber and Faber Ltd.

Capote, Truman *Breakfast at Tiffany's* © Truman Capote 1958. Reprinted by permission of Penguin Books.

Chancellor, Alexander *Some Times in America* © 1999. First published by Bloomsbury Publishing. Rights reverted to author whom we have made every effort to contact prior to publication.

Clarke, Stephen, *Merde Happens*. 2007 Published by Black Swan. Reprinted by kind permission of the Random House Group Ltd.

Cole, Teju *Open City* © 2011. Reprinted by permission of Random House Inc. and Faber and Faber Ltd.

Colin, Beatrice *The Songwriter* © 2010. Reprinted by permission of John Murray Publishers.

Cooke, Alistair *Letter from America* © 2004. Published by Allen Lane. Reprinted by permission of Penguin Books.

Crisp, Quentin *Resident Alien* 1996 Reprinted by permission of HarperCollins Publishers Ltd. © 1996 Quentin Crisp.

Cunningham, Michael *The Hours* Reprinted by permission of Harper-Collins Publishers Ltd. ©1998 Michael Cunningham.

DeLillo, Don *Underworld* © Don DeLillo 1997. Reprinted by permission of Pan Macmillan, London.

DeLillo, Don *Falling Man* © Don DeLillo 2007. Reprinted by permission of Pan Macmillan, London.

Díaz, Junot *Drown* © 1996. Reprinted by permission of Faber and Faber Ltd.

Doctorow, E. L. *City of God* © 2000. Reprinted by permission of Little Brown.

Doctorow, E. L. *Ragtime* © E.L.Doctorow 1974. Reprinted by permissions of Pan Macmillan, London.

Dos Passos, John *Manhattan Transfer* © 1925. Reprinted by kind permission of A. M. Heath.

Edmunds, Marian 'Blue, blue sky' © Marian Edmunds 2011.

Franzen, Jonathan *How to be Alone* © 2002 Reprinted by kind permission of HarperCollins Publishers Ltd.

Frazier, Ian *Gone to New York* © 2006 by Ian Frazier. Reprinted by permission of Farrar, Straus and Giroux, LLC, and the Wylie Agency on behalf of the author.

Gopnik, Adam *Through the Children's Gate* © 2007. Reprinted by permission of Quercus Editions Ltd.

Gornick, Vivian *Approaching Eye Level* © 1996 by Vivian Gornick. Reprinted by permission of Beacon Press, Boston.

Heller, Zoë *The Believers* © 2008. Reprinted by permission of Penguin Books.

Hughes, Langston *The Big Sea* © 1940 by Langston Hughes. Copyright renewed 1968 by Arna Bontemps and George Houston Bass. Reprinted by permission of Hill and Wang, a division of Farrar, Straus and Giroux, LLC and the David Higham Agency.

James, Tania *Atlas of Unknowns* © 2009. Reprinted by kind permission of the author.

Acknowledgements

Janowitz, Tama *Area Code 212* © 2002. Reprinted by permission of Bloomsbury Publishing.

Johnson, Joyce *Minor Characters* © 1983. We have made every effort to contact the author prior to publication.

Keller, Helen *Midstream: my later life* © 1929. We have made every effort to contact rights holders before publication.

Koeppen, Wolfgang 'Amerikafahrt' (1959) in *Gesammelte Werke in sechs Bänden* (Vol. 4, 1986). Published by permission of Berghahn Books (English translation forthcoming from Berghahn Books, Oxford.) This translation © Susan Thorne.

Leavitt, David *The Lost Language of Cranes* © 1986. Reprinted by permission of the Wylie Agency on behalf of the author.

Lethem, Jonathan *The Fortress of Solitude* © 2003. Reprinted by permission of Faber and Faber Ltd.

Markovits, Benjamin *Either Side of Winter* © 2005. Reprinted by permission of Faber and Faber Ltd.

Marshall, Paule *Brown Girl, Brownstones* © 1959. Dover edition 2009.

Matthews, Anne *Wild Nights* © 2001. Reprinted by kind permission of the Cynthia Cannell Agency on behalf of the author.

McCann, Colum *Let the Great World Spin* © 2009. Reprinted by permission of Bloomsbury Publishing.

McEwen, Todd *Who Sleeps With Katz* © 2003. Published by Granta Books. Reprinted by permission of A. P. Watt, on behalf of Todd McEwen.

McInerney, Jay *Bright Lights, Big City* Reprinted by permission of HarperCollins Publishers Ltd. © 1985 Jay McInerney.

Morris, Jan *A Writer's World: travels 1950–2000* © 2003. Reprinted by permission of Faber and Faber Ltd.

Morris, Jan *Manhattan '45* © 1987/2011. Reprinted by permission of Faber and Faber Ltd.

Nash, Juliana C. 'Snow' in *True Tales of American Life* (ed. Paul Auster) 2001. Reprinted by permission of Faber and Faber Ltd.

O'Neill, Joseph *Netherland* Reprinted by permission of HarperCollins Publishers Ltd. © 2008 Joseph O'Neill.

Pilkington, Ed 'Back on the Waterfront' © Guardian News & Media 2011.

Plath, Sylvia *The Bell Jar* © 1963. Reprinted by permission of Faber and Faber Ltd.

Puzo, Mario *The Fortunate Pilgrim* © 1965. Reprinted by kind permission of the Random House Group Ltd.

Rossant, Colette *Madeleines in Manhattan* © 2007. Reprinted by permission of Bloomsbury Publishing.

Rotolo, Suze *A Freewheelin' Time* © 2009. Reprinted by permission of Aurum Press,

Rubenfeld, Jed *The Interpretation of Murder* © 2006. Reprinted by permission of Headline Publishing Group Ltd.

Rutherfurd, Edward *New York* 2009 published by Arrow Books. Reprinted by permission of the Random House Group Ltd.

Sante, Luc *Low Life* © 1991. Published by Granta Books. Reprinted by permission of the Joy Harris Literary Agency.

Shteyngart, Gary *Absurdistan* © Gary Shteyngart 2007. Reprinted by kind permission of Granta Books.

Shteyngart, Gary *The Russian Debutante's Handbook* © 2003. Reprinted by kind permission of Bloomsbury Publishing.

Smith, Al *Up To Now* © 1929 by the Viking Press, © renewed 1957 by Walter J. Smith. Used by permission of Viking Penguin, a division of Penguin Group (USA) Inc.

Stainton, Leslie *Lorca: a dream of life* © 1999 by Leslie Stainton. Reprinted by permission of Farrar, Straus and Giroux, LLC.

Threapleton-Horrocks, Vanessa 'The Frick: from frivolous to fabulous' and 'Opera-Nation' © 2011.

Thurber, James *The Years with Ross* © 1959. Reprinted by permission of the Barbara Hogenson Agency on behalf of the Thurber Estate.

Tippins, Sherrill *February House* © 2005. Reprinted by permission of Simon and Schuster.

Updike, John *Odd Jobs* © 1991. Reprinted by permission of Penguin Books.

Vega, Bernardo *Memoirs of Bernardo Vega* © 1955. We have made every effort to contact the rights holder prior to publication.

White, E. B. *Here is New York* © 1949/1976. Published by the Little Bookroom.

White, Edmund *City Boy* © 2009. Reprinted by permission of Bloomsbury Publishing.

Wolfe, Tom *The Bonfire of the Vanities* 1988. Published by Vintage Books. Reprinted by permission of the Random House Group Ltd.

Every effort has been made to trace and contact copyright holders before publication. If notified, the publisher will rectify any errors or omissions at the earliest opportunity.

An exciting and unique travel series featuring the best-ever writing on European and World cities

A selection of reviews

city-lit PARIS

'It's terrific ... all the best writing on this complex city in one place'
Professor Andrew Hussey, author of *Paris: The Secret History*

'A great and eclectic set of writings ... an original book on Paris'
Sylvia Whitman, Shakespeare & Co, Paris

'It's like having your own iPad loaded with different tomes, except that this slim anthology contains only the best passages, bite-sized chunks just perfect to dip into as you sip that pastis in a pavement café.'
The Times

'The ideal book for people who don't want to leave their minds at the airport'
Celia Brayfield, author of *Deep France*

£8.99 ISBN 978–0–9559700–0–9

city-lit LONDON

'For those visitors to London who seek to do more than bag Big Ben and Buckingham Palace, this is the ideal guide, a collection of writings that expose not only the city's secret places but its very soul ... I can't imagine a more perfect travelling companion than this wonderful anthology'
Clare Clark, author of *The Great Stink*

'The latest offering in this impressive little series concentrates on the spirit of London as seen through the eyes of an eclectic selection of writers. Part of the joy of this collection is that the writers span several centuries, which means that multiple faces of London are revealed. It's an exciting selection, with unexpected gems from novelists, travel writers, journalists and bloggers.'
The Sunday Telegraph

' ... a frenzied orgy of London writing. You'll love it'

Londonist

'The second volume in this enticing new series includes extracts from the work of 60 wonderfully diverse writers, including Will Self, Monica Ali, Alan Bennett, Dostoyevsky, and yes, Barbara Cartland (writing about a West End ball)'

Editor's Pick, *The Bookseller*

£8.99 ISBN: 978–0–9559700–5–4

city-lit BERLIN

'A gem ... an elegant, enjoyable and essential book'

Rosie Goldsmith, BBC Radio 4

'This wonderful anthology explores what it is really like to be a Berliner by bringing together extracts about the city from a range of genres, including some specially translated. This was the city of Einstein, Brecht, George Grosz, and Marlene Dietrich. It was 'the New York of the old world', a melting pot of new ideas and lifestyles ... This collection is timely: on 9 November 20 years ago, Berliners tore down the hated wall'

The Guardian

'*city-Lit Berlin* gathers more than a hundred extracts from writers on aspects of Berlin's conflicted heritage ... the editors have trawled widely to try to capture the modern city's rule-bound yet permissive tone, as well as its persistent state of cultural and architectural renewal. The result is an eclectic pillow-book ... a stimulating intellectual tour of the idea of the city that would complement any guidebook's more practical orientation'

Financial Times

'This is a sublime introduction to the city'

Sydney Morning Herald

city-pick DUBLIN

' ... an elegant, incisive and always entertaining guide to the city's multitude of literary lives.'

Lonely Planet Magazine

'*city-pick Dublin* is the latest triumph of distillation. There's everything here from David Norris' defence of the significance of Joyce's *Ulysses* to Iris Murdoch's fictional treatment of The Easter Rising. You'll read about walking and drinking, being poor and being poetic, new wealth and newcomers, old timers and returning natives."

Book of the Month, The Good Web Guide

'From Sean O'Casey to Anne Enright – the best ever writing on Dublin has been specially published in a new book entitled *city-pick Dublin*'

RTE

'Bite-sized beauties ... You won't find pub recommendations or directions to art galleries in this little guide, but you will get a taste of Dublin's most important natural resource: stories.'

The Dubliner

£8.99 ISBN 978–0–9559700–1–6

city-pick AMSTERDAM

'This engrossing book ... Some of the names in city-pick Amsterdam – such as the historian Simon Schama – may be familiar to British readers, but there are plenty more contributions in translation from Dutch writers.'

Lonely Planet Magazine

'This latest addition to the excellent 'city-pick' series of urban anthologies weaves together fiction and non-fiction, including more than 30 specially translated extracts, to give an intimate portrait of one of Europe's most distinctive cities.'

The Guardian

'It's a simple idea, presenting a metropolis in all its multifaceted glory through the words of great writers; and it's one so good it's astonishing it hasn't been done before. Split into loosely thematic sections, one of the nicest features of this collection are the 70-plus contributors – novelists, journalists, travel writers – who span the centuries. There's a thoughtful selection of Dutch writers including not only literary heavyweights like Mak, who are widely known in translation, but also lesser-known authors – Meijsing, Stefan Hertmans, Jan Donkers – some of whom are translated into English for the first time. It makes for some delightful discoveries – even for those of us who think we know this city well'

Time Out Amsterdam

city-pick VENICE

'Composed of over 50 of the very best writers on Venice, this book is so much more than your average pocket guide ... the perfect companion'

Real Travel Magazine

'This welcome addition to the excellent city-pick series ... with more than 100 extracts, this is a delightful literary guide to *La Serenissima*.'

The Guardian

'The latest addition to this admirable series ... makes any visit to La Serenissima more flavoursome'

The Bookseller, Editor's Pick

' ... the latest literary treat from the city-pick series ... as a guide to the atmosphere and spirit of the city, it's unmissable.'

Lonely Planet Magazine

'For those who love Venice, this book is genuinely unmissable ... short extracts are seamlessly blended into a compelling narrative.'

Sydney Morning Herald

www.oxygenbooks.co.uk

257